Answering Back

Answering Back

Girls, Boys and Feminism in Schools

Jane Kenway and Sue Willis with Jill Blackmore and Léonie Rennie

London and New York

First published in the UK 1998 by Routledge
11 New Fetter Lane, London EC4P 4EE

Simultaneously published in the USA and Canada
by Routledge
29 West 35th Street, New York, NY 10001

Typeset in 10/11.5pt Palatino by DOCUPRO, Sydney
Printed and bound in Singapore by KHL Printing Co. Pte Limited

British Library Cataloguing in Publication Data
A catalogue record for this book is available from the British Library

Library of Congress Cataloging in Publication Data
A catalogue record for this book has been applied for

ISBN 0–415–18191–7 (pbk)
ISBN 0–415–18190–9 (hbk)

I have dreamt in my life dreams
that have stayed with me ever after,
they have changed my ideas:
they've gone through me, like wine through water,
and altered the colour of my mind

EMILY BRONTË

Contents

Acknowledgements

We wish to express our gratitude to the Australian Research Council which funded much of the research upon which this book was based. We wish to thank the many principals, teachers, students and policy-makers who shared their ideas, time and daily activities with us. The following people worked with us: Daphne Bastow, Janine Collier, Shirley Dally, Merilyn Evans, Andrea Fulton, Linda McGuckin, Vanessa Reynolds, Pauline Richards, Shirley Tucker and Maggie Woodhead. We express our sincere appreciation to them all. We also wish to thank Elizabeth Weiss and Bob Lingard for their advice, encouragement and support as editors. We thank Deakin, Murdoch and Curtin universities for providing us with the institutional bases from which to undertake this research. Finally, we thank our families for living the values we value.

Introduction

We know a lot about some aspects of gender and schooling and precious little about others. This book will address a topic that we know very little about. Indeed, it will begin to fill a rather embarrassing gap in the literature on gender and schooling. What is this gap? In a nutshell, it is as follows. We do not know what happens in schools when people try to remake gender in more life-enhancing ways. We do not know whether feminism has made any significant difference to teachers or to boys and girls in schools. When people make the case that there has been a feminist revolution in schools and that boys and men are schools' 'new disadvantaged', we have little systematic qualitative data which would allow us to assess adequately such a claim. Further, we have little data which would allow us to judge the merits or otherwise of feminist work in schools. This is a strange state of affairs—particularly given that we know so much about other aspects of gender and schooling.

We know a lot about gender differences in such things as retention, subject choice and achievement and about the ways in which these have shifted marginally over time. We know about the ways in which schools contribute to these gender differences in educational outcomes. And we know about the ways in which they also contribute to the construction of gender identities and gender relations. As our research methods and our theories become more sophisticated, we are learning more about the subtleties of this process—although we do not know nearly enough about the differences within and across the sexes. We know that the ways in which schools deal with these differences often constrain rather than enable certain students and contribute to educational and social inequalities and injustices. We know that the need for change within schools and beyond remains.

We know that, for over twenty years, policy-makers, bureaucrats, researchers, teachers, curriculum developers, teachers' unions and professional and parent associations have sought to address many of the injustices arising from the differences between and, to a lesser extent, within the sexes in schools. We know that all of this has led to the production of many policy frameworks, action plans and accountability mechanisms, research projects and publications, conferences and workshops, inservice programs for principals, teachers and even parents, curriculum packages and kits, videos, journals, registers, newsletters, bibliographic guides, promotional materials, bridging courses, access strategies, professional and research networks and the appointment of committees and personnel to effect gender reform in systems and schools. We know that there are different feminist theories and that these have different implications for educational policies and practices. We know that the theories which have informed these many efforts for change have evolved over time. Finally, and paradoxically, the sting in this tail—or tale—is that we know that feminist educators do not necessarily agree about what we know and need to know. We know that our preferences for action and our knowledge are situated, partial and interested. They arise from our own biographies, our different theoretical, institutional, geographic and time locations. As the issues have become more subtle, the theories designed to address them have become more complex. This has had costs and benefits which we will point to.

One effect of all this has been the development of a critical mass of teachers, researchers, curriculum developers, educational administrators and policy-makers who make matters of gender analysis and reform a central feature of their working lives. This is well and good, but what have the effects been on gender identities, relationships, inequalities and injustices within schools?

To put it bluntly, we do not really know what all of this means for schools, teachers and students. While there have been some attempts to identify the educational outcomes of all of this work, these have usually been based on quantitative measures and on input–output, cause and effect metaphors of educational change. To the extent that such data show that things have or have not changed and point to problems requiring attention, they are helpful (Collins et al. 1996). They have their uses, but also their limits—just like all research. They do not point to why things have or have not changed, suggest ways of doing things differently or shed light on the process of gender reform in schools. And this is what is most absent and most needed in the field at this time.

What happens when people who normally work in schools try to remake gender identities and relations in more humane and just ways? How does it look and feel and what does it mean to those involved—and, indeed, to those who don't want to be involved? Does it make a difference, and if so is it making the sort of difference that its instigators hoped for? To our shame, after twenty odd years of gender reform policies and after untold numbers of curriculum advice manuals on what needs to be done and how to do it, we still have very few published answers to these questions. Indeed, the field lacks an adequate empirical base which shows how people in schools go about the process of gender reform and what happens when they do. It is our view that we cannot enhance the lives of girls and boys in and beyond schools through gender reform until they have a much better sense of what it looks like in the flesh.

Anyone who has attempted gender reform in schools knows that it is much easier said than done. Gender is deeply and often unconsciously ingrained within people's psyches and behaviour and deeply inscribed within school cultures and education systems. Therefore, changing girls, boys, teachers and school curricula and cultures is no simple matter—indeed, as we will show throughout this book, it provokes complex and often unexpected reactions. Gender reform in schools is a process fraught with difficulty, and attempting to document its processes and effects is also difficult. Just as the quantitative methods noted earlier have their limits, so too do other research methods.

We have opted for methods which sought out the fine grain of gender reform—its niches and nuances, singularities and subtleties, difficulties and dilemmas—in all their spectacular ordinariness. We have developed a collection of vignettes around critical incidents of gender reform which pointed to its gender and educational politics. We wanted to give teachers, and particularly students, a voice in policy—to 'voice the unvoiced', to provide them with the opportunity to answer back. We also wanted to see for ourselves which things turned students and other teachers on and which turned them off gender reform. We were frustrated with the feminist theorising which seemed to feel no obligation to connect substantively to empirical referents. We were also frustrated with the research which was so gender reductionist and microanalytic that it could not see other and broader patterns of power within and across schools. Consequently, this book is about gender reform in the flesh—its many forms in many circumstances.

However, we must acknowledge that the stories we tell here are situated, partial and interested. The 'truths' we offer are in a sense our and others' stories. How could they be otherwise?[1] Further, we know that in telling these stories we destabilise many previous feminist truths about what is right and proper practice. 'Truth' has always been problematic for those feminists who acknowledge the constructedness of knowledge. We often want to challenge others' truths but tell our own, to test others' truths rather than our own. Here we have tried to contest our own truths as much as those of others.

In this book, we offer answers to these sorts of questions: What do teachers do when they address gender issues in their schools? Does it look anything like the ideal models found in advice manuals and policy documents? How do different teachers and students respond to such attempts to change them and why do they respond in the ways they do? Which programmes for reform gain or lack support and why? What social, cultural, personal and educational factors shape the 'choices' made? What can we say facilitates gender reform and what reshapes and inhibits it?

These questions have guided a number of research projects which we have been involved in together and separately since 1990 and all of these informed our ideas for this book.[2] Collectively, these have included research in five Australian states, each with rather different policies for, and orientations to, gender reform. However, the major source was a research project funded by the Australian Research Council, which continued for five years. For the latter project, we collected qualitative data from a range of types of schools, each with a different approach or approaches to gender reform, with a view to building rich narratives of the processes and practices involved. We aimed particularly to consider two things: how did gender reformers read and rewrite policy and how did others in the schools read and rewrite the work of gender reformers? As we will show, there was many a slip between the cup and the lip!

Our other two objectives were theoretical, aiming firstly—from an empirical base—to build theories which adequately accounted for the process of gender reform in schools and, secondly, to contribute to the development of feminist theories of and for educational change. In the general literature on educational change, matters of gender seldom rate a mention. Yet, as gender is such a feature of our lives and because an understanding of gender offers useful insights into educational issues and problems, it seemed to us that theories of educational change should not remain gender blind. It also seemed to us, however, that gender reformers did not necessarily have answers to the perennial questions about how to effect change in schools. Further, we felt that gender reform had its own specificity—that ideas developed in order to effect other types of changes could not necessarily and easily be transposed to gender reform. After all, most educational change efforts are directed to teachers and principals as professionals or to students as students. In contrast, gender reform works on their gender identity as well. This book rests on the premise that changing schools, teachers and students is a complicated and even messy enterprise which can best be understood and assisted by theories and policies which recognise the complexity of the process.

The field of cultural studies helped us to structure our investigations. Cultural studies is concerned about social and cultural processes and products, particularly the ways they work on people's subjectivity and the ways in which people work on them. It is concerned about how such processes and products are produced, circulated and consumed: the struggles and compromises involved. It is further concerned about the material, social and cultural conditions which have an impact on such production, circulation and consumption (Johnson 1983). We conceptualised the gender reform 'policy trajectory' (Ball 1994, p. 26) as a cultural process and the policy documents and curriculum materials associated with it as cultural products. In our view, gender reform consists of at least two intersecting sets of cultural processes.[3] The first is that which exists at the macro level of the wider gender order, and of governments, as policy and curriculum are produced and circulated by policy-makers and their agents and as they become part of the garrulous world of education policy. The second set of processes exists at the micro gender-political level of the school itself. Here gender reformers, key mediators of policy, bring their readings and rewritings of policy into the school and, through such policies, read and seek to rewrite its gender regime. This second set of processes also includes others' various responses to gender reformers' efforts and gender reformers' responses to them. Our focus in this study was on the consumption of state-generated gender reform policies in schools rather than on their production and circulation—or what is called the moment of policy formulation. Our interest was in 'policy as practice'; in policy as it is enacted in local settings and in the ways in which it becomes part of the 'wild profusion' of the local (Ball 1994, pp. 10–11). To focus thus is not to deny the systematic power of the state or the power relations which sustain and change it. Equally, to focus on gender reform policies is not to deny their intertextuality with other policies. Where pertinent, we allude to these. However, we are concerned with the ways in which the hopes of policy are expressed in happenings in schools. This sets this study apart from those which privilege policy-makers' views of reality.

Let us offer a little more detail about theory. We began this project with the belief that the theories which had hitherto informed many attempts to effect gender justice in and through schools had run out of energy. We turned to feminist post-structuralist theory and to post-structuralist theories of policy. They offered new conceptual lenses which provided different ways of looking at things and put provocative new questions on the agenda. We will not offer a full beginner's guide to feminist post-structuralism or to post-structuralist policy analysis. Instead, we will offer an example of what Wexler (1992) calls 'descriptive analysis'—that is, our theory in use. We will embed our reading of its imperatives and concepts in the text, thus grounding them and enriching their empirical and social meaning for those new to the theory. This is our way of dealing with the challenge to make post-structuralism both accessible and practical. However, a few quick words are apt.

Post-structuralism is a term applied to a very loosely connected set of ideas about meaning, power and identity. It is concerned with the way in which meanings are made, the way they circulate amongst us, the way they are struggled over, the impact they have on our identities and actions. Post-structuralism is particularly interested in the connections between meaning and power. Meaning is influenced by power and vice versa. For post-structuralists, meaning, power and identity are always in flux. They shift as different linguistic, institutional, cultural and social factors move and stabilise together.

The emphasis in post-structuralism is on the discourses which make up social institutions and cultural products. Discourse is a key concept drawn from the French philosopher Michel Foucault, who understands it to mean 'practices that systematically form the objects of which they speak . . . Discourses are not about objects; they constitute them and in the practice of doing so, conceal their own intervention.' (Foucault 1977, p. 49) Foucault uses the term 'discourse', then, to point to the relationship between power and knowledge. His studies of discourse point to the ways in which knowledge influences what can be said, who has the right to speak and who is silenced. Finally, as Foucault further explains, discourses also gain and assign power and control through their inscription in institutional structures and practices and in cultural products. Overall, then, it is through discourse that meanings and people are made and through which power relations are maintained and changed. A discursive field is a set of discourses which are systematically related. As Weedon (1987, p. 35) points out, however, discursive fields may 'consist of competing ways of giving meaning to the world and organising social institutions and processes. They offer the individual a range of modes of subjectivity.'

Such a view of meaning and power raises questions about notions of 'truth' and promises of 'enlightenment'. Both are seen to be the products of particular peoples and cultures, times and places and the relationships of power which run through them. This view of meaning calls attention to the particular rather than the general; to discontinuity and instability rather than continuity and stability; to plurality, diversity and difference rather than to similarity and commonality; and to the complexity rather than the essence of things.

The focus of post-structuralists is on the 'myriad of power relations at the micro level of society' (Sawicki 1991, p. 20). But of course the politics of discourse are always a reflection of, and in tension with, the power relationships which exist beyond the moment and the specific locality. Times and places cannot be isolated from the wider politics of the state and civil society. When post-structuralists widen the lens, they show the ways in which the micro-physics of power contribute to wider power relationships. However, understanding the local is what is considered important strategically.

Where and how do individuals and groups fit into the above picture? As they are located within a complex web of discourses, they are offered many ways of seeing and being themselves and many positions to occupy—some more powerful than others. They will draw, both consciously and unconsciously, on the discursive repertoire which resides within them and, in differing ways, either take up or reject the positions offered. According to this view, people's identities are shifting and fragmented, displaced and positioned as they are across the various discourses which historically and currently constitute their lives and their sense of self.

Such a view of post-structuralism becomes feminist, firstly, when matters of femaleness and maleness and the differences and dominations between and within them are made a central feature of analysis and, secondly, when analysis implies a challenge of some sort to any inequitable relationships of power which involve gender or sexuality. These concerns are similar to those of other feminist theoretical traditions. However, feminist post-structuralism stands in stark contrast with other feminisms because it rejects many of their basic premises. For instance, feminist post-structuralists reject the logic of binary oppositions (e.g. male and female = oppressor and oppressed) and ideas associated with free will, fixed identity and fixed truths which can inevitably enlighten. Paradoxically, post-structuralism opposes the notion that one theory can fit all circumstances (see further Kenway 1991).

Social institutions such as education bureaucracies and schools, cultural products such as policy documents and curriculum texts, and interpersonal processes such as pedagogy (teaching/learning) are made up of many different and often contradictory discourses and discursive fields. Some of these are dominant, some subordinate, some peacefully coexisting, some struggling for ascendancy. Ball (1994) calls this 'policy *in* discourse'. In contrast, the efforts by policy to control meaning and truth, to construct positions for readers, to provide discursive possibilities and limitations, he calls 'policy *as* discourse'. Whatever the terminology, policy processes in systems and in schools consist of fragile and uneven settlements between and within discursive fields. Such settlements are open to challenge and change through the politics of discourse directed towards the making and remaking of meaning and power relations. The policy process is unruly but patterned at all stages, its writers and readers variously constrained and enabled by the patterned and by the unruly. Predictably, one such pattern is that gender reform is always a subordinate discourse in Australian education systems and schools. In schools, the dominant discourses are associated with the profession and culture of teaching, but these and gender reform are increasingly being redefined according to the logics which dominate systems in the 1990s—that is, those associated with economic rationalism, corporate managerialism and technical rationality.

The most useful lessons from feminist and other post-structuralism for education policy analysis are as follows. First, gendered meanings are unstable and constantly struggled over. Second, feminism in education is involved in a struggle over the meaning of gendered identities and relationships in and around schools. Third, gender reform seeks to offer new 'truths' about both. It offers alternative ways of being and valuing. Fourth, at the same time, feminism acknowledges that these 'truths' are situated, temporary and political and will change over time. They will change as feminism develops and as the meanings and purposes of feminism change as a result of struggles over the meaning of feminism itself from within and without. Today's dreams may well be tomorrow's nightmares and this means that feminists must be sensitive to the possible dangerousness of their truths—they must trouble themselves as much as their 'others'. Nonetheless, to have some political credibility in schools, feminists must also speak with some certainty and authority. This book represents our attempt to manoeuvre our way through the dilemmas that are inherent in speaking with apparent certainty in the age of uncertainty.

Let us now mention some matters of method. The study involved a mix of qualitative and quantitative research methods. Six major case studies involving visits over two or three years and eight cameo studies involving several visits over a year were conducted in Victoria, Western Australia, the Australian Capital Territory and the Northern Territory in schools catering for widely differing class and ethnic populations. Each involved interviews with key gender reformers, their school principals, their supporters and opponents and the observation of them at work in various meetings, classrooms and other school locations. It also involved interviewing, shadowing and observing students as individuals and in groups. Analysis of pertinent policy and curriculum documents and of students' writing on set topics was also conducted. In order to ensure that the understandings we were reaching in our case and cameo studies had some wider applicability, we conducted surveys of 100 schools in Victoria and Western Australia and from the data generated from these we selected an additional sixteen schools in which to conduct snapshot studies to further flesh out our perceptions. Predictably, this generated a massive body of data.

Our primary purpose in this book has been to bring to life the gender politics of gender reform in schools—its successes and failures, pleasures and disappointments, complexities and confusions, tensions and temptations. Our tales will tell what happens when feminist ideas come into contact with the everyday life of schools. They will identify the range of ways in which teachers have worked with various feminist ideas in developing new curriculum and classroom practices and discuss the various responses of girls and boys and other teachers. They will concentrate particularly on the subtle ways in which girls and boys interpret and reconstruct different feminist agendas. In addressing issues of curriculum and pedagogy, we hope to attend to the interests and concerns of teachers, to recognise their difficulties in addressing the sensitive subject of gender and to point to new possibilities for bringing about gender justice in schools. But we expect to surprise and provoke.

The research which informs this book took the first five years of the 1990s and during that time a great deal changed in education policy and administration in Australia.[4] Over these years, the different theoretical and practical orientations and emphases of gender reform policies changed. So, too, did the educational and political grounds upon which these policies were developed and with which they sought to contend. This is not the place to go into all these changes except to say that, with regard to their support for gender justice policies, governments became more mean and more lean as time went on. Gender justice policies, programmes and personnel were restructured and 'downsized' along with much else. At the time of writing, in early 1997, uneasy relationships existed between economic rationalism, corporate managerialism, and matters of gender justice. The gender reform ideas that were most fashionable in government policy circles in the early 1990s were no longer fashionable in such circles.

When we started our research, the dominant emphasis was on encouraging girls into 'non-traditional' areas in curriculum and the workplace (see, for example, Commonwealth Schools Commission 1987; Australian Education Council 1992; and for a discussion see Kenway and Willis 1996). At this time, a great deal of effort and money was put into changing girls' subject and career choices, into the development of single-sex classes and into changing science, maths and technology curricula and teaching to ensure that they were 'gender inclusive' (Kenway and Willis with Education of Girls Unit, SA 1993). Also at this time there was a growing concern about 'sexual harassment' and about the development of procedures for dealing with sexual harassment in schools (see, for example, Australian Education Council 1991). These fashions superseded those about sex-role socialisation, sex stereotyping, self-esteem and role modelling which tended to dominate policy in the 1980s. In the mid-1990s, they have all been superseded by emphases on the construction and reconstruction of gender within school cultures and across the curriculum and on the education of boys (e.g. Australian Education Council 1993; O'Doherty Report 1994). Of course, many other issues have been on gender reform policy agendas, including the need to attend to the educational issues associated with poverty, ethnicity, race, disability, sexuality and locality. However, they have never dominated policy circles.

It is difficult to pinpoint what caused these shifts in policy. An argument could be sustained, however, that they arose as a result of the uneasy compromises between developments in the wider field of feminist ideas, the takeup of such ideas by leading feminists in educational circles, the ongoing documentation of gender issues in schools, other popular discourses in government circles and the tolerance limits of the state. For the purposes of this book, the general and important point to be made is that these changes did not tend to happen as a result of research either about gender reform in schools or into teachers' and students' experiences. Feminist policy was to inform feminist practice, not the reverse; teachers and students, feminist or otherwise, were to do as they were told; they were not to answer back. However, in this book students' and teachers' voices will come through as we address five central concerns of gender reform: success, knowledge, power, emotion and responsibility.

Answering Back

1

That mysterious gap 'between hope and happening'

At first glance, schools appear ordered, controlled and predictable—and, indeed, in many ways they are. This is so with regard to matters of gender and much else. As a result of feminist scholarship it is now possible to predict with some certainty a great deal about who does what, where, how and why, with and to whom in schools. Schools have their gender patterns of difference and dominance and, as we will show throughout this book, these are increasingly being questioned and challenged. Gender orders schools in quite systematic ways. However, to focus only on the ordered and patterned within and across schools is often to miss the fact that schools are also different, complex, contradictory and often confusing places where the unexpected happens just as often as the expected, particularly in the fine grain of the everyday. To be open to surprise is to be open to the richness of schools and the people within them. It is to acknowledge that, because of the many forces at work and interests at stake both within and beyond them, schools are as fluid as they are fixed, as different as they are similar and as surprising as they are tediously predictable.

Of the 60 schools we surveyed in Victoria in 1993, 29 had gender reform programmes underway, although some were quite modest. In Western Australia, Australia's biggest and most isolated state, seven of the 40 schools we surveyed described specific gender reform programmes. All of the 30 schools in which we conducted case, cameo and snapshot studies were undertaking some sort of gender reform. But across these schools there was enormous variation, even with programmes focusing on the same issue. Further, within each school, gender reform was manifest in ways that were both predictable and surprising. There was seldom a perfect match between 'hope and happening'—between the aspirations of gender reform policies and practitioners and the processes and effects of their proposals for change. The purpose of this chapter, then, is simply to tell some stories about this imperfect match. These stories offer some insight into what goes on in that mysterious gap between 'hope and happening'.

But first, a brief outline of the patterns of gender reform across the schools we studied. (All schools, teachers and students have been anonymised.) Some schools had a wide range of programmes, others only one, two or three isolated initiatives. Bettleford was at one end of this spectrum and had the following programmes: single-sex maths classes, self-defence for girls, gender and personal development classes, girls and careers, projects for boys in mixed classes and for changing boys' attitudes, a project for girls in technology studies and a staff development project looking at curriculum development in terms of gender and students with English as a second language. To take another example, Nerringo had a girls and physical activity plan, an action plan to produce a gender-inclusive commerce curriculum to encourage more boys to do keyboarding, personal development classes addressing harassment and violence, a girls and middle school physics curriculum project and a gender awareness staff development programme for maths, science and technology teachers. In contrast, Neerbin had a special, one-off programme called 'Gaining the Edge' which sought to enhance students' life chances and attended to gender and geographic isolation. East Barton had single-sex classes in science. Birrilup's main programme was aimed at stigmatised high-achieving boys and girls.

Some schools identified gender issues that were specific to their school and locality and tailored programmes accordingly, while others took a more generic view. Draymill, for instance, is a small rural town where sexual abuse and domestic violence are quite prevalent and so the school decided to make this the focus of its gender reform programmes on gender and violence. Stowley, a school in a depressed rural area, was concerned about the needs of students at risk and the under-achievement of rural boys. Kennetton, on the other hand, adopted the generically popular strategy of single-sex classes for maths and technology—largely because the impetus for gender reform came from only one mathematics teacher. Some schools closely followed government gender reform policies; others took a more divergent view. Those who took the latter path tended to be schools with populations which were not well addressed in government gender reform policies. Thus it was that Mt Mullin, the high school in a remote town in Western Australia, developed a programme for its Muslim girls seeking to attend to issues associated with their geographic and cultural isolation. Other schools in this category— and their numbers were not great—sought to attend to the connections between gender and Aboriginality, homelessness, ethnicity and social class. Most of the schools in Victoria followed Ministry of Education policy and built gender reform into their staffing, through the establishment of Equal Opportunity (EO) Coordinator positions, and also established EO and/or Social Justice Committees. In Western Australia, where policy did not require it, few schools had formally established such positions or committees. Where special programmes existed, some schools drew on the normal school budget; others were funded through government initiatives. Certain schools were particularly skilled at gaining grants for projects. Meadowlands had cut its grant-application-writing teeth in the 1970s and 1980s with such Commonwealth government funding programmes as the School to Work Transition Program and the Participation and Equity Program. Fleming had gained considerable government and private funding for several projects. The sponsors for its Girls in Science Project included The West Australian Women's Trust, The University of Western Australia, the Commonwealth Government and Zonta International. Across our schools, approaches included the use of single-sex classes, visiting speakers, camps, visits, drama, student action plans, curriculum topics, morning teas or breakfasts, changing timetables, classroom checklists, changing textbooks, changing language codes—the list goes on and on.

Some gender reform programmes in schools were addressed particularly to teachers who were encouraged to reflect both on gender issues in their subject areas and in their own teaching, and to develop gender inclusive teaching practices and curriculum. However, most activities were addressed to students. Of these, most addressed girls, but many addressed girls and boys and quite a significant number addressed boys particularly. Most did not distinguish amongst girls or amongst boys, though some did target particular subgroups—students thought to be 'at risk', for example. Programmes for girls included: attempts to encourage girls in maths and science, the trades and physical education;

encouraging girls to use more linguistic and playground space; self-defence classes; truancy prevention, and Aboriginal health. For girls and boys, programmes included: attempts to ensure gender balanced classrooms; careers days; anti-sexual harassment curriculum and policy; exploring 'gender socialisation' (e.g. gender and work, gender and advertising, gender and popular culture); examining sexuality and human relationships; improving communication between girls and boys; and lunchtime activities which were gender neutral. Programmes specifically for boys included those which focused on: personal development; addressing violence through the use of conflict resolution and emotional management; encouraging the entry of boys into 'non-traditional' subjects and careers (e.g. home economics, commerce); enhancing boys' self-esteem; and changing their views of maleness through special events and positive male role models.

In some of our schools, gender reform was a very contentious issue; in others it seemed accepted and uncontroversial. In some it was woven into the fabric of the school as a whole and in others it appeared and disappeared either regularly or irregularly. In some cases, many teachers were committed to it and in others, one or two gender reformers worked alone. Some were men, but most were women. Also, within schools things often changed over time. Sometimes teachers left, money ran out, programmes finished, senior staff changed and either boosted or slashed particular programmes, government priorities changed and put pressure on schools to do other things or, as one teacher says, 'We all just got sick of it'.

Collectively, our schools were a rich mix. Across the range we had inner city, outer city, provincial, country and remote schools, rich and poor, traditional and progressive, monocultural and multicultural, hierarchical and democratic, academically and university oriented, technically and vocationally oriented, and the two in one. We had schools on the move and in decline, schools where the atmosphere was hostile and repressive, schools where apathy, boredom and defeat pervaded, schools with a strong sense of caring and shared commitment between staff and students and those with a relaxed friendly style.

As the following stories will show, even though some schools were more open to gender reform than others, there was invariably a gap between intentions and effects.

4

It doesn't happen all the time but it does happen

It was the middle of July, it was wet and muddy and they
wanted to play football. The first thing they wanted to do was
get out and push each other around and roll around in mud. That
was all they were interested in doing. [Sally, physical education
teacher]

Until recently, all physical education at Nerringo was coeducational, but last year the school began to offer single-sex electives. At
the first class meeting, Sally asked the girls what they would like
to do and they said 'football'.

They were rolling around the ground tackling each other and
laughing because it was so funny and they loved it. They'd never
had that kind of experience before. Girls who usually stand back
were right in there pushing each other around in the mud. They
weren't threatened, they knew they wouldn't get hurt by mistake,
that was very important. When the boys are there it's 'don't hit
me', 'don't touch me', 'don't get mud on me'.

By week four, the girls were confident and challenged the parallel
boys' class to a match.

Karen Marks who doesn't play any sport turned up with her
father's old 1940 boots and the big jumper. The ball was bounced
and she came charging through, grabbed the football under her
arm and ran straight ahead. Everyone stopped, stunned, 'Karen!'
We're dispelling myths. [Keith, physical education teacher]

Keith umpired a somewhat rigged game.

We had about 25 girls on the field. If a girl even looked like
getting two hands near the ball, even if they dropped it, it was
still a mark. But they loved that and the boys thought it was a
big laugh. [Sally]

But it wasn't simply a laugh. It was part of a much broader
agenda within the physical education department and the school
more generally.

As part of its Girls in Physical Activity Action Plan, the school
requires all students to participate in four periods of physical
education (physical education) each week and offers some single-
sex electives. The thinking that led to these decisions was
stimulated by the EO officer, Alan, who noted that sport had a
high profile within the local community, with most social life
centring on it. Over recent years, local girls have been champions
at netball and hockey and are heroes amongst the younger girls.

Nevertheless, there is a big drop in the number of girls choosing physical education once they reach puberty and many fewer girls than boys continue to play community sport. Alan provided reading material to members of the Physical Education Department, who were already concerned with what they observed in their classes.

If the class is dominated by the boys and the girls are not getting involved, their skills stay at a low level. And with the body changes occurring, the girls pretended not to have their uniform and didn't participate. The body changes don't seem such a big issue with the boys. They tend to prefer to show it all and the girls to hide it all. It's a Catch 22, because they need to participate to improve their body image, but they don't want to show it to start with. [Keith]

Based on the belief that all students should be supported to 'take up an active life role', the physical education units emphasise participation, skill development and improvement of body image. Teachers try to be 'gender inclusive' but don't find it easy: 'You usually pick sports that you're familiar with,' says Bob, 'but now, in the theory component, when I'm about to use football to display mechanics, I say, "No, no, I should use netball."' Also, 'we're taking the emphasis off competition. You can have games along the way and have winners and losers but everyone must be involved and be supported rather than put down.' The physical education programme tries to be explicit about its intentions to both girls and boys.

We look at influences on participation and the large dropout of women once they get to adolescence, and discuss corresponding fitness levels. We consider possible reasons and what could be done. And we try to help the boys understand why everybody needs an active life and to feel good about using their body. So while we're encouraging the girls we're also trying to help the boys see the need for justice to be done in terms of the media and the views that are held. [Bob, physical education teacher]

Sally explains that within the school there is a conscious effort to make girls' activity visible:

Our lunchtime practices are outside on the netball courts so that the boys see the girls training because you know the old thing that the girls sit around in the yard and do nothing but talk. Four out of five lunchtimes there will be girls out on the court training. We deliberately did that rather than having training inside where the others don't get to see it happening.

They also encourage the boys' involvement in what have traditionally been girls' sports. Indeed, according to Sally, now the boys 'love playing netball, they love it'. Girls will organise a team, not only of their girlfriends but also with boyfriends and other boys in their form. She comments:

> And of course the boys are still learning and the standard of the girls' netball is so high that the girls are going to be above their standard for quite some time. So they are not taking over . . . Also the boys have had to learn a whole new behaviour code . . . They find it difficult and frustrating because they can't just pick it up right off . . . They really look up to the girls too.

The school has also introduced shorts and slacks into the girls' regular uniform. Tanya, the previous EO Coordinator, suggests that many teachers and parents were supportive on the grounds 'that it's about warmth', but she felt it important that they understood that the real issue was one of girls feeling more comfortable about being active. She adds:

> It's a very traditional community here in terms of gender roles, so we've got to try to enlighten the community as well. There's not a lot of people who are aware of the issues and I suppose it's our responsibility to show them how it works. So I think you've got to push the changes you want but also try to raise the understanding levels at the same time.

Girls are generally supportive of the Girls in Physical Activity Programme and are appreciative of its purposes. Thalia, in Year 10, says:

> It's good in this school because the pressures of being a girl and the pressures from boys of being girls has reduced in a lot of ways. Things like not having to wear skirts to school gives you more opportunities to be active, like choosing to do things you wouldn't normally feel comfortable doing. The last few years some of my friends have gone to kick the football at lunchtime. It doesn't happen all the time but it does happen. It's just the confidence to do stuff.

It is not, however, all easy going. Consistent with the commitment to ensuring justice in the treatment of women's sport, the school makes an effort to get girls' team successes into the media, but this has resulted in complaints from some parents.

> We get irate parents coming 'my boy competed in this why wasn't it publicised?' Well we did give it recognition but they only see that suddenly all these girls' things are coming. We're

trying to make sure that we don't make a conscious effort *not* to recognise the boys' achievements. Any achievement is recognised, but we're making sure that the girls get equal recognition. [Keith]

There is also resentment amongst a number of boys at the attention given to the girls. Clifford, in Year 10, describes the sentiments of some of his friends that, because of 'equal opportunities' things have 'gone a little bit too far'.

> There's sports, the perfect example, because with the girls—like you've probably heard of the hockey team—they're the Victorian leaders. Well we won the cricket by miles and we weren't allowed to take it any further . . . They say to us that the cost is too much to send us away, but we feel it's just that girls are basically favoured in this school.

Whether their anger is justified or not, it has to be dealt with. This is the challenge Nerringo now faces.

Some chicks just take it too far

> Some years ago we invited an expert speaker to talk to the staff about girls' education. A few of the men got quite belligerent. At lunch two of them decided that they would go and get dressed in women's clothing and then proceeded to parade around the staffroom. Fortunately many of the male staff told them where to get off and they didn't get the reaction that they had hoped for. [Patsy, English teacher, Banksia]

In terms of gender reform, Banksia is a school of extremes. At one end of the spectrum are fierce opponents, largely from the Technical Faculty and Mathematics and Science Faculty. At the other end is a small, cross-faculty group of reformers and in the middle is a large group of 'swinging voters'. The gender politics of the school revolve around the struggle for the middle ground.

The impetus for gender reform comes from government policies and from several progressive and dedicated staff members but from one in particular, Joan, the school's officially appointed Equal Opportunities Coordinator and Chair of the EO Committee. Joan, a human dynamo with more energy and charisma than most, put gender issues 'up front' but with the support, behind the scenes, of several of the school's quiet reformers—mainly women. However, over time, the ranks of supporters have included more male teachers and parents whose support Joan has carefully engineered.

She has gained their support through the use of argument augmented by statistics, compromise, persistence, some bloody-mindedness and unfailing good humour. She has researched the gender composition of the school, showing how subject and career choices are strongly coded by gender. She has spoken powerfully, but 'non-threateningly', to staff, parents and kids about this, and about the need to change. She has drawn on a range of discourses with 'selling power'. For example, she pointed to the need for students, including girls, to study Maths so as to 'keep their options open' in times of high unemployment. She argued that if the school wished to attend to the dropping ratio of girls to boys (40:60 from 50:50) and restore its gender balance, it needed to attend more properly to the girls' needs. She has built up the EO Committee so it has representatives in all faculties—'infiltrators', one member jokingly calls them. She has planned several very successful careers days for girls. She arranges celebrations for International Women's Day. She has organised professional development sessions and turned around a few 'diehards from the hard core'. The speakers have adopted 'the gentle approach rather than bludgeoning people on the head'. Witness the following remark after a compulsory inservice course for the maths and science staff:

> I've really learnt a lot. I felt it was interesting and they spoke nicely and they introduced it and explained each thing. I've been to some of these conferences when the women are quite overbearing. But they asked, 'How are you changing your learning environment? How are you changing your approach to this subject?' And I was prepared to listen because of the questioning, 'hands on' approach. [Jeff, mathematics teacher]

Along with others, Joan points to the effects of timetabling, which blocks off alternative options for girls and boys, she has co-opted the librarians to mount displays and get in resources to assist students to explore gender issues. She is developing strategies to attend to the problems of sexual harassment. Joan works hard with others and, through Australian Studies courses in particular, is aiming to raise the students' awareness of gender issues in society.

Like many staff, however, she feels that encouraging students to be socially critical is an uphill battle. The school catchment contains a social range from wealthy to 'very poor students who have been through a lot of hardship', but many staff refer to the majority as WASPish members of the 'hire purchase set', materialistic and inward looking—preferring, for example, to spend money on their children's clothing than their education. This remark is typical:

> Our students have an attitude of, 'Oh what's all that about? Oh that's not important, it doesn't affect me,' or, 'It will be alright, not to worry.' That is very hard to fight against, it's very hard to raise their consciousness above that level. [Anita, social studies teacher]

Despite many attempts, it is not clear to Joan or the others how best to encourage this range of students—particularly the 'rogues', as Joan calls the school's rebels—to attend to gender issues in society. Nonetheless, it did not help when Australian Studies was dropped as a compulsory subject in the final years of schooling.

In a short space of time and with a difficult staff, Joan has made remarkable gains. She has come to symbolise EO in the school. Many of the women support her even if they do not say so publicly or always agree with her. As she says, 'The female teachers are well and truly behind me with one exception. I think they can see the inequalities in every classroom, they're not hard to convince.' Joan also feels that some of the antagonistic men are coming around.

> Maybe there would be ten to fifteen men who wouldn't do anything but the rest would lend a hand. I go around and badger them into it. I got a lot of the guys who I knew weren't supportive to supervise the ex-students' talks last year, and that brought a lot of them around. I put them in with the girls because the girls gave a little blurb about labour statistics. That opened their eyes.

Many girls are also fully behind Joan. The school's 'naughty girls', from whom we will hear more in Chapter 5, are fiercely loyal.

> Shannon: You know, like if someone is paying you out.
> Erin: Sexual harassment.
> Madeleine: You go to Mrs Ginsberg [Joan] and she just stuffs them right up.
> Erin: She'll sort them out.
> Shannon: If a guy in our History class says something to us that is sexist, she'll be putting the thumb right on him.
> Madeleine: If you say, 'they're harassing me', she gets out her little book nearly.
> Erin: That's good because someone is actually doing something about it. Most of the other teachers aren't as interested and they just sort of mumble.

Even in the trade workshops, things are changing. In the Automotive class in Year 10 there are three girls.

Sarah: It's good. Last year when I first did Auto they sort of said, 'Oh it's a girl, there's a girl in the class, there's a girl in the class!' But they think nothing of it any more.

Janine: It was a guys' profession, a guys' trade and a girl was doing it.

Did they give you a hard time?

Amanda: No, because they were told right from the start, any harassment of the girls and I'll fail you straight away.

Who said that?

Janine: The teacher, Mr Hickey. He's good.

Amanda: He's more impressed with our work than he is with the guys' work. Half the guys are only passing because of Sarah, Janine and myself.

Sarah: They get us to do it for them. [laughter]

The general outcome of Joan's and the committee's work is, as one woman says, 'Overall, a much greater awareness of girls' needs, the need for teachers to expose them to more things and to review our courses.' Another observes that 'the girls now have a bit of faith in the system as they see us following through on complaints of harassment.' And, Jan from Year 11 says:

There'll be people who'll be sexist but that's going to be anyway, you won't change these people's opinion, but everyone's equal, everyone feels equal and that's always been brought out at our school, not that the girls can't do this or that.

The predictable paradox is that the more visible and apparently successful Joan and the EO programmes become, the more gender becomes a touchy subject, the more those in the middle stand still on the matter to avoid a backlash, the more the opposition mounts and the more compromises are called for. As Joan says, 'I've made a lot happen but I've had a lot of flack.' As Joan moves into her third year, the opposition no longer takes the form of male teachers parodying the feminist cause 'in drag'. It comes from many corners of the school. For example, many of the humanities, arts and social science teachers are resentful of the maths/science push in EO and believe that they lose students and status as a result of it. However, the general target is the concept of justice embodied in the EO programme. Most opponents think the concept 'Equal Opportunity' means 'the same treatment'. As one student says 'equal for both sides'. Many argue that boys are now 'disadvantaged', 'missing out' and that 'girls are getting too much attention', EO is seen as 'sexist', 'discriminatory' and 'going overboard'. Boys and male staff, parents and girls and female teachers make these sorts of claims—not all, but enough to cause some noise. Witness the following regarding the careers days:

> The boys feel that they are being left out because we have never had a special day for them. They ask why do the girls have this special day and we don't have one? It wouldn't hurt to have some days for the boys and let them know that they can go into some of the girls' sort of jobs too. Give them some encouragement. [President, Parents and Friends group]

Some boys have become particularly hostile and suggest that Joan 'must be a lesbian' and that she 'should be shot'. As the outcry has grown, Joan has decided, in the first instance, to organise careers days for boys too.

'Equal Opportunity is alright but some chicks just take it too far,' says a Year 10 boy. Asked, 'Do you think women have equal rights now?' he replies, 'Not really, but they're too close to what they should have.'

Speaking out in a big loud voice

Karrawong has a truly multicultural profile. Over 70 per cent of students have non-English speaking backgrounds and about half do English as a Second Language (ESL) rather than English. There are large proportions of students with Indo-Chinese, Turkish and Arabic backgrounds and smaller but significant proportions of several other ethnic groups, including Spanish speaking. According to the Principal, Heather Bennett, many students are recent arrivals, often refugees and poor. Their parents generally 'place a high premium on education' but the families have often experienced considerable dislocation and the children intermittent schooling.

Asked what are the gender issues for the school, Paige, a curriculum coordinator, deflects the question, suggesting that the key equal opportunity issue is racial tension. However, she then talks about the interaction between race and gender:

> Consider equal access to time in classrooms or use of space. The gender issue is complicated and given more weight by the culture issue on top. I mentioned before about stereotyping but consider your Macedonian male as opposed to your Vietnamese female.

She continues, 'It is really more about nationalities than that people are different but I suppose that's making a broad statement isn't it because we are different individually too.' Linda, an ESL teacher, observes, rather sweepingly, that:

Because many of our students come from non-English speaking backgrounds, their parents have different cultural expectations for girls. For example, Vietnamese students whose parents value education highly still see a boy's education as being more important than a girl's and this is the girls who are telling me this.

A number of teachers are worried at what they see as the essentialist/racist tendencies in such remarks. Jana, the Language Centre Coordinator, argues that culture is not the only issue.

I think there's many more things in it than that. I think family upbringing is almost more important than culture, because you can get two or three kids from the same country, speaking the same language, presumably sharing a very similar culture but they've got very different outlooks on gender. So I don't think you can categorise it like that, and it's very noticeable sometimes.

Conceding this point, Linda suggests that placing a priority on the education of boys also applies to 'Australian' families. 'It's not just them, many Anglo Saxon background people feel the same way and some of the Australian-born students in the class still feel that their parents feel that way as well.' Heather agrees, suggesting that what appears to be lesser value placed on girls' education can often be explained by economic circumstances, poor English and the loss of a network of family or friends who can take care of children or ill relatives.

Traditional Australian families also expect their girls to do more of that sort of thing than their boys but the girls aren't as likely to have to stay home from school to do it when Mum has to go to the doctor or whatever. And here the boys also get kept home to translate at the Housing Commission or whatever. What I find is that happens less and less as the English skills rise in the community.

Nevertheless, students are regularly described by reference to their race and gender, 'your loud Malaysian boy', 'your shy Cambodian girl', 'Vietnamese boys don't harass', 'Muslim girls . . .', 'Spanish boys . . .'

A concern of many teachers is the 'extreme shyness' of many of the girls and their unwillingness to take part in anything that might appear immodest. Brian, a teacher of Year 10 single-sex classes in mathematics, comments:

> I think girls are more confident in single-sex groups. In the group that I have there are a number of very quiet girls and it is only because their English is poor. They are relatively new arrivals and have come into what we call pre-VCE [Victorian Certificate of Education, Year 12]. I would not get a word out of them in a mixed class. I think one of the differences in the approach is that you can afford to wait for a response in the girls' class, especially from those very quiet girls. You can afford to say, 'Look so-and-so would like to contribute, can we give her a break?' The boys are too impatient.

An interesting twist on this is that at the time of our visits there are two boy-only classes in Year 7 science because there are many fewer girls in the year level than boys and it is Ministry policy that schools try to ensure that girls are not in a small minority in classes. The boys' science teacher is now convinced that *they* are more confident and less afraid to say they don't understand when they won't lose face in front of the girls!

A number of teachers in the Language Centre think that, although poor English is a problem for both girls and boys, and means that both are often reluctant to speak out publicly in class, language competence does interact with gender because the boys are generally 'more outgoing'. The school has many new arrivals throughout the year and girls in particular 'will sit there absolutely silent' and not 'learn English or much of anything'. The school has just reorganised Year 10 classes to place all students who have been in Australia less than three or four years, both boys and girls, into the same classes. This is how Jana describes it:

> None of them are allowed to hide in the class. All of them are asked questions, they're all expected to respond and participate and they're all doing it and they're all quite enjoying it. Their language level is improving—it's just improved amazingly—just in five weeks. They're really coming on well and they're getting so much more confidence. I don't think they would have got it, if it had not been for this process.
>
> Now, they're actually speaking up in class and volunteering information and actually even disagreeing sometimes, which is amazing for girls who were sitting there, very quietly, unable to say anything. And [they are] holding to their opinions when someone has disagreed, which is a huge breakthrough.
>
> We were putting them into groups—and one of the girls turned around to Kerry and said, 'No!' Like it's a little

Vietnamese girl who usually wouldn't even have eye contact with you, and Paige was just so astounded and really thrilled to think that this girl has got so much courage in the last five weeks, that she was prepared to speak up. But she laughed immediately she said it, 'Wow, that was me.' [She was] speaking out in a big loud voice and saying that she wasn't happy with something—yeah that was really good.

Several physical education teachers commented that while participation in sport was an issue for girls generally, ethnicity did make a difference. Marlene said, 'It is a tough one to deal with,' and commented particularly that Muslim girls were too embarrassed to do sport. Aisha, the Multicultural Liaison Officer and herself a Muslim, laughingly offered a different take on the matter.

When I first came here they had all these excuses for the teacher. These were all excuses because they really didn't want to do it. Other girls—when they don't want to do it—pretend they have their period, some get it every week. They can't pull that one over a woman teacher but they can a man. These [Muslim] girls were pulling it over women and men teachers . . . Kids!

I said, 'No, all you have to do is cover your hair, put a scarf around there and wear something like a tracksuit. Then there is nothing wrong. You can now do any sport except perhaps swimming. You can do running, you can do all sorts of things.' Now they do it!

The physical education teachers set their Year 10 female students an essay topic on why they were not enthusiastic about participating in sport. According to Marlene, a number of Vietnamese girls said that boys didn't think it was attractive or that they felt themselves that it was not attractive to be active and strong, 'and some of them said that if you are too active, in a way it is like losing your purity. Girls aren't meant to be like that.' In order to provide a setting where the girls can engage in some 'rough and tumble' without embarrassment, the school arranges a girls' camp. The girls who go on the special camp, many of whom are new arrivals, clearly get immense pleasure from it.

Helena: We went to girls' camping—yeah, it was very nice and I liked.
Trei: Oh well, the camp was very, very good. I enjoyed it. Because the first day, when we came there we feel very happy. Yes and we play many, many game and climb on the mountain and climb on the hills. And play the big games, as we find . . . the things which was lost . . . Yeah, that is good game, I like it.

15

Rani: I enjoy for that camp. That is good camp we had here.
Trei: With my Mum and Dad, they happy for me to go
          without them, because when we went outside, we can
          understand more about outside and join more in
          English. Yes, they happy about that.
Rani: Mine too.
Trei: And we enjoy for myself. And with some idea from
          another people and they have some idea from another
          people, and that help us more better, you know, better
          for thinking. In that it can help us with the games and
          speaking and dancing or something like that.
Helena: Yeah, I still think about it. I hope for this year or next
          year, we can still go together and learn more about
          that, I love it.

A transcript is unable to convey the delight in the girls' voices. They are able, in the camp setting, to admit their difference and differences, to find what they have in common, and to struggle with a new life with other girls who are struggling similarly. Who could deny its value?

And yet deny its value some do. In particular, it has attracted considerable negativity from some males on the staff and some boys. 'Why are you doing this for girls but not for boys?' they ask. Heather's response is that, 'we are not doing it for girls we are doing it for girls who would never be allowed to go on a mixed camp. There is no way that the Muslim girls would be allowed to go on an excursion where there were to be boys and this is also true for many of the Greek and Indo-Chinese girls.' As Trei says, 'I think if we are go with boys sometimes people, they can't keep their self and they might with the boy and girls, they do something it's bad.' This doesn't appear to carry much weight with certain male members of the school and the displeasure is shown in a number of ways.

Sadly, when we visited the school the next year, it was to find that the camp had not been repeated. 'A combination of factors,' Merri Kerry the EO Coordinator said, 'including government cutbacks and industrial action' but mainly it wasn't worth the 'bad feeling' it generated amongst staff. Strangely, asked what she believes to be the main gender issue for the school, she says 'trying to get the girls to consider non-traditional career options and to consider non-traditional subjects including maths and science'.

It's different being a girl than a boy in this school

At sixteen, Georgie regards the small rural township of Draymill, and her parents, as old-fashioned and sexist. 'For a boy it doesn't matter if you stuff up. They say "boys will be boys" and it's almost expected. Whereas if a girl does anything wrong, suddenly it's big news.' The town is rife with gossip and 'once your name gets in there it sort of keeps going around and around,' says Angela, who would like to get right away. 'Not that I've done anything,' she laughs, 'but just in case I have and haven't heard.' David Styles, principal of Draymill Secondary College, describes it as 'very much a sporting community, which is a bit male dominated—certainly there's a separation of males and females.' Jessica, a student, agrees and believes the school reflects the town, 'It's different being a girl than a boy in this school. Well, in a small town it's different being a girl, so when you come to school it's the same. It's still very old-fashioned.'

Apparently it wasn't always so. David Styles was attracted to the school by its innovative reputation but, in the time he's been there, the school has become more conservative. 'I mean, all those radical teachers were up here doing strange things that local people couldn't really understand. Also, we had a large number of very experienced and quite innovative teachers—risk-takers—they leave for a whole variety of reasons.' Now, as Jessica and Georgie explain it, 'there are a lot of male teachers that have lived here for years and years and years, and they're the same as the town. Some of the females tend to be a bit younger than the males or have a younger point of view anyway.'

The community suffers from high unemployment and, recently, a bitter industrial dispute. Family breakdown is rife. Aware of the high incidence of domestic violence, sexual assault and incest, the school has appointed a full-time student welfare worker and developed a policy on procedures to be adopted when it becomes aware of abuse and on ways of helping such students. A number of key teachers and progressive parents supported the initiative through the School Council although, says David Styles, most parents are apathetic and, 'of course, some members of staff think it's a load of rubbish but they don't actively oppose it'.

Girls outnumber boys two to one at Draymill, as many boys attend the local technical school. Students suggest that this puts girls in the dominant position, but then proceed to describe how girls' movements are restricted by boundaries laid down by boys—with 'no go' areas for girls, how boys occupy more than their fair share of 'airspace' in the classroom, how teachers respond to the boys first, and how sexual harassment—although rarely named as such—is commonplace and a daily occurrence for some.

Georgie and Jessica, with two other girls, were in Year 8 when the harassment began.

> We were sexually harassed by three boys in our class for three years. A group of us were singled out for it. There were only those three boys in the class, most of the time. [Georgie]

Initially, it was relatively 'mild' and they put it down to the boys' immaturity but, by Year 10, the intimidation had escalated. Jessica recalls:

> It got really, really detailed and graphic and very distressing for all of us—I mean, some of the girls stopped coming to school and one even left school. It wasn't tiny little things and it was constant. Very personal things. Some of the things they said were absolutely *disgusting*. Made your stomach churn. They were very graphic. About what they could do, what we could do, what they wanted to do, and all. Right in the classroom. We were so scared. I mean it was already so bad and we were scared that if we went that one step further and told someone, they'd get worse.

Out of class, the girls were tripped and slammed into lockers although, as Georgie adds, 'it didn't happen as much outside the classroom because we kept our distance.' Unavoidable in the classroom, 'it was like walking on a tightrope.' Incredibly, she says:

> The teachers in our classroom didn't know about it. It was happening right under their noses and they did not know anything about it. We used to say some of the teachers had selective deafness.

After three years, the girls finally reported it to a teacher who, according to Georgie, reacted with disbelief, 'Oh, but surely not . . .' Furthermore:

> They did nothing. I was quite surprised that some of the female teachers didn't understand and weren't willing to help us. I thought it would have been the male teachers who didn't understand how we felt but it was actually a few of the female teachers that we approached who didn't understand and just weren't very supportive at all. In the end we wrote everything down because we couldn't say it, it was just too painful for us to actually come out and say it . . .

Georgie adds:

> We had one teacher that really helped us, and I was really quite
> surprised, 'cause he's a male. Originally we went to our
> Coordinator and then it went to the Vice Principal and then
> straight to the Principal, in a very short space of time. But then it
> went a long time without anything happening. You know, to get a
> reaction from them. And the same things were still happening.
> But it wasn't until parents—someone's parents came in and said,
> 'Look, we want something done about it now!' And legal action
> was threatened—and then the school took notice and said, 'OK,
> we'll do something about it.'

Their peers were unsympathetic. 'The boys took the boys' side
and most of the girls took the boys' side as well.' The four girls
had broken the rules of peer culture by 'dobbing in' the boys. The
principal held a meeting with all the girls in the class to find out
how widespread the harassment was. Many girls laughed and
said the whole matter was 'stupid' and not important, but 'they
knew it was happening. I felt they'd betrayed us.'

A teacher and counsellor then brought each of the boys in
individually and the four girls had to confront him with their
claims. They were required to repeat the verbal abuse to the boys
in front of other students and to explain why they thought it was
wrong. The girls were in tears as they recounted the 'terror' and
'humiliation' they felt during this. 'Then we had to walk into the
corridor and everyone was talking about us.' The boys' reaction
was to sit silently and smirk. Jessica said, 'I felt really violent, I
just wanted to thump him and get the smirk off his face'. 'I felt
like saying, "How dare you smile! How dare you!"' cried Georgie.
The boys were not required to respond but were warned.

The harassment continued with the boys becoming 'cleverer'
and 'more cagey' in producing smarter forms of harassment, such
as waiting until a teacher left the room and then subjecting the
girls to a barrage of comments. Eventually, Jessica experienced a
further blatant incident and told the Vice Principal, 'Look, I am
not going to take this.' With the threat of legal action by her
parent, the Principal called up the boys' parents. Ultimately two
of the boys were suspended for two days.

Many students, teachers and parents defended the three boys,
constructing them as victims of female paranoia and incapacity
to deal with normal student peer cultures in which 'boys will be
boys'. Thus sexual harassment was psychologised as the girls'
problem, an attitude exacerbated by the procedures adopted. A

psychologist was brought in to counsel the girls, but not the boys. It was as if 'there was something wrong with us'.

A year later, however, Jessica laughs, 'It's been a growing experience.' Georgie has learned 'that I don't have to take that sort of *shit* any more. I would never let it happen again.'

The paradox is that many boys attend the school because they believe they would get 'eaten alive' at nearby Braydon Tech. The boys at the school are described by the Student Welfare Coordinator as being 'milder and meeker'. They would be lost between the 'bad boys' and the 'high achievers' at the Tech but are protected in the environment of this school. As Angus says, 'You don't get hassled here, we sort of stick together.' The three boys involved in harassing Jessica and Georgie attend the school because, 'there are few other boys to pick on you' and the 'girls are friendly'. It is 'small', 'caring' and a 'community'. Indeed, they appreciate being in the minority because when other boys are there they 'run amok'. The girls encourage you to be a lot quieter, work better and, 'at the same time', says Robby, 'you can be yourself'.

Robby is now deeply ashamed of his behaviour. Recently he came to Jessica and Georgie and apologised. 'We forgave him and now talk to him,' they say.

I understand gender heaps well now

Teachers at Kingwood describe the school as very 'gender aware'. By this they mean that there is awareness of gender as an issue in education and general acceptance of the importance of gender-equitable practices. Given this, it is surprising how few are able to point to anything that the school is doing or has done relating to gender.

> I'm not aware really of any particular things that have been done—I just know that we've been made aware that these things have to be looked at. [Jessica, mathematics teacher]
>
> I suppose girls now do subjects that used to be exclusively for boys and vice versa. I don't really know that I can see anything else that's particularly visible or different from when I was at school myself which is some time ago. Not really, I honestly can't. [Carol, languages teacher]

A number of teachers show considerable sensitivity to matters of gender and education and the great majority express commitment to treating girls and boys equally. This apparent consensus, however, masks a wide disparity of views on what 'equality' means and on the school's responsibility to undertake gender reform. It must be said that a disconcertingly high proportion of teachers make a simple equation between achieving gender equity and providing 'equal opportunities' which in turn is equated with 'not discriminating'. All three are regarded as rather straightforward matters. Equitable practice involves removing overtly discriminatory barriers to participation and success by reforming timetables and opening up subject choices, using non-sexist texts and language, and becoming gender blind.

In Year 8, right from the beginning, it has been compulsory for boys and girls both to do home economics and industrial arts. [Steve, manual arts teacher]

Ten years ago I put the boys in blue and the girls in red in my marks book. These days I don't tend to do that. They are just a group of students. All have the same chance. [Tom, mathematics teacher]

There's been the guide to textbooks to check that everything is non-sexist and I think that's worthwhile. [Jessica, mathematics teacher]

We are now fairly aware of things like setting exams—so when asking a question we would normally use 'he', but now we try not to use that—we would use 'she/he'. Also, because of all this literature coming through, when a girl asks advice you try not to slip into the old habit of saying, 'That course is much easier, probably you might like it.' [Will, computing teacher]

Two teachers in the English Department, Ted and Beth, reject the idea that schools generally, and their school in particular, might be inequitable places.

I would like to think that . . . teachers, be they male or female, would give the same opportunity to any student. I can't pinpoint any teacher I know, if they found a student who was enthusiastic, of either sex, wouldn't give them support . . . If somebody's good, male or female, we'll encourage them . . . This perception that might be going around that we discriminate in favour of boys, it's barking up the wrong tree. [Ted]

I think we're all aware of gender as an issue and people are making an effort to ensure there's no blatant discrimination. In terms of any other discrimination which may occur, it is a value judgment and depends how far you want to go . . . I think it's just about time to stop talking about gender. [Beth]

And what of their responsibility for bringing about gender

reform? 'If the occasion arises we'll have the students pick up other students about sexist language,' says Beth, 'it's done in an informal way.' In something of a role reversal, Ted suggests that, 'some of the kids that I teach are very aware of what can be classed as sexist comments and keep me on my toes. They have caught me a number of times this year but the more they catch me the more I become aware of it.'

Stereotyping in the media is part of the lower school English curriculum, says Beth:

> We talk about stereotyping in advertising—male and female roles as portrayed through the advertisements—and look at the changing role of men and women in advertisements because of the changing role of men and women in society.

According to Ted, the teacher 'tends to take a devil's advocate role' in the ensuing discussions although, given his previous comment, it isn't clear what this might mean. Almost all of the Department's staff consider that any more would be inappropriate in the lower secondary years:

> You're more concerned with just developing basic concepts of characterisation. To take a gender approach is to ask a level of sophistication beyond the lower school. [Paul, English teacher]
> There are no gender issues in English really. We just jog along. Kids bring their attitudes from home. We have a lot of little male chauvinists here and also some little radical feminists. If they want to have a debate, they're quite welcome to but I wouldn't bring it up as a matter of course. English shouldn't be that kind of sexual political discussion. [Kerry, English teacher]

Jenni disagrees, to the surprise of the others. They appear not to have discussed this before. Jenni believes English should help students work through the gender issues in their own lives. 'Maybe society is not changing as quickly as we would like it to and we have to wait for it to catch up,' she says, but, 'when we have these discussions in class, what we're doing is planting the seeds.' She adds:

> It's a difficult area. Adults find it hard to come to terms with. One can talk about gender issues intellectually on a certain level, but then emotionally one comes to a stalemate. Exactly the same thing happens with kids, except their life experience is not as wide as ours. They can argue it to a point and then they hit that wall again. We find it a struggle to deal with our lives because we have to work things out not always in the ways we were brought up with. That's the role of the school; helping kids, not

necessarily to come to any conclusions now, but at least to be a little better prepared than we were.

Andrew Renault, Head of Department, agrees with Jenni. It was his particular wish that the school should choose 'Gender and Literature' from the three elective components in the externally examined Year 12 Literature course. The unit addresses gender in terms of critical theory which sees a piece of work as influenced by the culture in which that work has been written and is read. Students learn about dominant readings, says Andrew, and that 'any minority or less powerful group, women, homosexuals, etc., are marginalised and so we need to redress that imbalance' and one of the ways to do this is to 'take a gender reading'. He tries to relate it closely to students' own lives and help them see that 'it's not so much what we see—rather what we don't see'. Andrew believes that the unit is working very well but, he points out, this is 'the high end of the English courses and the bright kids gravitate towards it so you're getting a pretty select group of young men and women in the Lit. class'.

The thinking about gender and power presented in the Literature course appears not to have influenced the thinking or teaching of most of the English Department, although Ted suggests that he has 'found teaching the Lit. course quite useful because it's changed the way that I approach literary text and has translated itself into the way I approach my work'. Somewhat disarmingly, he offers an example, 'probably now I make more of an effort to use non-sexist language in the classroom'.

The major gender preoccupation of this school is subject choice. Gender issues are framed almost completely within an individualistic, liberal discourse and the language of access and choice predominates. Gender reform is seen to require the provision of role models, improved advice about subject and career choice, and encouragement for girls to broaden their horizons and take non-traditional pathways.

Teachers at Kingwood consider the school to be progressive and active in gender reform and to have gone 'far enough' or even 'too far', even though it has not been particularly successful even in these terms. In Year 9, for example, only five out of 120 students enrolled in manual arts are girls (all in Jewellery Making) and only two boys have enrolled in childcare courses although a significant number enrol in food and nutrition. The proportions of girls in physics, chemistry and the higher status mathematics courses have remained at under 30 per cent, with mathematics participation sometimes dropping alarmingly low. (One year, only four of 35 students in the highest status maths course were girls.) Ironically, equal numbers of boys and girls now enrol in Literature, the higher status English course. Nevertheless, while some teachers do not agree, the broad consensus of opinion is that the school is successful because girls and boys are now equally free to make their choices. Gender differences, they suggest, simply reflect the cumulative result of individual differences.

> I think our school here is doing quite a good job in giving an open choice. [Lili, French teacher]
>
> I believe that if they want to go into these careers, the options are open. Whatever career they want to choose, if they make up their minds that they want it then they can pursue that career. The trouble is, I feel that girls don't always want to. [Franco, mthematics teacher]
>
> I'm not sure why it is there are fewer girls than boys. I don't think it's a case of girls not coming into the course because of any gender issue. I think it's just a case of their own personal situation. [Alana, Transition Studies Coordinator]
>
> I still regard it more in the area of an individual difference. I've always tended to see all these equity problems from the individual differences standpoint. [David, Principal]

Some of their students, however, have learned different lessons from feminism and do not agree. An insightful discussion about the quite different pressures acting on girls and boys to influence their subject choice, was summed up by sixteen-year-old Daniel:

> I don't think we should be considering personalities or how individual people are able to cope with the pressures applied to them. We should be looking at the pressures applied to them.

And how did he, and his peers, come to this understanding? They attributed it, in considerable part, to their English teacher, Andrew. According to Saul:

> The course is alright but it really depends on how the teacher wants to take it. Mr Renault's really into it. He used to talk a lot about it. So we developed attitudes from what he said—pointing out certain things about gender and power.

And Rebecca says:

> Because of my English teacher, I understand gender heaps well now.

Getting rid of some of the distractions

> Single-sex was in vogue. It did seem like quite a credible
> experiment. People could see the problems with silly girls making
> out with silly boys. [Bruce, Head of Social Studies Department]

Single-sex classes were the flavour of the month in Western
Australia in 1993 after the Minister for Education attended a
breakfast at which Dale Spender spoke. The Minister immediately
announced to the press an 'initiative' to provide girls with boy-
free learning spaces in maths and science. Many schools became
involved, some drawing from the spirit of the government's
intentions and others forming single-sex classes for reasons of
their own, but nonetheless under the umbrella of gender reform.
We visited Blackstone during this period and it is to its story we
now turn.

Blackstone's single-sex experiment has little to do with conventional understandings of gender reform. As Bruce says:

> It's addressing social justice issues, in a way, because we're really
> after quality output from as many students as we can target.
> We've got problems with self-esteem, usually we're looking at
> boys in that group, to be honest. Not because the girls don't need
> self-esteem, but usually the boys' self-esteem is bordering on
> criminality and so that's the real problem.

The strategy of single-sex social studies classes for Year 10 is
devised mainly as a means of combatting behaviour problems
associated with the school's 'difficult customers' where 'as high
as 10 per cent of the boys have police records' and are on
probation. A secondary motivation is the problems associated
with 'a large number of girls who are very, very highly motivated'
and 'a bunch of girls who are significantly underachieving and
have been reporting troubles with boys and with other girls'.
More specifically, Ken—inexperienced, young, and with a subordinate masculine style—is having difficulty managing the 'problem' boys who are 'running riot' in his classes and making it
impossible for him to teach. The classes are rearranged so that
Ken ends up with a small class of 22 consisting of the 'tamer'
boys. Shirley has a class of 36 girls and Geoff has a class of 26
consisting mostly of 'tough' boys. According to Bruce, everyone
is happy.

> He's [speaking of Geoff] got rid of some of the distractions. This
> has just reduced the number of reasons the boys have to play up.

Not that they need many reasons The teachers are humming along, yes, I'm getting the feedback from the teachers, they're all very happy with it.

Geoff is particularly happy being with the group of tough boys. 'It's very relaxed in here,' he says:

> Prevents ulcers. Far more relaxed, incredibly relaxed, in the classroom. Rule number one—look after yourself, bugger the kids. [Laughter] There's no behavioural problems whatsoever. The academic performances haven't improved at all but their efforts are fine.

Having an all-boys class means that neither he nor the boys feel the pressure to perform in front of girls and women.

> I think it's well known that boys of all ages, even cranky old fools, tend to perform in front of females. Yeah, they perform. But, when I'm there, I'm relaxed and I'm also one of the boys. You know, if you had an inexperienced man or an effeminate man or a bloke who's too academically inclined or something like that, then that might not work. You might end up with a them and me situation.

Geoff enjoys being 'one of the boys' and clearly the boys also now enjoy Geoff and the 'boys own' atmosphere of his classes. They also make some other rather astute observations. Danny, in Geoff's class, argues that this strategy makes the teachers happier. He implies that it is actually the teachers, and not the boys or girls, who benefit most because, 'Then they can concentrate more on teaching than separating the boys from the girls.' And further, says Danny:

> He's getting somewhere with the kids . . . and he likes having a joke around with them. 'Cause when the kids are arguing, like the boys argue with the girls and all that, then he tells us off. That means we don't like him 'cause he tells us off. And he doesn't like us because we backchat him for telling us off and all that. A big chain reaction. But then, when it's just the boys, you know, that's no hassle.

Danny and his mate Lindsay also implicitly show how successful this strategy has been in encouraging a macho culture to become the accepted norm in Geoff's class:

> Danny: If a Year 12 was walking past our room, a nice looking one, he could say, 'Ooh, she's pretty good, eh? Quite good looking.' But, if there were girls in there, he wouldn't.

26

Lindsay: He just makes fun of them. He goes, 'All the girls in the world, you won't be out of work.'

Danny: Without girls in the class I can swear more.

Lindsay: If we had a female teacher and a nice woman walked past, like we couldn't say, 'Ooh, look at her' like that. 'Cause if we did she'd look at us and say, 'That's sexism' and all this. But with Mr Blaney, he'd just laugh and say, 'I'd buy that for a dollar'.

Geoff and the boys enjoy the freedom to be sexist. It has become a bond between teacher and students.

Unfortunately for Ken, he is the sort of 'inexperienced man', the 'effeminate man', the 'bloke who's too academically inclined', whom Geoff believes is unable to generate the sort of male bonding required for such classroom camaraderie. Yet, in his class of 'tame' boys, even Ken seems to feel that he is 'one of the guys'. As he says, 'As I was talking to guys, I could use a lot more of the language that perhaps they would be using, perhaps some of the slang that they'd be used to using.' So, in the first instance, Ken is happy too.

The only one who is not happy is Shirley. Her class is too big, she is unable to teach properly, she is getting bad migraines. So, the solution to what has come to be seen as 'Shirley's problems' is to reallocate six girls to Ken's class. Now Shirley says. 'Well, for me it is great [laughter]. Even within myself I am feeling very comfortable with it . . . I am just enjoying it now.' Shirley is certainly enjoying teaching the girls' class. She stresses the cooperative nature of the classroom and how the atmosphere allows them all to be more open, honest and sharing with each other. They talk a lot more but she believes this enhances the work ethic and progress of the class. She has been more adventurous in her teaching strategies as she knows they will be listened to and not 'rubbished' which was her experience in mixed classes. And, as Bruce said, 'Shirley hasn't been ill since.'

In Ken's class the story is confusing. Ken and the transferred girls are no longer impressed. Ken believes that he coped really well with managing the tame boys' behaviour until the girls came in:

When I first had the boys, they were really good, they were working really well, we had really good discussions and everything . . . All the guys just really seemed to enjoy just being in that classroom by themselves actually . . . They were joking towards me before and they knew I'd have a bit of a joke with them about things, and it was good. Then, when the girls came in, I thought a lot of the students, particularly the boys, just started misbehaving a great deal more.

27

In Ken's view, mixed gender is the source of the problems.

> Now we just have to change the whole approach . . . I mean, I
> wouldn't have minded another five or six boys in the class, but
> having five or six girls meant that the whole classroom has
> tended to slip.

Ken feels that, since the girls have come in, the boys have:

> . . . all slipped back to their levels, and yeah, it's a bit
> disappointing . . . they just don't hand up assignments and they
> don't come to class. And when they do they're not interested or
> in the mood to do anything.

However, from the point of view of the bemused boys in Ken's
class, the opposite is true. 'No, the first couple of days, he couldn't
keep anyone under control, then once the girls came in, it got a
bit easier for him.' They are all very clear that they try a lot harder
academically with girls in the class. They feel that had the class
remained single-sex then their marks would have fallen as they
would have just 'mucked around' all the time. Now the girls are
there they have settled down more, are working harder. Here is
how they expressed this view:

> Charlie: I suppose you try a little bit harder, put a little more
> effort into what you're doing.
> Patrick: Yeah, you don't joke around so much. Like, with all
> boys, you just joke around. With girls in there, it helps
> you work a bit harder I guess.
> Rodney: Yeah, they settle you down a bit, they're a bit more
> mature than some other people.

Ken has been replaced by Alison in Term 3 and it is her belief
that the girls who were added to Ken's class have been disadvantaged by the process. Alison has noticed with alarm that she is
hardly aware of the four remaining girls:

> I'm not really sure whether it's because they're girls or because of
> the type of girls they are. My time seems to be taken up more
> with the boys than it is with the girls. Just last week, one of the
> girls came up to me and said, 'Look, I won't be in your class for
> two weeks because I'll be on work experience.' I honestly didn't
> realise that she was in my class. I think they're definitely
> disadvantaged.

And what of the girls' academic achievement which has taken
something of a backseat to the problem of the boys' behaviour?
Interestingly, it is Bruce's belief that some of the girls were

actually being disadvantaged in the all-girls class. These girls he classifies as the 'cute, favoured, teacher's pet types' who get noticed in a mixed-sex class, because they are more cooperative, more helpful, but who get ignored in an all-girls' class.

> There is a lot of non-verbal interaction in the classroom and a lot of the good girls get that. They get the attention, the ticks, the teacher smiles. If they're trapped in a big all-girl class, perhaps they might miss that because they're no longer contrasted. Also, some very low-achieving girls will always be above the base in a co-ed class because there's always some boys who get less marks, maybe because they don't hand their work in. I wouldn't want to trap them in an all girls' class, because they would probably always be down the bottom.

Given that Bruce holds this view, it is difficult to see why he was prepared to sacrifice these particular girls. While Bruce had some concern about how Shirley would manage such large numbers, there was no similar concern about how the girls might fare in either the big class or as a significant minority in the 'tame' boys' class. It was left to the girls to raise these concerns. As Shirley notes of the girls' class of 36, 'One student said to me, "How are we supposed to get more attention and help when there's so many of us in here?"' It is difficult to avoid the conclusion that Bruce was less concerned about the girls than the boys and the teachers. So the fact that the girls who remained in the all-girl class felt that they benefited significantly from this experiment in terms of both being more vocal and interactive in the class and also being able to work better without disruptions from the boys is something of a surprise bonus.

In terms of gender relations and gender reform, this is a story rich with ironies and ambiguities. The boys who caused the original problem are rewarded with a class which allows them to continue to behave in an offensive manner with regard to girls— except this time behind their backs and with the teacher's encouragement. Nonetheless, from the teachers' point of view, the boys' behaviour problems have been addressed and thus the experiment can be judged successful. (At what cost is apparently not at issue.) And certainly there appears to be little concern about the sexist atmosphere encouraged in the boys' class, let alone about the flow-on effects of that elsewhere. Ken's adoption of Geoff's mateship model with his class is filled with ironies, not the least being the fact that he felt it appropriate in a class of 'tame' boys not generally considered behaviour problems. The boys disparaged his attempts at mateship and were rather pleased to have the girls back with them as they helped them get on with their work. Because Ken had convinced himself that it was working, he felt able to blame the girls who came into the class for spoiling what he had built up with the boys. Interestingly, the girls who he saw as sufficiently powerful to disrupt the class were the same girls that Alison was barely aware of in class. Another irony is that the females remaining in the girls-only class, who were not a prime consideration in this exercise, consider the experiment to have been a big success for them.

Gender reform seeks to rearrange schools' gender patterns and ultimately to make gender irrelevant to the patterns of life in schools. And, because it tries to unsettle the settled, it takes many schools by surprise. It messes with institutional and community traditions and cultures and individual psyches. It wants to rearrange things—and people. It is thus not necessarily welcome, and its criticisms, ideas and imperatives are often ignored, wilfully misinterpreted or vehemently resisted. However, more usually—as we have shown—they are reinterpreted, revised and rewritten. When gender reform becomes part of the rich and messy mix of the everyday life of schools, it represents only one of many often competing sets of interests—some more powerful than others, of course. It not only works against different forces for school-as-usual, it is one of many competing forces for change. Work for gender reform always operates in tandem and tension with whatever else is going on in classrooms and staffrooms, playgrounds and sports fields, libraries and lavatories, corridors and canteens, topics and texts. As a result, it constantly gets challenged and changed, selectively appropriated and applied. Hence many schools take gender reformers by surprise, and not always pleasantly. Equally, the results of some of their gender reform efforts take schools by surprise, also not always pleasantly. The process of change in schools is always non-linear and messy. Schools do things to proposals for change that may seem puzzling unless understood in the context of the politics of the institution and of the field of education more generally. Gender reform is no different in this sense, except to the extent that its proposals for change often touch raw nerves at the institutional, group and individual levels. Let us now consider the different meanings of success which gender reform has mobilised and the passage of such meanings through schools and systems.

2

Success

Tan is Vietnamese. She and her family arrived in Australia as refugees three years ago. Now she attends Bettleford High. Sharon Roberts, Maths Coordinator at her school, visits the Year 9 single-sex maths class to talk about careers and maths and the changing position of women in work. She and their teacher, Colin Masters, see this as broadening the perspective of ethnic minority girls who come from backgrounds 'which position women as unequal to men and restrict them to more traditional roles'. When Sharon arrives for the second talk, most girls seem pleased. Tan, however, continues to work on maths. Colin quietly asks her to stop and listen but she keeps working, head down. He does not make an issue of it because she is usually so good. For the third talk, a fortnight later, the class is asked to shift to another room to watch a video. Tan's earlier passive resistance becomes overt anger. She gets up, throws her chair against the wall and stalks out of the room muttering, 'All this girls' study is a waste of time.' This is remarkable and distressing to her teachers since it is the first time they have ever seen her express aggression. It is seen to be 'culturally inappropriate' and differs from the usual attentiveness and diligence of Indo-Chinese girls—'good' students who sit passively and uncritically absorb.

Tan is happy with the school and likes all the teachers; they are very helpful and 'explain things carefully until you understand', but she doesn't like Ms Roberts' visits.

> I want to learn maths. I need the time. But sometimes she comes in and talks about girls and I don't like it. She could do it in

32

health or history. I wouldn't like her to come into maths or science or English as they are very important for my future. She just comes to talk about girls.

Having not listened to Ms Roberts, it is not surprising that Tan has misheard.

She said that men have to do the hard work and women can't. But no! She is wrong! Women can do anything men can do. Women don't have to have babies or stay home and look after the baby. Men have got to go out and work for money, women can too.

She does believe that Ms Roberts has her best interests at heart and 'wants girls to get a good job' but Tan doesn't need to be told this. 'My father and mother wants me to go to university. No different for my brother or me. They think it depends on how they go in their studies.' Indeed, Tan is torn between her parents' wishes for her future and her own.

I want a part time job and save my money to travel to Hong Kong to see my boyfriend who is an actor and singer. I wish . . . My dream when I finish high school is to send to another country—England or Canada—to learn English better. I want to be myself, to be free. I would have to save, my parents could not afford it. I like pop music.

Brightening up, Tan starts to smile and laugh.

If I can I would be a singer or an actress. If I can't I would be a hairdresser. My favourite subjects are drama and drawing. You know why I like drama—because I can have fun. I learn about how other people think. I really like acting. After I leave school I would like to go on with what I want. Drama. To take a drama course. It is my secret but I told Mr Miller. He says this Drama School will not have classes for nothing. So I am scared because my parents could not afford.

Mr Miller tells us that Tan takes on a new life when she is in his Drama class. She is the centre of attention and hardly recognisable as the self-effacing person who goes to other classes. She is also very talented. Nevertheless, as we have seen, Tan is anxious to do well in mathematics and science.

I only do maths and science if I have to. I need maths because my father and mother wants me to go to university. I do it in case I'm not an actress. I'm not very good at maths—just half and half. I need to study hard.

The meaning of success has always confounded teachers, parents, schools, education systems and society. What is it? Does its meaning change over time, in different places, amongst different groupings? Does it have lots of different meanings and if so which meanings matter most? Who says so, what values inform their judgments, and why should teachers and students believe them? Whose meanings become institutionalised, why and how can this be changed? Is success necessarily a zero/sum game? Must success for some involve failure for others? Do some groups always succeed? If so, why? And would they if the definition of success or the ways in which we assess it were changed? Every day of their working lives, teachers and students live with the ways in which the powers that be have answered these questions. Whether they like the answers or not, oppose them or not, their lives are heavily influenced by them. Many teachers grapple with these questions and try to come up with different answers. Yet, as we will show, the systems within which they work make doing so extraordinarily difficult. Simon Marginson (1993) points out that education performs many often conflicting roles in society. These include the custody, care and academic development of students, the preparation of a democratic citizenry, the construction of a more productive economy, and social selection. All these roles have implications for the ways in which educational success is understood. But, as we will also show in this chapter, together academic development and social selection overshadow other roles and absorb within their ambit other definitions of success which contest their supremacy. Gender contests do not escape their co-optive power.

Teachers are inscribed within educational, economic, cultural and social systems which define success at school largely according to academic performance. Within that narrow band of understanding, such systems value and reward certain types of performance in certain subjects more than they do others. When success is associated with academic performance, high marks are often not enough. 'Real' academic success depends on the status of the subjects that are taken. The high status subjects are the 'hard' sciences, physics and chemistry, and the higher levels of mathematics, including calculus—subjects which are regarded as prerequisites for entry into tertiary education for training relating to high-status careers, like medicine, engineering and some sciences. Educational success plugs into other sets of values too, so the mental is valued more than the manual, the mathematical, scientific and technological more than the artistic, historical, literary or sociological, the physical more than the emotional, public knowledge over private knowledge, high culture over mass culture, and the list goes on. Success is defined accordingly.

The socially powerful put their full weight behind such definitions of success and ensure that credit, and later material, status and power rewards, are accrued and distributed accordingly. Across time, there are regular winners and losers. The constants are a complicated and ugly blend of social class, race, gender, ethnicity and 'disability'. Teachers and students live with the problems created by this educational zero/sum game. They see its inhuman face, they deal with its inhuman consequences. Many, particularly those who teach the likely 'losers', strive to develop other ways of understanding success for students, other sets of values, other systems of rewards. Predictably, this isn't easy. Seldom do such alternatives become anything more than alternative. Hence teachers invariably walk a tightrope between encouraging students to succeed in conventional terms and encouraging them to succeed differently—always with the knowledge that difference seldom wins out over dominance. Success is a minefield not easily negotiated.

In the 1970s, gender reformers entered the success minefield and since then they have been trying to find a way through it. They took different routes—all difficult, some particularly tortured, some dead ends. Most gender reformers accepted dominant versions of success, observed that more males than females succeeded in these terms and thus had access to more rewards. They argued that girls could do equally well if gendered barriers were removed and if they were given the right encouragement and environment. This resulted in an intense push to encourage girls to change their choices and to participate in high-status subjects dominated numerically and in other ways by boys. The dominant driving ethic was equal opportunity and access.

Another and more difficult route through the success minefield taken by other gender reformers was to reject dominant versions of success and to offer alternatives which were more in tune with girls' and women's educational and other experiences. Those who took this direction sought to remake the meaning of success, to value the under-valued, to recognise, celebrate and reward what girls did well at—the 'feminine'. They wanted girls to feel good rather than be good; indeed, successful girls were not necessarily good girls, rather they were girls who developed a strong sense of self and who recognised that 'girls' things' were worthwhile. Boys were to change their view of what was worthwhile too. Given the stranglehold on definitions of success gained

35

by the 'masculine', this was a big ask. But it led to the concept of the gender-inclusive curriculum.

The idea of success became more subtle here and more difficult to sell. In all fields the school curriculum was seen to be written largely by, for and about males, to inscribe within it their learning styles and to work in their interests. For girls to succeed, they had to learn knowledge which implicitly oppressed them. Such success came to be seen as a double-edged sword. Paradoxically, for girls, to succeed was to fail. In contrast, the gender-inclusive curriculum required all teachers, including those in subjects dominated numerically by girls, to rewrite the curriculum in ways which gave all students access to gender balanced knowledge— women in history, art and music, for example. This conceptual turn led those involved in the mathematics and science fields to place curriculum and assessment under closer scrutiny and to rewrite them in more gender-inclusive ways. In turn, this led them to revisit the idea of girls' success in these fields relative to boys'. Some surprising and rather embarrassing things emerged. Such lines of argument pointed to the fact that, even when girls did succeed in such subjects, it often went unnoticed or was understood as a lesser form of success than that achieved by boys (Walkerdine 1989; Willis 1989). This understanding had significant strategic implications, because in some ways it raised doubts about the earlier claims that girls were failing at such subjects.

However, despite these rather drastic shifts in the discourse associated with encouraging girls to take 'non-traditional' pathways and despite the doubts, it was the changing choices, curriculum-as-usual route, rather than the changing curriculum route, which achieved the greatest profile and gained greatest acceptance amongst teachers, parents and policy-makers. Already, towards the late 1980s, there were signs that gender reformers may have made some strategic errors.

For some gender reformers, gender-inclusive notions of success weren't enough and the gender and success storylines dispersed in several directions. Some argued that success meant learning the skills as well as the knowledge which allowed girls to be agents in their own destinies—they had to learn the process skills which allowed them to be critical or deconstructionist readers of knowledge, to effect change rather than to accept the status quo, to be active citizens in their own and other girls' and women's interests. Successful girls were those who could negotiate the curriculum, the culture, their lives. Anything less was a failure for gender reform.

Some 'heretics' also argued that success should be redefined for boys and that reworking masculinity and its power relationship to femininity was also important. The aim here with regard to both girls and boys was gender education—educating students about gender and its implications, educating them for change. The successful gender reform programmes were those which assisted students to recognise, challenge and change injustices based on gender. 'Successful' students, then, were those prepared to remake themselves and their world.

Others argued that the gender and success story needed to be broken down yet further. They claimed that some girls were always more successful than others according to all the above criteria and that even the gender reform story was biased in favour of certain girls, namely middle class, Anglo—the normalised 'normal girl', against whom all others were judged unsuccessful, even by feminists. Calls went out for gender reformers to be more democratic and inclusive and to work towards the success of all girls. Difference became the catchcry and success came to be understood in multiple ways, all contingent. As we write, this is the way in which success is understood—by the purists, at least. However, complexity, contradiction and contingency are difficult ideas to sell and to buy, to use as rallying cries, to convert into policy and practice. Currently gender reformers in academic and certain policy circles are trying to work through these difficulties by using post-structuralist theories about the construction of gender in schooling's multiple discourses and in individuals' multiple identities. Again, this is a big ask. And it has to be said that success has eluded the difference discourse within gender reform circles as well as within wider educational circles. Nonetheless, its moral imperative is that all approaches to success should be sensitive to difference. But as our leading story of Tan and other stories to follow show, many are not.

Meanwhile, in the mid-1990s, gender reformers' naive early notions of educational success and the strategic errors made in relation to them have come back to haunt them in the form of a discourse about the under-achieving boy. We are currently seeing a curious reversal of the gender politics of the 1970s. Boys are currently being constructed as the ones with the educational problems, the ones suffering injustice. Regularly calls are made in the press and in government circles for schools to restore the balance, to offer boys equal opportunities for success. Things have come full circle, it seems.

In our research schools, constructions of success both within the gender reform programmes and more generally are multiple and often contradictory. They are influenced by local social, cultural and geographic contexts and the ways in which they operate within the wider constraints of the educational system, its academic expectations and its available resources. There are inevitably tensions between teachers and between teachers and students about what counts as success. Ideals and dreams constantly clash with everyday pragmatics. In the stories which follow, we take up some of these different constructions and the contradictions within and between them.

Broaden your horizons

Possibly the most pervasive and persuasive gender reform story of the past decade or so has been that girls and young women should 'multiply their choices' (by succeeding in male-dominated school subject areas), 'broaden their horizons' (by, for example, overcoming stereotyping in planning for paid work) and 'reach for the sky' (through, for example, improved confidence or self-esteem). Within this narrative, a major sub-plot has been the one about mathematics.

While the 'facts' of girls' achievement and participation in mathematics vary with time and the narrator (Willis 1989), the gendered pattern of participation and achievement in mathematics has been presented in a series of national and state education reports as a major and direct cause of gendered patterns of participation in further education and employment. Mathematics is imbued with an almost mystical power to make and remake futures.

In 1991, a major television, radio and print media campaign, *Maths Multiplies your Choices*—perhaps the most expensive single educational intervention strategy ever mounted in Australia—was funded by the Department of Industry in Victoria. The advertisements, timed to appear as students were making their Year 11 and 12 subject choices, exhorted parents not to 'pigeonhole your daughter' and told girls that 80 per cent of all jobs require mathematics so they would have 400 per cent more choices if they took mathematics. Schools were provided with kits of materials— posters, stickers, talks, class activities—with which to back up the campaign message. Later that year, in Western Australia, the television advertisements were screened for a few days, although there was no radio or print advertising and a considerably more modest package of posters and brochures were available for schools which requested them.

Gender reforming teachers in many of our schools took up the message with some enthusiasm. The programmes they initiated typically involved advice to girls on subject choice and careers and activities designed to encourage girls to take up mathematics-related options, perhaps visiting role models or girls-only maths problem solving workshops or role plays and games involving envisioning futures. A considerable number of schools also offered girls elective single-sex classes in mathematics at some stage during the compulsory secondary years; indeed, almost one-third of the schools we visit have offered some single-sex classes in mathematics at some time or other in the past five years and a few offer them consistently.

If you want to be different then you're out of it

And how do students interpret the efforts to encourage girls into mathematics? A number of girls, particularly in those of our schools which define themselves as 'more academic' with a high proportion of tertiary bound students, are rather dismissive of the media campaign. We interviewed students at Kennetton, Banksia and Kingwood. 'It was stupid,' said one, 'it must have been meant for parents.' They don't need to be told that mathematics is important, they tell us, 'most of us realise we want to do maths because it's going to help us,' and anyway, 'Everyone knows you need it for your score [for admission to tertiary education].' The producers of the advertisement, they think, must have been thinking of the past.

> It was a bit silly. It was sort of interesting because it showed that the government was kind of concerned about it, but I think it was directed more at times before when parents said, 'I don't want you to do maths, it's a boy's subject', and that sort of stuff. But now it's changed. Maybe there still are some older parents who, I don't know, expect girls to do girlie things, maybe people do still think that way. I don't think there is any harm in the ads. [Year 10 girl, Kennetton]

Such girls, while accepting the good intentions of the campaign, say they felt belittled, 'I didn't really think that I couldn't do maths until they brought it to my attention,' and offended by the suggestion that *they* are ill-informed, that they don't know what is good for them and, worse, that girls but not boys need to be told.

It's just kind of assumed that guys will make the right choice, that they know what they want to do and they'll make the right choice. But girls are sort of waylaid, they're wandering off the track and they've got to be pushed back on to the right line. [Year 10 girl, Banksia]

This is particularly irksome to those girls who consider that they have made more sensible choices than boys who are inhibited by their need to do mathematics because it is expected of them. One fifteen-year-old girl from Kingwood tells us how sorry she feels for the boys because 'they have no choice—it's a macho thing. Teachers, parents and other boys expect them to do it.' This may reflect a rather naive understanding of the different constraints acting upon boys' and girls' choices and of the unequal and gendered effect of those choices, but surely no more naive than the campaign itself which both homogenised girls and their families and placed the responsibility for change with the individual choices that girls and young women make. Indeed, the campaign in its entirety offered little to such young women that might take forward their understanding of how they come to make the choices they make or what they might do about any associated issues.

As it turned out, many other students were far from sanguine about their choices. A girl in Year 10 at Kennetton, who decided to do two mathematics courses in Year 11 rather than the one she had planned, becomes agitated when asked why. 'If you don't know what you want to do it leaves your options open, we were told. I don't know how, that's just what we were told. Not to get pigeonholed.' And indeed, in the television advertisement, the 'before' scenes have girls curled up in pigeonholes—colourless, confined and almost catatonic. According to the advertisements, without mathematics you'll be stuck there. Many girls and boys alike feel anxious and intimidated by this 'new' knowledge.

I wanted to do maths for my TEE [Tertiary Entrance Examination] but because I didn't have the background it wasn't recommended I do it. So when I saw the ads I nearly had a heart attack. [Year 11 girl, Kingwood]

I wasn't sure what I was capable of doing, I was really worried. I was just thinking about it for a whole week, thinking what should I do—which one. And I ended up doing all of them, not all of them, I picked two. It was only going to be one and I ended up doing two, because I wasn't too sure. [Year 11 boy, Banksia]

Others reject it, knowing that mathematics won't open any doors for them.

It didn't influence me. It doesn't multiply your choices if you can't do maths. Considering I only get an average of a D in maths, I don't think it's going to multiply my choices. [Year 11 girl, Kingwood]

Some, such as Kelly in Year 10 at Kennetton, answer back, 'It probably turns you off more than on. I'm not going to do maths and science—stuff these people.'

It has to be said, however, that quite a lot of girls comply and so too do quite a lot of boys! In Victoria, in the period immediately following the media campaign, a number of our schools experienced huge increases in enrolments in mathematics in Year 11. Indeed, enrolments in other subject areas fell dramatically. At Kennetton, we were told, 'our figure for Year 11 economics next year is only two, whereas this year it's a class of twenty.' At Banksia, 'When these figures came back, there were very few humanities subjects, very few commerce subjects, very few physical education subjects that could even go ahead. The students *en masse* chose mathematics—also science but particularly mathematics—which of course created problems with staffing in the school.' Kennetton and Banksia each undertook an almost panic-stricken 're-counselling' of students, telling them they didn't need so much mathematics and science. Many students, with parental support, insisted on and persisted with their choices. They heard the message loud and clear. A successful gender reform programme? Perhaps.

We discerned amongst many young women in our research schools a deep resentment at the push to change their choices which is directed less at the message than at its means of delivery.

I didn't want to do maths at all. They say, 'You should give it a try. You can always change. I'm sure you can do it. Do it.' Eventually I was talked into doing just Foundations, not because I wanted to do it, but just because I wanted to get her off my back. I just couldn't handle it any more, them saying, 'You're cutting out all your choices if you don't do it.' They say that they're advising you—but I think that they force you. They make you feel really bad if you don't do what's expected of you. [Year 11 girl, Kingwood]

It was as though they were saying even if you don't want to

41

do it, do it to prove yourself, like prove a point by doing this. Just because we're a girl. Show that we *can* make it. That's what they're trying to say, we can make it. But if you don't want to do it . . . [Year 10 girl, Kennetton]

One girl captured the irony nicely:

And so what they're saying is if you don't want to [do maths] then you're virtually out of it. Before we were told not to do it, now we're told we have to do it and if you want to be different then you're out of it. Like back then if you did do it you were strange, but now if you don't do it you're strange. [Year 10 girl, Banksia]

These girls consider that they are being told that they are in the wrong for the choices they wish to make and that they are being used simply to make a point—someone else's point—and they do not appreciate it. On the one hand, they are positioned as passive recipients of this feminist rationality; on the other hand, they are positioned as possessed of the complete free will to 'make their choices'. For such girls, the voice of feminism, even in its most 'liberal' form, is authoritarian and insensitive even when—perhaps *especially* when—they feel compelled to comply with its message.

In the vignette with which we began this chapter, Tan's choices can be seen as a victory for the (liberal) feminist message that mathematics is powerful. But it surely is a hollow victory; for Tan, this is not an emancipatory message. Neither Tan nor, it seems, any of the five other Indo-Chinese girls in her class needed to be told that 'maths multiplies your choices'. They and their families knew this long ago. And, contrary to what their teachers know about ethnic minority girls, these girls expect to be in paid work for most of their adult lives and know that their parents expect them and want them to 'broaden their horizons' and 'reach for the sky.' This is not to suggest that Tan's teachers at Bettleford were uncaring or even insensitive to matters of culture and circumstance, but rather that the dominant discourse that gender equity is about moving females into male-dominated fields leaves no space for attending to differences between girls. Institutions position certain cultures centrally and others marginally and gender reform programmes tend to do the same. Let us illustrate this point by visiting another school.

Everyone was giving you support and urging you to try for what you want

Mt Mullin is a small mining-industry based town, geographically isolated with a harsh climate. There are substantial communities of Aboriginal people, Muslims from the Cocos Islands and Yugoslavs. The 'town is characterised by high pay, low status jobs with high turnover' and education is generally not valued highly. Alcoholism and drug abuse are serious problems. Over 40 per cent of the unemployed people in town are Aboriginal, amongst whom illiteracy levels are high. Mt Mullin is, we are told, 'a man's territory so for girls there are some parameters that are very clearly set by the social structure of the town'. Strong gender role distinctions are described as a feature of all the major cultural groups within the town, albeit presenting themselves in different forms. There are 39 different ethnic groups represented in the 850 students in the school. Many of the almost one-quarter of students who are Aboriginal come from tiny remote communities and experience severe culture shock in their transition to town and secondary school; truancy is high. Across the whole school, retention to Year 12 is approximately 50 per cent of girls and 30 per cent of boys.

Anita, a literacy support teacher, and Zoe, the Deputy Principal, plan two activities for girls. The first 'event' involves 270 girls and some 80 women, including teachers, support and ancillary staff and visitors, in a short, one-hour 'talkfest' at which a number of women from the local community come and tell their stories. The second is a two-hour breakfast with a similar agenda. Anita describes her and Zoe's thinking:

> In Mt Mullin there is often a problem that many people, like teachers, who come in from outside, act as if Mt Mullin is the pits and everything here is worthless and to get something of value you have to go away. Whereas I actually think that every community has heaps of valuable things in it. So what I thought would be a good idea was to look at the women, the local women, and help the girls develop gender esteem through women they could relate to. We wanted to help build rapport for women across and within the local communities.

The speakers included an Aboriginal woman who talked bluntly but humorously of institutionalised racism and about what it is like to move between two worlds; in one world she sees her place as a woman as clearly defined and highly valued and in the other world she finds her place as a woman much more ambiguous and as a black woman much less valued. In her forties she returned to secondary school and has just become a teacher. Also speaking were: an Aboriginal girl doing a trade through BHP; an Anglo woman who has disabling arthritis but eventually completed a diploma in horticulture and now owns her own nursery and has taken on an apprentice; a 'Filipino bride' who is on the Community Advisory Council; a woman who fosters many children; a Yugoslavian woman who set up a carpet-laying business and only employs women; and an ex-student who is at university. Kate, the school psychologist, describes how the two functions made her feel:

> Women told their life stories and because it was local and it was community, it was really wonderful. I felt really proud because I don't think that one of them had come from the top down. Maybe a couple had but the stories that stay with you are the ones about women who had persevered. They were all so good humoured and funny and hopeful. They were just grand stories and I suppose you could hook into them.

And the girls shared her enthusiasm. On the feedback sheets an amazing 83 per cent of the girls said the programme was great or good and their comments were overwhelmingly of the following kinds:

> After listening I had faith in myself.
> I know that if I fail I am not useless, I should just try again.
> I found it comforting that you can achieve an education at any age, that there are no boundaries.
> I really admired the women. It made me feel even I have a future.
> I enjoyed hearing that girls can do boys' stuff too and better.
> Debbie's speech gave me a positive feeling about my future.
> Everyone was giving you support and urging you to try for what you really want.

The women's stories are stories of hope and the girls' responses are also hopeful. As Kate describes it, the girls know that it is worth 'hanging-in there'.

Enthused by the success of these two events, the following year, the District Office organised a Girls in Education Conference for Mt Mullin. According to Anita:

> Their philosophy was a bit different to Zoe's and mine because they felt the girls needed to see that there was more than Mt Mullin. That there was bigger and better things out there. So they

flew up women from Perth who were more, sort of, impressive. They were all great but—I'm not sure . . .

The women visitors were almost exclusively Anglo and, whatever their origins, they were now well-groomed, middle-class city women. They clearly made considerable effort to prepare talks and workshops to enthuse the girls and the girls appreciated it, but their message was the more conventional message of 'broadening post-school options'. They were largely chosen to represent 'non-traditional' careers and they promoted maths, science and technology. Their anticipated audience was girls like they once were or now knew.

The feedback was reasonably positive from the Year 12 students, but much more muted from other girls. Many enjoyed the day but found they were over-awed by the visitors, the distance between the speakers and girls was too great, the speakers couldn't quite connect to the girls' worlds and the girls couldn't really relate to the message. The problem with the conference, Anita thinks, is that it failed to recognise differences between girls, except possibly as a problem to be overcome:

> It isn't helpful to, in effect, tell Muslim girls that the only hope for them is if they leave behind their families. They need to hear Muslim women and other women who have similar values to their own, who accept some restrictions on their options, but who find that there are other things that they can and want to break through and move on.

No one believes that any of these events alone will change futures, but the first two more modest occasions appear to have considerably more potential to tap into the girls' lives, fears and dreams. They resonate with the girls' local communities while challenging the view that they have to be restrictive. For Anita, the aim is to help the girls see that, 'even though they are working within certain parameters, opportunities are there if they want to pursue them'. They are being encouraged to broaden their horizons and reach for the sky, but it is *their* horizons and *their* sky—in many cases reasonably harsh, to be sure, but nevertheless where they are. That different girls will experience different constraints upon their options and that each girl will experience them differently is understood without demeaning who they are.

It seems to us that a sense of agency in girls is the real strength of many of the programmes which seek to broaden girls' post-school options, but the knowledge they need is the kind which will help them to understand how their choices come to be the way they are and to articulate the constraints—material and social, real and perceived—on their choices. It is the kind of encouragement that will enable them to understand that, while actions are socially constrained, they are not socially determined, and to develop strategies for changing the things they want to, and can, change. This is clearly a rather large agenda but, in the absence of such education, exhortations to 'broaden your horizons' and 'reach for the sky' are dishonest and often even cruel. The following story may seem modest even mundane, but it represents precisely what we mean.

The girls who had never lit a match

When new Ministry of Education curriculum frameworks came out, science teachers at Edgecliffe seized the opportunity to reorganise and plan the Junior School Science curriculum. Their first effort included a 'whiz bang' unit in Year 7 to develop observation skills and teachers were amazed to find there were girls in their classes who had never lit a match and couldn't light the bunsen burner. Staff discussion developed about differences between boys and girls in science classes. They applied for a small external grant to purchase equipment including Lego and various tools and Don developed a tinkering unit which involved working with and manipulating things that many girls hadn't used in the past—for example, using a soldering iron when taking apart a video recorder. At first, Don found that the boys 'just raced in and grabbed. They had a quick look at it and said, "Oh this is baby stuff" and gave it to the girls.' Rather than simply instructing the boys to get on with their work, Don says:

> I stop the class and point these sort of things out and say, 'Do you realise that this is happening and why is this happening?' so there's a lot of values stuff in it. Just looking at the way we interact with each other. I suppose it's a lot more than a science class.

Don finds it hard to tell whether the unit is successful in terms of immediate spin-offs:

> My gut feeling is that it's a valuable exercise and the majority of kids enjoy doing it and they also enjoy the discussions that go with it about gender and things sexist . . . One of the activities I did with them, I gave them a tool box and, without any explanation, said write down the names of all these things, now

put down next to them whether you think they are male or female tools. Then we had quite an interesting discussion about that. And we talked about things around the house, whether they were male or female and just the role that kids believe that people have, it's just I suppose opening their eyes as much as anything.

The girls enjoy the tinkering unit and talking about sexist things. They also describe the boys who say girls shouldn't be fixing things—that they would 'break a nail'. But, they say, girls can be sexist too, like having a go at boys doing cooking and sewing.

The tinkering class is seen as part of a longer term strategy to redress the imbalance of girls in physics. But success for students is defined more broadly than participation and achievement in physics: it also includes enabling them to understand and possibly break down gender boundaries. This school does not simply exhort girls to change their choices; rather, it seeks to enhance the skills both girls and boys require for progress in science and, at the same time, offer them opportunities to analyse the reasons why there are differences in the kinds of skills boys and girls bring with them to school. The course links students' skill development to the way gender is traditionally constructed through the use of tools, and asks students to question why it is so. The goal is to assist students to understand how they come to have the skills they have and make the choices they do. It is a success story on success within the non-traditional storyline.

Boys are the new disadvantaged

'Strutting and fretting' at the centre of the gender reform stage in the mid-1990s is the 'under-achieving boy'. Statistics on girls' and boys' academic achievements in their final year of schooling in certain prestigious subjects are being widely aired in the press to show that girls are out-performing boys. This story gained considerable coverage in the press in Australia, Britain, the United States and some parts of Europe in the mid-1990s; it also played a dominant role in our research schools from the late 1980s to the present. It has come to dominate government policy on gender reform and also holds considerable sway in the popular consciousness in many Western countries. The boys' story has become gender reform's biggest dilemma.

Once all the complexities are taken into account, however, the evidence about the 'under-achieving boy' is not as clear cut as it would seem. This point is well demonstrated in the insightful and revealing study by Teese et al. (1995) which concludes that, across Australia—despite girls' increasing participation and continuing achievement—certain boys still top the high-status subjects and stay on top in post-school life as a result.

The study also flies in the face of another widely held assumption, that girls overall are gaining more success through their schooling than boys, indicating that boys rely less on school because they have stronger vocational educational pathways outside it. It concludes that girls' patterns of subject success and choice offer them less tertiary study and career payoff than those of the elite boys because they are less coherent, less vocational and less mutually supporting, *but* that these actually prepare girls better for 'life' more broadly. Teese et al. also argue (1995, p. 108) that:

> Boys, too, are disadvantaged. Their school careers, on the whole, seem to be less successful, to terminate earlier, to be characterised by failure at an earlier point in time, and to be more frequently accompanied by motivational and behavioural problems.

However, they then make the significant point that the gender gap narrows the higher up the socio-economic scale one goes, and the differences 'become sharper the more socially disadvantaged their parents'. They conclude by arguing that 'the real question is not whether girls as a group or boys as a group are more disadvantaged but which girls and which boys' (p. 109).

What about all the poor boys?

Despite this and other widely and carefully researched studies, the perception that girls are out-performing boys remains and the debate continues to rage. We will not enter the debate here because frankly we think its questions are ill-informed and that educationally it is unhelpful. What we are concerned with is the general perception about the truth of girls' success, the ways in which this perception has been mobilised and its effects.

It is fascinating in itself that girls' alleged success has not been greeted with acclaim. It has not been welcomed by schools and systems as an educational achievement or even as a welcome sign that things are evening out between girls and boys—if indeed they are. Liz, who teaches English at Wattlehill, comments that more girls are now receiving awards at the Year 12 graduation ceremony, and continues:

> This year it was overwhelming, to the extent that the audience was muttering and mumbling and some teachers said things like, 'Oh they think girls are having a hard time. What about all the poor boys?'

There is a definite air of apology about. A zero/sum mentality has led many to argue that if girls are succeeding, then boys must be failing. As Liz remarks, boys' apparent failure is immediately and unquestioningly assumed: 'If girls are doing well, boys must be being hard done by.' Then, boys' 'failure' is converted into boys' disadvantage, and this is then converted into an equity issue which schools and governments must address. And so this has occurred, in one way or another, at the national level and in several states of Australia (e.g. O'Doherty Report 1994).

The case about the under-achieving boy has a number of features worth noting. First, it seems to have come out of the blue. Although comparative figures about changing patterns of partic-ipation and performance have been around for some time and are by no means as stark as they have been portrayed (Teese et al. 1995, pp. 1–19), suddenly there is consternation, suddenly there is the smell of scandal. Suddenly the girls are said to be beating the boys at the most prestigious end of the educational success spectrum. Suddenly gender is an issue in education after years in the doldrums, suddenly there are gender wars in the classroom. As we will go on to demonstrate, there is nothing sudden about many of the concerns expressed about boys' education.

Another feature of the discourse is the way in which it gath-ered momentum. It is clear that the core issue is that girls appear to be out-performing boys in those high-status knowledge domains which high-status males generally like to keep to them-selves. For some this is shocking. However, it is not a matter that is likely to shock many. So suddenly, as if to bolster the case, statistics on boys' and girls' comparative performance in *other* areas are being widely aired. Whereas once it never mattered much to boys, and to men generally, that girls succeeded at things they despised, suddenly it matters that boys are not as successful as girls in the less prestigious subjects. Then further figures are mobilised to reveal that schools are punishing boys more than girls and helping them less through welfare and counselling support. We also learn that, in the rest of their lives, boys have more problems than girls—they commit more crimes, have more road accidents, are more likely to suicide. Further, they do not have the social and emotional skills that girls have. And, as a function of single-parent families, absent fathers and largely female teachers, they have no role models, so they are not even in the position to help themselves. The general process at work here is the mobilisation of a 'competing victims' discourse (Cox 1995) and boys are constructed as the new disadvantaged, much worse off than girls—failing at school, failing at life.

A remarkable feature of the debate is that it is couched in terms reminiscent of the gender reform discourse of the 1970s. It is naive and simplistic and consequently unlikely to be helpful to boys. Few, if any, of the issues about success so painstakingly explored by gender reformers over the intervening decades have been addressed. The notion of success is seldom made problematic or challenged, even though dominant notions of success and their accompanying knowledge hierarchies seriously disadvantage significant numbers of boys, encouraging them to over-enrol in mathematics and science and hence to under-perform. This striking absence leads to another, which is the issue of difference. Boys generally are constructed as failing. Which boys and why these particular boys is not asked, at least not in the popular version of this discourse. So the problems of specific groups of boys cannot be adequately aired.

Another moment of recycling has occurred when solutions to the problems of the failing boys are offered. Role models, single-sex classes, non-traditional subjects are all suggested, and these are the very same strategies invented by leading gender reformers in the 1970s and early 1980s and subsequently recognised as inadequate. Alternatively, suggestions are made for a return to the good old days prior to the supposed feminisation of the curriculum. A striking difference from the 1970s is that, by and large, a blame-the-victim model has not been mobilised. Rather, blame has been sheeted home to programmes for girls. So much has been done for girls that boys have been overlooked, neglected. Too much has been done for girls, thus giving them an unfair advantage.

The central 'truth' of the debate is not true and the ideological forces driving the debate are not new. But, if it were true, would it matter in terms of girls' post-school success and life chances? How readily can girls convert education success into 'success' in tertiary education and the workplace? If the past is anything to go by, educational success for girls does not necessarily translate into workplace success (Kenway and Willis 1996). This is partly because many workplaces are heavily coded by traditional gender conventions and partly because of the relationships between family work and paid work. Grades are only the start, not the end of the story. Does girls' alleged or actual success at school still mean their failure after school and does boys' actual or alleged failure still mean their success? This is a rhetorical question because it is undeniable that males continue to be more powerful than females in broad structural terms and this makes the idea that the boys' issue is an equity issue rather laughable. Clearly educational equity issues are involved, but for particular groups of boys—Aboriginal, working class, 'under class', homeless, rural and so on—not all boys. To say it is not a general equity issue is not to deny that boys have problems, nor is it to deny that there are educational issues involved. Of course there are. But what are they and how is boys' gender pertinent? These are key questions and we will seek to shed some light on this throughout this book.

Let us now go back into our data and see what it shows about the construction of the discourse about the under-achieving boy. We will explore three themes in the current discourse on boys: first, the idea that (suddenly) boys are under-achieving second, the idea that the girls are getting too many programmes and that boys are thus being neglected; and, third, the conclusion that, as a result, more must be done for the boys.

Successful failure, unsuccessful success

According to the criteria of academic performance, schools always fail some of their students and invariably this cohort of 'failures' includes girls and boys—although their patterns of failure differ (Teese et al. 1995). Our schools are no different in this respect and none, at any point during our research, gave any indication that there has been a dramatic change in boys' performance relative to girls. Certainly, many teachers compare boys' and girls' performances: some suggest that girls are out-performing boys; others, roughly equal in number, say the reverse; yet others say that overall, things are probably about the same. However, boys' low achievement is usually regarded in our schools as more of a problem than that of girls because, on the whole, girls fail quietly, while boys' failure is more noisy and noticeable. As Lynn, from Riverside, comments, it is often accompanied by visible and disruptive behaviour:

51

Girls don't tend to act out their problems in the same loud, violent way as the boys. So the girls are left at the back of the classroom while the boys are directed into special programmes. For lots of teachers, it's a battle for survival and the loss of a quiet, well-mannered, almost obsequious in her manner toward you, girl makes space for another loud, bumptious, non-achieving boy who is likely to treat the teacher like last night's garbage.

In our schools, the poor achievement of some boys was most often talked about in these terms. In contrast, boys' success was naturalised and went unremarked and girls' success—at least in the elite subjects—was seen as exceptional and thus remarkable. It was also often seen less as a function of ability and more as a function of diligence. Quite frequently, in discussion, teachers juxtaposed the academically successful girls against the academically unsuccessful boys. Notably the reverse never happens; failing girls are never compared to succeeding boys. But the point to be made here is that comparisons are being made between chalk and cheese. High-achieving girls are not usually compared with high-achieving boys and, strangely, neither are low-achieving girls compared with their male counterparts. Further, girls outperforming boys at the same level is not usually seen as a problem unless boys behave badly as a consequence—and they usually only do this when girls' achievements are associated with a gender reform intervention. Otherwise, boys 'take it on the chin'. Witness the remarks of these boys from Neerbin who, like many boys, imply that they are less attached to school than girls and that this affects their success:

Julian: Girls, I reckon have more fun. Generally boys don't enjoy being at school—they just can't wait to get out. Like girls come to school and they socialise a bit more.
Wayne: They do, generally in this school. Do you reckon they get better grades?
Matt: Yeah. They kind of dominate everything.
Julian: Yeah, I would say they do.
Matt: In the classroom and in other things like grades, behaviour and all that.

The Year 11 girls at Wattlehill make similar points about girls' and boys' comparative attachment to school:

Tracey: In more cases, girls have got more motivation to be at school. Boys can't be bothered.
Jody: The boys don't have to work. Most boys don't have to work at their grades. It's a week before exams when

they start studying. Us girls start studying like four weeks before thinking, 'Oh my god, oh my god, we gonna fail,' and we panic.

This, they suggest, reflects differences in boys' and girls' views of the relationship between success in school and success in work.

Tracey: They think they're just gonna get a job anyway. See the girls, we've got to pull our grades up to get a job because it's all equal rights. The females are trying to take over, not take over, but join the men in the workforce. So we've got to get our grades up to get in there.

Jody: Actually get in there and be part of the workforce.

Do you think your grades have to be higher than the boys to get in there?

Jody: No, but we have to work at it to get there.

Tracey: Yeah, I don't think you have to be higher, I think you just need to be equal. But we are always thinking that if I don't do good on this I can't get into what I really want to do. With most guys they just think, 'Oh yeah, I'll just find a job somewhere and that will do.'

Jody: There are a few guys around who are into study. They get quite a few top marks in most of their classes. Dedicated to their studies and that. But most of them got this attitude that, well I'm a guy and I'm meant to sort of not get stuck into the books and I'm meant to play it cool and all that.

Tracey: They don't mind if they fail, they don't mind if they get lower grades.

Jody: I think girls worry more about getting a particular job. They set their goals for particular jobs. With guys they just think, 'Oh, I want to get that job but if I can't get into it I'll just get whatever comes along.' Most girls are determined, I want to do that, so I'm getting my grades up to actually do that.

Tracey: I reckon most guys don't get bothered getting a particular job, just as long as they get one.

These girls' comments imply that they are more focused, dedicated and anxious about post-school possibilities than boys. This can be read as meaning that boys are disadvantaged because they lack motivation, but it can also be read to imply, as the literature would suggest, that girls have more of an investment in schooling because their options in training and core labour market employment outside it are fewer (Kenway and Willis 1996).

For most teachers the interpretation of success usually has an academic flavour, particularly in their subject area. In relative terms, the vocational pathways that more boys than girls tend to take are not generally well regarded by teachers and boys' success is defined accordingly. They hope that students will take the 'most academic' subjects that they are capable of and that they don't 'drop out'. Thus, at Edgecliffe—described by teachers as a competitive school which is successful by conventional criteria—a major concern is what to do with the students who are disaffected by the academic push for success—most of whom are boys. Peter, an English and history teacher, says:

> The expectations are for success and by far the majority of kids here want to go to a tertiary institution because that's the avenue to success . . . there's a fairly strong emphasis on it, but there are a lot of kids here who have no interest in that sort of thing and even though the VCE was set up to address those kids' issues . . . we're going to have to build an alternative programme basically . . . just to deal with problems of discipline . . . there's a great preponderance of males in a group like that.

Peter also recognises that there is a large middle group, mostly female, who seek invisibility as a defence against the competition. Jan, a past EO Coordinator at Bridgeforth, comments:

> We have the boys in a non-achieving mode and we have girls in the passive quiet mode who do their work most of the time quietly. They are achieving probably more than the boys but there is a whole dimension to their education which I think is not being addressed—the personal confidence to be able to say what you want. We are rewarding them for being nice, quiet and cooperative. Well I think that we need to challenge that a bit more. As for boys, their academic under-achievement is very strong at this school because they are involved in disruptive power game behaviour. We have a lot of programmes to address that in terms of personal development but it is also a very hard culture to defeat.

Nonetheless, no alternative is proposed for the nice, quiet, cooperative, undemanding girls.

While all our schools seem locked into the cruel logic of academic winners and losers, they also try to offer other avenues through which success can be defined and achieved. Sport is one such avenue, especially for boys. There is a well-documented and strong connection between sporting cultures and dominant and dominating forms of masculinity. At many of our schools, particularly in rural areas, the successful students—in the eyes of the other students, at least—are the high-achieving, sporty students. However, in nearly all schools, girls' sport is less highly regarded than that of boys and constantly marginalised. Both boys and girls play competitive sport in and outside of school, but boys' dominance of the playing areas and equipment at school denies many girls the opportunity of practising their skills. Attempts by girls to join in are usually rebuffed. The Mt Mullin boy summed it up when he said, 'girls should stick to netball and let the boys have the basketball court'. As our tale of Nerringo in Chapter 1 and many of our stories show, gender reformers are eager for girls' and boys' sports to share equal status. But, when they do, this becomes quite a sensitive matter among the boys.

For some students, sport is the only avenue offering any opportunities for conventional success at and after school. This is particularly so in schools in country towns with high levels of unemployment. In such schools, teachers promoting success in terms of academic excellence find themselves at odds with the students' perceptions about what is worthy. The Rullinga boy who misses school to go shopping during the week because he plays football on Saturday expresses this eloquently. Success in schools like these is a particularly complex notion, the dominant culture of the students often cuts across the teachers' perceptions, leading to multiple readings which vary for different groups of people within the school. As the following remark by the Principal at rural Neerbin indicates, the difficulties of reaching any adequate compromise are profound, particularly when matters of race, rurality, gender and generation come together.

> Boys opt out in the primary area. They have lots of days off school, they'd rather be out kicking footies. Schools seem to cater better for the Nyoongah [Aboriginal] girls—they seem to be more stable and mature than boys. Boys want to do what their dads do—kangaroo shooting . . . For Nyoongah kids, if their marks are reasonable and they have had a go, I'd say they were successful. There's not an academically capable Nyoongah boy in the school, unfortunately. For the other students, I look for success in their work, participation in the school, polite, well-mannered, attend school. That's success for me. If they're good at sport, we encourage it as well. In District High Schools, to be academically successful is not cool—across the board, boys and girls. It is improving, perhaps with more emphasis on presentation of work, rewarding students academically and making it more of an issue than being good at sport. But we must keep a balance, because

sometimes sport is the only thing the Nyoongah students are good at.

While it is not at all the case that sport is the only thing that Nyoongah students are good at, it is often the case that what they *are* good at is not considered worthwhile by schools.

Success through the students' eyes is shot through with as many contradictions as success through the eyes of teachers. 'Squares', 'swots', 'nerds' are amongst the terms used to derogate the hard-working male and female students, particularly those who prefer books and computers to sport and social life. Such terms were commonplace in nearly all the schools we visited. In many senses the use of such terms can be understood as a defensive strategy employed by the least successful against the most successful and used as a way of reclaiming positivity in a climate which defines them as failures. Nonetheless, students willing to aim for academic success are presented with the dilemma that sacrificing their social life to do well academically often results in harassment.

Getting good grades is especially problematic in schools like Rullinga, a rural school where life revolves around the skate-boarding 'skegs' and the 'footy-heads'. And, as one boy observes, 'Girls are more tolerant of their squares than boys are of boy squares. They let them do their work.' The strength of this male-dominated culture is evident by reference to girls who participate as 'skeg girls' or 'footy girls'. In this school, the high achievers are mainly girls, many of whom live out of town and who are regarded as strong and independent. Most look to university as a passport out of 'this gossipy town' which holds little chance of employment for them. Marjory, the EO Coordinator, notes that some girls 'are very, very academic and they do very well but then again, I think there is a hidden problem that, when they do, they're worried about not being socially or physically acceptable.' In contrast, but with notable exceptions, boys are described as academically very poor, often 'gross underachievers'. This is con-sidered by some teachers to be entrenched, but with no obvious reasons for it. Other teachers attribute it to the high unemploy-ment in the area, and the consequent lack of motivation. Accord-ing to Sandra, the Year 9 Coordinator:

> The boys who tend to be problems in the classroom, if you look at their achievement levels, are just so far down they can barely write. I wonder what has happened to those kids to make them

so bad because I have never seen such devastatingly low standards from girls.

The issue of academic success has many contradictions, some of which are manifest in the post-compulsory years. Although not wanting to draw attention to themselves as high achievers, many students try to avoid being labelled as low achievers by enrolling in higher status subjects. Thus many—predominantly boys—enrol themselves in physics and chemistry with little chance of success. In contrast, a lack of confidence or ambition—or both—are perceived by many teachers to prevent girls from enrolling in physics and chemistry when they *are* able to cope with them. Gender policies and programmes which define able students' choices as acceptable when they are based on physical science and high-level mathematics, and less acceptable when they are not, serve to privilege success in male and academic terms and to devalue success in other areas. Overwhelmingly, this works against girls, who recognise that their futures beyond school are not likely to be the same as those of boys. Less obviously, it also works against 'less able' boys, who inappropriately choose subjects which are not likely to match the kinds of post-school options which will be available to them. These ambiguities were rarely addressed in the schools involved in this study.

Resource-rich girls, resource-poor boys?

Let us return to the arguments about the under-achieving boy and consider the ways in which they articulate with those about the 'over-supply' of girls' programmes. It must be said that some schools did not mobilise the discourse that boys were under-achieving at any point during our research. Amongst these respondents were teachers who did not believe that boys were under-achieving and were comfortable with the development of programmes for girls; teachers who did not believe that boys were under-achieving but still felt that too much was being done for the girls; and teachers who believed that boys were under-achieving but did not connect it to what girls were getting. There is no uniform picture. Kingwood provides us with an example of the second group.

At Kingwood, a number of staff argue quite explicitly that gender reforms in schools have 'gone too far' and are now unfair to boys.

At some stage we have to sit down and say exactly where is the balance. Are we pushing girls to the detriment of guys? [Matt, Vocational Education Coordinator]

I just feel there's too much being done for them [girls]—when the ones who will be disadvantaged in the end will probably be the boys—well I sort of feel that's what some of the boys could envisage. You know all these girls being pushed along—there's no pushing on our side, so it's a little bit unfair. [Franco, mathematics teacher]

I think it's a bit of an over-kill, particularly at this school. [Beth, English teacher]

Yet no one at Kingwood, least of all the boys themselves, suggests that boys are the new disadvantaged or that boys' education suffers as a result of the attention given to girls. Boys are regarded as the high fliers in this school.

Most boys would be fairly happy with their education. All I'm saying is that there is a big push to promote the girls' side, and there hasn't been the balance on the boys' side. [Franco, Mathematics teacher]

There haven't been any requests to broaden the boys' range of options, not really. The background antagonism among the males in the school, in particular, is a reaction to the push to have girls treated in a different way, given a little bit more resourcing. [Matt, Vocational Education Coordinator]

Deidre, the Deputy, considers that the school has more 'bright girls' who under-achieve at the upper school level than boys who under-achieve. She convinced the school to set up an intervention programme for high-ability under-achieving girls. Matt, who developed the programme, broadened it to include both boys and girls and focuses it on the post-compulsory years. He comments that, 'Deidre's idea was that I would automatically include gender as a consideration but I felt quite strongly about not doing so. The way I saw it was not just helping the girls along but assisting students who are capable but are under-achieving.' The programme had run for two years at the time of our visits and, said Matt, 'there are more boys than girls who under-achieve according to the parameters we set—kids who have reasonably high IQs but are getting two or three grade levels below what we anticipate they should get.' That the parameters themselves might be gendered is not contemplated; to do so would undermine the very basis of the ideology which permeates the school—that equality is about girls being treated as equal to boys, like boys. With unconscious irony, Irena, the Guidance Officer, sums up the programme: 'If there weren't boys in the programme, it would be an intent to redress issues for girls.'

Apart from the above programme, the total of all gender equity initiatives at Kingswood during the five years preceding our visits was as follows:

- A two-year trial of single-sex mathematics classes undertaken as part of one teacher's study requirements.

- A gender equity committee set up to provide advice to teachers of the single-sex mathematics classes and to advise high-achieving girls on their subject choice. It developed a gender equity policy, but no longer functions.

- A new school policy requiring equal numbers of boys and girls on school committees introduced because girls had previously dominated.

- Occasional visits by women in non-traditional occupations.

- The distribution of brochures supplied to the school on 'non-traditional careers'.

Overkill? We think not. At this and many other schools, calls for more for the boys did not arise as a result of girls' alleged sudden success, an over-supply of girls' programmes, or after such programmes had 'gone too far', 'over the top'. Indeed, calls for more for the boys were being made when we first entered the schools in 1990 and, according to reports from these schools, gender reform has always been accompanied by such calls from teachers, from the boys and girls themselves and from parents.

On the basis of our data, there are four points worth making with regard to the call for more to be done for boys. The first point to be made is that often what has been done for the girls under the gender reform rubric is grossly exaggerated and then criticised. The example of Kingwood illustrates this point well. In some people's minds, it seems, anything for the girls is too much. Some of the subtle 'niceties' of this are evident in the following story from Terri, a home economics teacher from Wattlehill. She explains that, for International Women's Day, they usually organise an inexpensive lunch for the Year 12 girls and bring in some past students to discuss the girls' futures. However, when this event is announced to the staff, the reaction is as follows:

> There is this amazing negativity from the male teachers towards the whole thing. I think this just stems from the fact that we are doing something for the girls and it's seen as unfair. Rather than saying, 'Well, you are doing something for the girls, what should

we do for the boys?' it's rather, 'You are doing something for the girls and not for the boys.'

The second point is that, as the list of programmes offered in Chapter 1 shows, quite a bit is done for the boys under the rubric of EO, as opposed to the rubric of 'girls' education'. In many schools, programmes may well have been developed for girls in the first instance, but then schools often decide to offer boys parallel programmes. Some have a gender reform agenda, some are simply boys' activities. Some are compulsory, some voluntary. The frustrating thing for many staff is that, despite their complaints about girls' privileged treatment, many boys chose not to avail themselves of gender reform activities when attendance is voluntary. And certainly attempts to encourage boys to go into non-traditional fields generally meet with little enthusiasm. For example, boys stay away from subjects like child care far more determinedly than girls eschew industrial arts and technology. Child care, we are constantly told, is 'girls' stuff' and boys who do it are regularly called poofters. Ray, an English teacher from Wattlehill, sums up the attitude:

> A boy wouldn't say, 'I can't do child care.' He would say, 'I *won't* do child care.' I haven't heard a boy say, I lack the capability to do that. They say, 'I *won't.*'

The third point is that few such claims take into account the resources already devoted to programmes and facilities which are dominated almost exclusively by boys. Literacy programmes are the most obvious of many examples. Indeed, many such programmes in our schools function effectively but unofficially as boys' programmes. They rely on arguments about boys' ability, behaviour, need, self-esteem and on girls 'not choosing'. Consider some typical examples. Blackstone has the *Breakfast Club* and *Challenge Programme* explicitly for boys. Mt Mullin has the *School House* programme which is for 'kids at risk academically and behaviourally and for those with literacy problems'—these are mostly boys. Riverside has the *Learning Centre* which is populated mainly by boys who cause trouble to their teachers. It also has the *Off-line Programme* which is considered no place for a girl as it is heavily oriented to machines. It has the *Living Skills* programme which was designed to address the gender imbalance of the other two but now involves a majority of boys and is controlled by the needs of boys. Fleming has developed two special programmes which attract a tiny minority of girls but which are implicitly for boys. These are *Aviation* and *Cricket*. These subjects have contributed to what is called the 'accidental gender imbalance'. While boys themselves are seldom invisible, often programmes for them seem to be.

The fourth point to be made is that complaints about too much for the girls and too little for the boys often come from men who have difficulty separating gender reform for students from the restructuring of the promotional system to facilitate the advancement of women teachers. Both have become tangible targets for the (usually male) protests of, 'we are pushing girls to the detriment of the boys', 'women are taking men's jobs', and 'she's in that position because she's a woman, not because she is capable'. We will return to this matter in Chapter 6; here we wish simply to point out that EO initiatives have direct implications for the successful working lives of women and men and colour many teachers' perceptions of what are and are not acceptable gender reform programmes for girls and boys. Clearly, programmes which critically examine the gender relations in the world of work are at risk while such ambivalence prevails.

Insupportable conclusions

The dominant discourse of gender reform interrupts gender-conventional ways of thinking about success while, paradoxically, confirming them. It is our view that gender reformers made a strategic error when they mobilised and popularised generalisations about girls' poor performance in the mathematics and science areas and when they allowed the idea of getting girls into non-traditional subjects and occupations to dominate the gender reform agenda. These two mistakes have had serious implications for the ways in which success and associated gender issues and reforms are understood in some of our research schools. For example, it is not uncommon for science teachers to say, 'Well, our enrolments of girls in physics have always been quite high, so we don't have any gender problems at this school.' And, as irrefutable evidence that this school has gender issues covered, they frequently add, 'Why, last year the top student in science was a girl!' Girls' success in these elite areas is often seen as a sign either that there never was a need for gender reform of any sort or that gender reform has worked so well there is no longer any need for it. If, as in many cases, girls' success is then seen to mean boys' failure, it becomes relatively easy to mount the case that girls' programmes have tipped the balance in favour of girls and that extra support should thus be provided for boys to 'even things up'. Add to this the indisputable evidence that some groups of boys systematically fail and there exists a clear recipe for confusion and resentment among boys, their parents and a general credibility problem for gender reform. Thoughtlessly comparing the results, social skills and maturity of particular groups of 'failing' boys with those of 'high-achieving' or 'well-behaved' girls has led many teachers to wonder about the relevance of gender reform to their schools. This logically leads to the conclusion that special programmes are needed for these particular boys. However, because the discourse is couched in girl-versus-boy terms, our teachers often take the logical next step and argue that special programmes are needed for boys, *per se*.

The idea of boys *per se* and girls *per se* makes it very difficult to ask sociological questions such as, 'What is it about particular masculinities and femininities and their relationship to certain aspects of schooling that leads certain boys and certain girls to systematically fail?' or, 'What is it that leads schooling to systematically fail certain socio/cultural groupings of boys and girls?' Further, because the dominant discourse is couched in terms of conventional academic achievement, it makes it difficult to ask questions about other forms of success.

The two main themes presented in this chapter point to the enormous difficulties which gender reformers face when they try to renegotiate the meaning of success in and through schooling. As we have shown, even when they stay within the tolerance limits of conventional academic understandings, it is hard to redefine the driving gendered logic. With the luxurious benefit of hindsight, we have demonstrated that it was a strategic error for gender reformers at all levels of policy to operate within that logic. We have pointed to the ways in which teachers and students reworked such logic in unanticipated ways, which ultimately meant that the policy subverted its own intentions with regard to both girls and boys. Indeed, we have implied that the discourse of the under-achieving, disadvantaged boy was able to gain a stranglehold on gender reform precisely because of the dominant gender reform discourse on success for girls. Our implication throughout has been that gender reform must mobilise other versions of success which have more purchase on the ways in which dominant versions of success reinscribe the dominant. Our view is that stronger ways of understanding the connections between success, gender, power and knowledge are available, and indeed some of these are evident in our schools. In the following chapter, we will explore further the relationship between gender, power and knowledge, point to other constructions of success within such understandings and show how teachers and students have grappled with the associated pedagogical dilemmas.

3

Knowledge

'The boys would rather cover their face and say, "I don't want to know",' says Yotta. She is referring to two elective courses, *Women and Change* and *Men and Change* offered to Year 9 and 10 students at Brookdale. Anne has taken both, while Yotta has taken only the former. Boys will not take *Women and Change*.

Yotta: Females can go and say, 'I want to learn about men.' So they will go to the *Men and Change* but males won't go to *Women and Change*.

Anne: I think that it would be good if guys did learn more about what is happening in society with women. It is good for us to see what is happening to men too. I guess it is kind of hard on the men. Like they have been dominant in society for a long time and I guess it is kind of hard when they see all these women saying, 'No, we don't want this any more!' We don't really know how they feel about it. We just know we want to do it. But the guys are thinking, 'Oh where are we going to end up in all this?'

Yotta: Gradually over the years men have come down and women have gone up.

Anne: And I guess that affects them a lot. That's why they try to hold to anything that they have got, especially in the sporting area. A lot of things have been changed and I guess some, especially the older men, in their forties, or something like that, they are really getting affected by it. If they are male there is nothing much they can do.

Yotta: Yeah, that affects a lot of guys. Men have got used to being at the top. But women shouldn't have to take a back seat.

Knowledge

Anne:	No, women should have as much to do with everything as men do. I am just saying that it affects the men more than what we really think it does. They just don't want to think or hear about it because it is like too much has been taken away from them too quickly. It has built up over a gradual period but women, we can't wait. It is not fair for us to wait. *Why should we wait?* But I think that it would be hard on them too.

And what do the boys have to say? Some boys were quite cross and most really weren't interested.

Theo:	We were put in *Men and Change* and we thought it was what men do in the world and stuff like that. Their jobs and that. Oh, we thought that it would be a change, we will talk about men. And then we go in there and all we talk about is women!
Dom:	Yeah, women's rights and all that, yeah. I am not interested in women's rights. I suppose we don't care. It is up to them. Sure they have got rights but I don't really want to know about it at this time. It was just boring. It just didn't interest me.
Chris:	I'd say that I have learned the same really as I would in any other class. It depends if you are interested. Like in maths you have to really pass that, so you have to get your work done but in these sorts of classes that you don't choose and you are put in it you don't really pay attention as much. So I am not that interested, but I aim to like it.

Armand and James understood the boys' irritation but they thought the unit was OK.

Armand:	When you leave school you can't be [sexist]. If you say something to someone that you don't know on the street they can charge you.
James:	Yeah, like you are in a club and you are trying to pick up you don't want to be sexist, like you say. That's not very fair.
Armand:	Like really, I thought that it was going to be about guys and stuff, but we did a bit about women and we watched the movie *Thelma and Louise*.
James:	We had to write and say what we thought of it. She just asked us if we thought it would matter if it was two guys or two women. It was alright. It was pretty good. Some of the guys, they thought, like, just because it is called *Men and Change* they thought that it was about men. Men and the changes they go through life, really, like, as they grow, puberty and stuff like that, yeah. So it probably caught them off guard, yeah.

Armand: All they wanted to do was get surveys about what every-
           body else thought instead of thinking about what they
           thought. They just went around surveying what everybody
           else thought and they asked teachers about what they
           thought about it too.
James: Teachers made up the courses so you can get to be more
           sensitive and they thought the school was desperate. There
           was a lot of sexism last year but it's getting better as things
           go on. Hmm, probably they thought we might, like, get an
           insight into what sexism is all about, I suppose. I think it
           worked, pretty much so, yeah. It saved us two.

Knowledge is the core work of schools. Teachers are expected to
know their subjects and to know about knowledge, learning and
learners. Fundamentally, the teachers' job is to enable students to
become knowledgeable. But what do we mean by 'know' and
what do we mean by 'knowledge'? And what do they have to do
with gender reform? What knowledge about gender are our students supposed to acquire and how are they to acquire it? And
what do teachers need to know and do in order to assist in this
process? What do students do with what we teach them in school?
And what do we teach them about gender that we don't know
we teach?

The inescapable, undeniable and unfortunate truth is that some
forms and fields of knowledge are more valued and powerful than
others. This truth has underpinned gender reform policies and
strategies for decades. The credentials associated with certain
knowledge enable privileged entry to more sought-after educational and employment opportunities and the reform agenda is to
ensure that girls gain access to this higher status knowledge to the
same extent as boys. Equal access to positions of privilege and
power should follow. Well, that's what they say. Claims for the
intrinsic importance of certain forms of knowledge assume that
knowledge is neutral. Again, we must stress that this assumption
has been consistently refuted by many differently minded feminist
scholars, revealing the ways in which knowledge—including that
in the school curriculum—has been shaped by powerful, white
Western men in their own image and interests (e.g. Alton-Lee and
Denson 1992). A number of feminist critics challenge dominant
conceptions of important knowledge as ultimately diminishing
girls' and women's power and seek to revalue feminine forms of
knowledge and construct gender-inclusive curriculum (e.g. Allard
et al. 1995). Nevertheless, in the absence of a profound transforma-
tion of the status quo, ensuring girls' and women's access to existing

valued fields of knowledge—at present, mathematics, science and technology—has remained an important element of feminist educational thinking since the 1970s. In the late 1980s, in Australia, encouraging girls into these fields became the dominant policy message driven by both feminist and other agendas associated with economic reform (Henry and Taylor 1993). And, as we suggested in Chapter 2, the major gender equity discourse in our schools during the 1990s is to ensure that girls gain access to the valued knowledge (and hence formal qualifications) they need for entry to male-dominated positions of power, as well as the confidence to enter and the desire to do so.

But this is not the only way 'important knowledge' is conceptualised within gender equity discourses. First, certain knowledge is deemed necessary for informed decision-making. Thus girls are provided with information about the prerequisites for certain types of jobs, the typical length of marriages, the pattern of paid employment for men and women and difference in incomes for different forms of work. In order to bring about change, sexual harassment programmes commonly rely on the provision of information to girls and boys on the means of redress and the consequences of infringements. The major pedagogy is transmission, the assumption being that the acquisition of this knowledge will directly improve the quality of students' decisions in desirable directions. Secondly, certain skills and understandings are considered powerful in personal development, enabling students to better deal with their world through increased confidence and competence. Programmes which seek to enhance self-esteem, literacy, interview skills or risk-taking are often remedial in flavour, but not always so. Other programmes may seek to enhance girls' physical fitness or skills in self-defence or assertiveness, they may seek to enhance boys' conflict-resolution skills or their capacity to express their emotions.

These conceptions of the role of knowledge in gender reform underpin many programmes that fall within the broad ambit of equal opportunities (Yates 1993; Weiner 1994) and, until quite recently, girls have largely been the recipient of such knowledge. 'What girls know' will determine how well equipped they are to deal with their world and so the focus has been on improving the knowledge of individual girls for their individual good—changing choices and changing chances.

And then there is knowledge about gender as such—gender education. Over the past decade, gender reform policy and advice literature has increasingly included as 'important knowledge' what students need to understand, value and be able to do in order to improve their world. The agenda is emancipatory and transformational—feminist, even when not explicitly so. 'Awareness raising' to help students see the unseen is an important strategy, ranging from work on understanding stereotypes to naming sex-based harassment and understanding its gendered nature, through to more socially critical work on gender and power. Students are to explore the role of gender in shaping their lives and their environment and the possibilities for a different future. The task is deconstruction; students are to become critical readers of their world. Whether at the level of policy or practice, gender reform strategies for schools often stop there. The knowledge needed for reconstruction—advocacy skills, courage education, negotiation—is sadly neglected.

And what of teacher knowledge? The faith that is placed in raising teachers' awareness as a major reform strategy suggests that many believe that there isn't much that teachers need to know that it is simply a matter of goodwill and good intentions. Clearly it is not. Understanding 'what's wrong' may be a start, but it certainly doesn't tell you 'what's right'. Often teachers are forced to call upon their everyday practical knowledge of teaching to turn awareness into action, but that very commonsense knowledge, as we shall see, is often part of the problem. Knowing teachers know this.

An implicit assumption in many gender reform strategies and policies is that the major cause of gender inequality is ignorance; therefore, it is believed that disseminating knowledge will overcome such injustice (Weiner 1994). Many gender reform strategies, whether directed at students or teachers, are described as 'awareness raising', as though that is all it takes (e.g. Commonwealth Schools Commission 1987). If one were to believe a great many professional development strategies and manuals, raising awareness *is* all it takes; teachers, once they know the facts of gender inequality, will have the desire and the capacity to change their ways and provide a more appropriate and equitable education. Girls and boys, once *they* know the facts of gender inequality, will also change their ways. If only it were so straight forward!

It's what you know about gender that counts

According to a great deal of the policy and advice literature of the past decade, what girls, in particular, need to know is more mathematics, science and technology and what they also need to know is *why* they need to know more mathematics, science and technology. If one were to accept the advice of that same literature, an important strategy for encouraging girls into and in these fields is to learn from the more pleasurable pedagogies adopted by those fields in which girls presently predominate, particularly the arts and humanities. In Chapter 2, we described the reactions of girls in our schools to the endeavours to change their choices. But what do teachers make of this same advice? And what do they do about it?

It's always alright to aim up

Programmes which seek to increase girls' participation in mathematics are often described with considerable enthusiasm by gender reformers. It seems to us, however, that the enthusiasm is about the doors that mathematics can open, not about what the girls will learn or experience within mathematics. There are exceptions. For example, Beth Norton, the Mathematics Coordinator at Kennetton who works hard to maintain a single-sex option in mathematics at Year 10 level, is convinced that mathematics is important 'beyond selection':

> Maths is important for their career paths. It can give them a sense of power and also access to jobs which will give them a better life. They'll have better wages, they'll have better working conditions, they'll have more interesting jobs, they won't be always in the secretarial, nurse type roles where they're helping some man to be wonderful. Hopefully they'll be learning along the way that they too can be wonderful.
> The second [reason why maths is important] is much more subtle and it's much more to do with self-esteem. Maths is about giving girls confidence in problem-solving and risk-taking. English is about making girls more articulate and more literate and more confident and enhancing female characteristics such as good oral skills. PE is about getting them involved in physical education so that they have better body image and the sort of confidence in their capacity to use their body well which becomes more powerful as they get older.

Beth tries to provide a mathematics education consistent with her views of what mathematics should bring to girls. But the efforts to encourage girls to take up more mathematics (and science) are read by many teachers as confirmation that 'the problem' lies with the poor choices girls make as a result of social and peer group pressure, home influence or lack of accurate information about their options and futures. Many hold the rather complacent belief that the curriculum itself is not an issue, that it is equally appropriate 'for all students' in content and pedagogy. 'It doesn't come from the school,' says Otto, who is Head of the Mathematics Department at Mt Mullin:

> I mean, there is nothing at all that would stop anybody doing anything in mathematics. There might be in some subjects. They don't have to wear safety glasses or big boots in mathematics. They don't have to have a certain body shape or lift heavy weights in maths. There is nothing like that. So I don't see that there is any impediment to anybody.

We initially interpreted this as facetiousness, but it becomes clear on successive visits that this is not so. Otto has always experienced girls as just as able in mathematics as boys and is concerned at the suggestion that they might not be 'freely' opting out of mathematics. Stimulated in part by our visits, Otto sets up a project involving the mathematics department and the local primary schools to investigate 'why girls don't choose mathematics'. He, however, remains quite bewildered by the notion that the subject itself might be gender inflected; the explanation of differences in participation must lie in 'social pressures'. Subject content, as many teachers see it, is neutral; it is organised and taught in particular ways because it is inherent in the 'nature of the subject' and is therefore unchangeable.

Although one of the feminist arguments for single-sex classes is that a more appropriate curriculum can be provided, in our schools we found little evidence that this was intended, let alone achieved, in single-sex classes. Indeed, many teachers were at considerable pains to assure us that the curriculum content and pedagogy are the same—curriculum-as-usual—although classroom management and discipline often change. Merrin from Kennetton says, 'I don't think I have changed my teaching . . . I really like to think I do the same,' and Peter from Banksia concurs, 'I don't go out of my way to teach mathematics to girls.' While the girls *may* learn mathematics better, it is not suggested that they will learn better mathematics.

Single-sex classes in mathematics are usually described to us as providing a hassle-free environment more conducive to learning in which girls will gain confidence in their own capabilities. The knowledge which will enhance their participation in mathematics is self-knowledge—'I can do this.' Many girls in our schools—although certainly not all or even the majority—value these opportunities to work in an all-female environment and indicate that they are more confident to speak out in class without the boys present. Almost none, however, suggested that they were more confident about mathematics as such. Rather, what many girls, boys and teachers appear to learn is that boys are very powerful. By their behaviour, they have the power both to create the need for single-sex environments and to ensure that the existence of such classes is continually challenged. What many girls, boys and teachers also learn is that girls can't cope. At Birrilup, the Head of Department remarks that the 'able' girls selected for the single-sex classes 'seem quite pleased about being identified as a discrete group who are at risk . . . and to have that extra support'. At the same school, the boys claim, 'We were told that it was just that the girls were too scared to answer in front of the boys just in case they are wrong or something.' These are just some of the gender lessons schools teach that they don't notice they teach.

It is only very occasionally that EO workers promoting mathematics to girls suggest that the ways of knowing of mathematics do, will or can—even potentially—bring intrinsic rewards to the girls, that they will become more able and knowing, or that they may gain personal power or pleasure through such knowledge. This is not altogether surprising given that, as with people generally, many EO workers do not experience mathematics as personally rewarding or empowering. Indeed, they may find the suggestion incredible. Nevertheless, it is in quite stark contrast to the ways in which many other gender reform programmes are described. Thus increased participation by girls in physical activity is seen to bring its own rewards in terms of health, confidence and pleasure. A socially critical curriculum in English or home economics is seen to enhance both boys' and girls' understanding of the way their world is. The knowledge—of self or society—is itself important. With mathematics, the credential is the thing.

None of this is to suggest that girls do not need mathematics. There are good reasons why girls and boys should be encouraged to continue with some mathematics (and English and physical education) throughout their secondary schooling. Mathematics and English, at their best, each provide the foundation skills which students need to critically read their world and possibly to change it. The awful irony of the *Maths multiplies your choices* campaign described in Chapter 2 is that it provides a classic, almost 'textbook', example of a misuse of statistics. (The figure of '400 per cent more choices', upon which the campaign centres, equates the number of occupations with the number of jobs so that an occupation which offers 30 000 jobs is counted equally with an occupation which offers 300. The campaign also makes no distinction between requiring, say, Year 10 mathematics and the highest levels of mathematics at Year 12.) A number of feminist educators tried to get the percentages removed from the advertisements before they went to air in Western Australia, but were informed that they would then 'lack punch' because 'people find figures very persuasive'. Thus mathematics is used to distort, intimidate and mystify. This knowledge is used *on* girls, not *for* them and certainly not *by* them. One goal of a feminist mathematics education would be to provide girls and boys with the knowledge they need to interrogate the advertisement, to ask what the percentages refer to and how they were determined, evaluate the sexist and classist assumptions upon which the advertisements were based, reflect on what it is about mathematics that encourages people to suspend their common sense and allow such nonsense to go unchallenged, and question whose interests are served when such programmes go to air.

Instead, lacking these critical insights, girls enrol in mathematics courses for which they are ill-prepared in numbers for which their schools are unprepared. Six months later, many wish to withdraw. Some are able to pick up alternative courses, others are not. This campaign serves to underline the authority and power of mathematics and to undermine the rationality and confidence of many girls. Such is the power of this particular knowledge about mathematics.

To an extent, this emphasis on the mathematics credential can be regarded as a commonsense acknowledgement of the knowledge hierarchy of the school curriculum. Thus, while many gender reforming and other teachers are critical of the privileging of mathematics, they nevertheless accept it:

> I think in upper secondary education people should be able to get breadth and this concentration on everyone doing maths and physics isn't good for society. Still I guess we're not going to change the tertiary institutions' selection system for a long time. You've got to play within the system and that means you've got to do maths. [Jake, mathematics teacher, Kennetton]
>
> The basic point is that they increase their options if they take on maths and science. You can't argue with that if they do want to go on to tertiary studies . . . it just offers them that much more

flexibility. I don't like it so much [laughter] as a history/social studies teacher, but I agree with it. [Kevin, social studies teacher, Kennetton]

This pragmatism acknowledges the knowledge hierarchy but fails to attend to what Miles and Middleton (1990) call the gender contouring of this hierarchy. The almost exclusive promotion of mathematics and science and technology accepts the dominance of masculine values and knowledge and reinforces what many students already know, that those subject areas most associated with the masculine are to be valued over those most associated with feminine. Far from breaking down gendered dualisms of hard/soft, male/female, powerful/powerless, it underlines and exaggerates them.

> Arts subjects feel like second-rate subjects. Like someone with an art/drama, English lit., studio art sort of course, it's like they're just doing Arts because they can't do the other. [Year 10 girl, Kennetton]

During our visits, claims gather momentum that, just as girls are disadvantaged by their relative absence from mathematics, science and technology, so too are boys disadvantaged by their relative absence from subject areas like art, history, languages other than English, child care and music. This assertion of some sort of symmetry in the disadvantage caused by gendered subject choice seems blind to the clear differences in status between different subject groupings and fails to acknowledge the asymmetrical consequences in power and privilege associated with them. As one perceptive 16-year-old put it:

> Women are on a lower level and the guys are on a higher level. You won't get hassled if you're going to a higher level, but if you're going down they'll hassle you. I think it's like that. It shouldn't be, but it is. [Year 11 girl, Kingwood]

Her friend said more succinctly and cynically, 'It's always alright to aim up.'

It's just the natural order of things

Colin, who teaches English at Kennetton, remarks that many students 'firmly do believe gender inequality is just the natural order of things, it's the way it is'. Colin thinks this belief should be challenged directly with students, but doubts that teachers themselves understand what it would entail.

> It's an interesting point, isn't it, because it is also naturalised in the curriculum hierarchy or power in the school which certainly is sympathetic with the degree of maths/science being taken. If those assumptions are going to be questioned then a great many other things in this school have to be reviewed by those very people who hold power in the school. It requires such massive consciousness-raising amongst staff that it's going to be a long time before we change the way students see it.

And, of course, many teachers have considerable professional and personal investment in existing knowledge/power arrangements. Clearly, there is some kudos in being associated with those subject areas popularly regarded as being most intellectually challenging and, when these are part of the core curriculum, some security in not having to compete for students. It is not only teachers of high status and mainstream subjects who have something to lose, however. For example, we are frequently told of the stranglehold that Manual Arts Departments have over the school timetable. This is explained by reference to the need to schedule the workshop spaces, but the 'female domains' of home economics and business studies, with equal demands on special facilities, are rarely privileged in the same way. Furthermore, many teachers of elective and/or more marginalised subjects are reluctant to lose the freedom they often have to do what they want without interference. Lorna, Head of the Home Economics Department at Wattlehill, points out that she has considerable autonomy, as 'no one would even know what you are doing in your own little area'. The sting in the tail/tale for those with a reforming agenda is that while 'you can make a lot of changes, they have to be done within the system that already exists'. In Lorna's case, the changes she makes are to 'try to use a critical theory approach to get students to question the gendered mores of society and to frame questions that give them opportunities to expand their thinking'. Other teachers, however, appreciate the untrammelled freedom which allows them not to change, not to take a 'gender perspective'.

Girls' numerical predominance in arts and humanities reassures many teachers that there are no issues in their subject area for girls' education. For example, at Banksia, Kennetton, Fleming, Kingwood, Mt Mullin and Bettleford, we were told explicitly by the Art Heads of Department, both male and female, that gender considerations were totally irrelevant to art and that there was no need to consider such issues if they were irrelevant. In each case, they said that art caters equally for both sexes and 'we treat the two sexes the same'. One female teacher at Kennetton disagreed and suggested that the models made by her students in ceramics were sex-role based and that girls were learning to 'read' art through male eyes. She was one of the very rare teachers in our schools who indicated any knowledge of the extensive literature on the role of art in producing the gendered subject or of the complex gender issues in school art (e.g. Collins 1995). When she tried to raise these as an issue, the Head of Department looked at her teaching methods and decided that she was worrying too much and that she taught even-handedly. By even-handedly he explained that he meant using things like flowers as a still-life subject, 'I call them plants and it hasn't worried the boys.' He concluded that the curriculum and the school were not the problem, that 'role development comes from home and the culture of society'. In any case, he and the other Heads of Department pointed out that Art suited the girls anyway or they wouldn't choose it.

Indeed, it is suggested—both within our schools and also in some of the policy and advice literature—that in the arts and humanities may lie the answer to gender inequality. Not only do these subject areas provide models which mathematics, science and technology should emulate in order to attract more girls (e.g. Lewis and Davies 1989) but, furthermore, the very 'feminine' qualities of these subjects which attract girls and distance boys are the ones which will turn boys around by attending to their expressive and emotional sides ('What about the Boys?' 1994). Poor literacy skills and the inability to express their emotions, attend to their creative urges and relate to others are often blamed for boys' aggressive harassing behaviour in schools and outside. However, as McLean (1996a) suggests, the notion that the answer to boys' sexism and violence lies in the arts/humanities subjects is rather curious, given the levels of misogyny evident in the works and lives of many artists, writers and other intellectuals. It also ignores the sexist, racist and classist records of many such fields (see, for example, Gaskell and Willinsky 1995; Gilbert and Taylor 1991).

In any case, quite a number of teachers, particularly women, do not accept that simply because girls like or choose a subject area, it must be working in their best interests. Leanne, a social studies teacher at Kingwood, regards history as gender inflected; 'In history there is an imbalance—it's mostly about men's exploits but the girls have just learned to accept that. The boys who do history really enjoy it, but I wonder if they would if it was all about women?' Her colleague, Terry, who only two minutes earlier firmly asserted that the *only* gender issue in social studies is that too few boys do history and too few girls do economics, acknowledged her point and offered the following anecdote:

> We ran a term assignment last year on China. We asked the kids to imagine that they were a Chinese person living in a particular time and to write about their experiences—living there, army's role, etc. Out of the whole hundred or so, only one person, a girl, wrote as a woman. The girls wrote from a man's point of view. All the history we have is about men.

The whole department agreed that 'in textbooks women just don't figure, what is mentioned is done by men', but there the agreement finished. Neville began with the patronising statement, that 'where there are significant women in history we really emphasise it—to show that women can be dynamic in certain situations.' He was immediately challenged by Leanne, but she clearly has an uphill battle.

Leanne: Women *are* significant but we are conditioned to accept them not being seen. In ammunition factories in World War I they weren't just supporting—they were really in there, weren't they?

Barry: Women in those times were out front in the forces—nurses.

Leanne: So basically we have a man's eye view of the world. How can we turn that around?

Terry: I think a valid question is how much it needs to be turned around. That's part of the debate. What is the role of the sexes within history? It hasn't been thoroughly debated. . .

Leanne: Reconstructing history would mean to see it from a woman's point of view or to reconceive history as the history of normal people.

Terry: It creates problems though. The kids by and large need to go through the great men, great event type syndrome so as to build up their own framework before they're ready to come to terms with history about lives of ordinary men and women: even though we put a fair amount of that in our courses. Kids find it very difficult to handle. It's a much more difficult thing to empathise with lives of ordinary people than it is to feel the shock and horror of wars and the romance of the great successes.

Leanne:	None of our upper school courses have as an objective addressing some of these deeper sorts of gender issues in the way history has been constructed.
Neville:	We don't touch the suffragette movement, Emily Pankhurst.
Terry:	Where we can bring them in, we do, but there's nothing in the syllabus that says you have to address these issues. Just something we do when we can. It's rather the way people go about teaching things, rather than a curriculum thing. Can't guarantee it.

This exchange isn't a simple matter of lack of knowledge or an inability to see each other's point of view—it is a refusal of certain knowledge as valid. Terry and Neville may be prepared to 'bring them in . . . when we can', but it is difficult to escape the notion that it won't be too often—there simply aren't enough significant women. Girls may assume that a request to write as a Chinese person of a particular period is a request to write as a male, but nevertheless Terry still feels a need to debate whether history should also become 'her-story' or 'our story'. That such views are not peculiar to Kingwood is clear from our data. A girl in Mt Mullin, for example, tells us that:

> We wouldn't normally do anything about women in Social Studies because mostly in Social Studies we learn about history. It would be pretty good if we did I guess but I don't really know if we could because I don't really know about any woman that was anything in history.

It's what you know and do about gender that counts

Students learn 'about gender' in some form or other in the formal curriculum of virtually all our schools, although the extent and nature vary widely. Discussing the stereotyping of men and women in the media is the most commonly cited example of teaching about gender—usually in English, health or personal development. Many teachers indicate that they 'do it incidentally' if it 'comes up' but it isn't a major objective. Some teachers, however, see the opportunity and the necessity to address gender regularly and often passionately in whatever they are doing. There are, in addition, a number of examples of units or courses in formal curriculum offerings which provide more systematic treatments of gender issues. In some cases, these form part of externally developed curricula—for example the *Gender and*

Literature unit at Kingwood referred to in Chapter 1—but many schools also develop their own units of work.

At Nerringo, the theoretical component of physical education courses seeks, amongst other things, to 'debunk myths about girls and physical activity', and 'analyse and change media coverage of women and sport', and to teach boys, in particular, that everybody benefits from an active life and that they have the responsibility 'to see that justice is done in terms of the media and views that are held'. At Wattlehill, the Home Economics Department takes a 'feminist stance' and encourages students to 'question issues of morals, values and ethics to look for inequalities, injustice, sources of domination and power, conflict, discontent and hidden assumptions'. Brookdale offers Year 9 and 10 students two social education electives, *Women and Change* and *Men and Change*, which seek to have students consider the range of options that men and women can have with respect to their lives. In each case, men and women are 'looked at through history,' including how education has been different for girls and boys. 'Contemporary issues' are also addressed, including workplace issues, such as 'non-traditional' jobs, sexual discrimination, pay rates and part-time work, and issues such as rape, domestic violence and gender relations generally.

And what do students learn from such courses? The story of Brookdale's two courses, which feature in the vignette at the beginning of this chapter, is instructive.

We haven't really learned about ourselves yet

Women and Change and *Men and Change* were developed with an explicitly stated reform agenda. Since reform occurs in the longer term, few teachers expect to see the results of such courses immediately and have to judge their success by students' immediate reactions. Not surprisingly, and as our vignette shows, these are mixed—ranging from enthusiasm and delight, to anger and hostility, with not a few students expressing a polite uninterest.

The girls we spoke to were able to describe the courses in considerably more detail and depth than the boys. The following comments about *Women and Change* are typical:

Anne: We are doing a court case where a girl has been raped. We have got to decide whether she asked for it or not. It gets you angry when you think about some of those things, but it is the way that the courts have been. As women, we are trying to learn to change it but it hasn't really affected us personally, because we haven't been in a court. But it is good to get it changed though. [laughter].

Yotta: We were talking about that guy who was killing everybody's friends and must have hated women. And were thinking about the things that you can do to help men prevent it from happening. Just to protect us. You know, things that we are interested in. Because it is not going to do us any good just to read through the history books and say, 'Yep, women should be interested in that sport, women did this, women do that.' We are actually learning about today and how we are in society not how they were. And how we are going to change things.

These comments from boys at the same school are also typical:

Stew: We sang a few songs.
Aaron: 'Botany Bay', 'Click Go The Shears'.
Stew: We were embarrassed. [Agreement and laughter]
Lester: Some of us sang. [Agreement]
Jarrod: I sang.
Stew: Is that right? [Shocked]
Jarrod: Yes.
Aaron: It was to learn about, well the song said a story.
Jarrod: 'Cause we were doing the First Fleet. 'Cause there was more men than women.
Aaron: Now we write our summary on it and probably talk about it for a while.

Some boys are a little more forthcoming, to be sure, but only just so. These differences cannot be explained simply as matters of style or articulateness since the boys become quite voluble a few minutes later when discussing behaviour in the schoolyard and a number of other topics. Rather, they simply don't seem to remember much of the detail of what they have done or to have engaged with the course very much at all. As Chris, from our vignette, suggests: 'it's just another class'. At first we found this rather surprising, considering the subject, but this may be the nub of the matter.

The flavour of *Men and Change*, it seems, has become much more factual and historical than that of *Women and Change*. Chris captures the sentiments of a number of the boys in the following remarks:

I am not really fond of the past. I live in the present. So I am not very fond of history. It doesn't really bother me but I don't really like it much. We haven't really learned about ourselves yet. Not yet really. We have just learned about other people. I was expecting a bit more, but. [shrug] It would be good to explore the man's world really. Yeah, but we really haven't done so.

A number of boys express their resentment that the course does not deal with the feelings that men have and what it means to be a male. Some expected the course to be about body changes and sexuality. Not all boys are negative about the course—indeed some, like James and Armand in our vignette, are quite positive, but few show the same level of engagement and enthusiasm as the girls. Chris suggests that something a little more stimulating may be occurring in the girls' class and that a woman teacher might be better at dealing with the things he would prefer the course to attend to.

A woman teacher would probably be exploring more on the men's side. They would probably be taking, um, more of the men's side of it, the *Men and Change* and *then* going on to history and things like that. They would probably bring it into the present day. Yeah, it might be a bit better, yeah. It would be better probably if they talk about something in this day and age, sort of like the rape case the girls are doing. It would be good to explore that.

Mike Bevan, the boys' teacher, said that the first time he taught *Men and Change* there was a bit of resistance to it from the boys, but 'that doesn't mean there was resistance to the concept really, I wouldn't like to think that'. He laughingly added that 'they're not more resistant than they are against doing any sort of work', and so 'I ended up doing a pretty structured course with lots of worksheets and short written assignments'. The boys are kept busy on their assigned tasks but we observe little effort to help them articulate or clarify their understanding and/or beliefs about the material. Indeed, what some of the boys now know would surprise their teachers.

Dom: In *Men and Change* we are learning that it is OK for girls to deal with their feelings. They go whingeing and crying all the way to the teacher. We don't, we just have to deal with it ourselves. That's how it has been all the time. Women are allowed to show their feelings. We learned men are not meant to! Like your mate said when you were little kids or whatever, 'Did you cry?'

> 'No.' 'Good!' 'Did you cry?' 'Yes.' 'Oh, what a wimp!'
> We have to deal with it ourselves. With our mates.
>
> Theo: I wouldn't show it to guys at school. I've got mates
> out of school and a few interstate which I can share it
> with.

A critical reading of the relationship between masculinity and emotion becomes an imperative but not one with which Mike feels prepared to deal. Indeed, he describes his strategy of trying to have 'a laugh about things' and not become too preachy or too personal.

> Like every time that sexism would come up I'd put it on the
> board, and we sort of had a look at it and it became a bit of a
> sort of joke. So I wasn't going to be saying, 'Oh, you shouldn't!'
> all the time. It was more, well, let's just acknowledge that
> something is going on.

Clearly students do not like being preached at and authoritarian pedogogies based on 'putting students right' are unlikely to do much good. Indeed, students often react by becoming more extreme in their behaviour and attitudes (Kenway, Blackmore and Willis 1996). As a result, particularly when boys are present in significant numbers, many courses lose their reforming agenda pretty swiftly. Volatility can be disruptive of the 'good order' of the class and the desire for order, together with the insecurity many teachers—particularly males—feel when dealing with gender matters, causes them to neutralise the subject matter so that it becomes non-threatening—both to students and teachers. Many teachers draw on their existing repertoire of commonsense knowledge, the knowledge which enables them to cope with the everyday life of classrooms, and avoid or smooth over anything which might disrupt the orderly running of the class. Unfortunately, gender reform requires upsetting and altering the 'everyday'—in schools as elsewhere. Managing the process is the challenge teachers face every day, as our following story demonstrates.

If they're uncomfortable they're going to reject it

Louise at Eden Park says that the whole issue of 'gender and power, and who's got the power whether in a classroom or elsewhere' has become a major part of her thinking about teaching and she struggles 'to find strategies to handle it'. She has designed a Year 9 and 10 English elective course on gender, ethnic and age stereotyping which encourages students to think 'deeply, perceptively and sensitively' about literature generally and the media in particular, and the part they play in 'constructing perceptions'. Louise recognises that 'teenage kids are preoccupied with trying to make sense of what it is to be female and what it is to be male'. She seeks to help them make sense of their gender by offering them identities as critical and resistant readers of the cultural forces which will shape their lives. She also works hard to keep them with her.

> I just keep it squarely in the domain of literature and the media so it doesn't become too personal and too uncomfortable for the kids. Because if they're uncomfortable they are going to reject it. And then you've lost them completely. They don't want to do it. It's hard. You can't just hit one sex. When you do it that way with a mixed group, the boys still have a dominant role. They still take over the classroom . . .
>
> I just spent two lessons in a row looking at song lyrics which focus on males. The girls put up with it, without comment, for two lessons but in the next lesson the girls said, 'Well come on Miss, where's the stuff about girls?' I thought this was a big plus because earlier on in the unit they wouldn't have asked that . . .
>
> So I said, 'All right, so the next lot of short stories we're going to look at, all have females in them, and I'm not going to apologise for that.' . . . And I said, 'Please if you feel uncomfortable with what's happening, either pass, don't say anything or if you want to challenge, challenge, but do it appropriately.'

The irony that a unit which seeks to be socially critical should demonstrate unequal gendered power relations in action is not lost on Louise, but Louise is in real classrooms with real kids and what is she to do? She believes that if she makes her students too uncomfortable she will lose them completely, but if she leaves them too comfortable nothing will change. Finding the balance is a real challenge—and Louise is knowledgeable, committed and experienced, which cannot be said equally of all teachers struggling to address these matters.

In our research schools, the balance tended more often to fall on the side of 'too comfortable', with teachers searching for 'non-disruptive' approaches. Some reassure themselves that maybe some of the things they say will influence their students 'in the future' but they rarely sound convinced—it is difficult to believe that a message that isn't remembered a week later will be a decade later. Indeed, the problem with non-disruptive approaches is that they cannot disrupt. Instead, what we often have is an attempt to change students by stealth. But this is not the only story—some teachers, like Jeanette, an English teacher at Mt Mullin, confront the issues head on.

School's a start for sure

Davey, in Year 10 at Mt Mullin, describes Jeanette as being 'really dead set against sexism and racism and things like that'. Maddy, in the top Year 10 English class, describes how, 'She asks us to wonder about things like, "Why aren't there many boys in this classroom, why do you think that is?" We try to think about it and she takes time out to talk to us about that.' Glen, a Year 9 student, tells us, 'She is a feminist. She was abused when she was married and all that and she was getting us to talk about how to deal with those situations.' Jeanette expects her students to consider gender at the level of their own lives and to act on their understandings, even if only in school. Unlike Louise, she declines to keep it 'squarely in the domain of literature', and she thinks her students need to be made to feel uncomfortable. Davey describes how:

> Anything racist or sexist in the classroom she will get on top of it. I mean . . . she'll put them on the spot, sort of thing and say, 'Oh, why don't you explain yourself?' or 'Why are you saying that?' It stops people from being sexist or racist in the classroom because they know that they are going to have to explain themselves which is something no one likes doing anyway. I don't know if that would be the same in private but school's a start, for sure. Yeah, it is really positive.

Their responses to her persistence blend affection and exasperation. Some are offended by her explicitly feminist stance—they think she just goes 'on and on' and 'doesn't listen to what we think' and 'doesn't do real work'. According to Glen, however, 'It isn't a problem, we just change our English essays to work on all that.'

A year later, Jeanette has moved to another school, but in our conversations with her ex-students she is ever-present. Alana, now in Year 10, sums up the sentiments of many of her peers:

> Some people found it really offensive but I don't see how. You know, it was really interesting, it was real life sort of issues. And

now that we've got another teacher, the people that didn't enjoy it are saying that they miss that. 'Cause they're saying that these other teachers are a little bit boring. She was really outrageous, yeah, she was really cool. She was one in a million, true.

That they miss her is clear but, perhaps more to the point, they still remember what she wanted them to think about and to act upon.

Wendy, another English teacher at Mt Mullin, commented that it is only when you expect students to begin to act on the things they have been learning and to change *now* that the real resistance shows but also the potential for real learning exists. She commented that, in her experience, approaches to stereotyping go little beyond having students identify examples of stereotypes or recognise sex role socialisation. Students are on the whole 'not too reluctant to join in such discussions,' but she said, 'the moment you pass any responsibility over to them for the problem . . . that's when you get this resistance.' She suggested to some male students that their stories about violence towards and mutilation of women might not be appropriate and 'that there might be a better, more subtle and sensitive way'. They were angry at what they saw as a restriction on what they had the right to write. She understood that it was a big step for them to take—after all they are fed a constant diet of such material—but she was in no doubt that if she avoided the issue, they would too and there is not much evidence that things will get better as they get older.

> I was trying to get them to understand why a person could react really badly and be offended by the films that are all the rage now. I gave my own personal reaction where I was just thoroughly appalled when I saw *Silence of the Lambs* and the kids were just astounded, you know, 'How could you react like that. It was a great film!' As if it was the best thing that they had ever seen. They raved about what a brilliant film it was. It took about two hours' careful discussion over a week or so before even the girls really began to see why films like that do damage.
>
> I said to the girls that as women we know that we are always looking over our shoulder. We can't go anywhere without feeling threatened. And the girls supported me and really understood what it was like to be a women in the 1990s and I think that it was quite enlightening for the boys to realise the girls they know have those feelings. A lot of the time the girls and boys don't share those feelings. But I don't know how many of the boys took it on. There were still a lot of boys who were very vocal and said that I was just being stupid and paranoid and who were trying to blame it on me.

Like many other teachers, Wendy does not expect the knowledge students gain in her classrooms to change them overnight—there are many it may not change at all. But the knowledge she expects them to develop is that they *are* implicated in gender inequality, it isn't something that happens to them or outside them; they are agents and not acting to change themselves and others is an action in support of the unjust status quo. As Yotta from Brookdale told us earlier, the good thing about about *Women and Change*, is that 'we are actually learning about today and how we are in society . . . [and] how we are going to change and how we have to change things.' The sense of agency in Yotta's remarks is surely what gender reform programmes in schools are about.

Peter, who teaches at Edgecliffe, comments:

> Some people say schools are separate from real life, but I think they are in fact an intensification of real life. I see that what a school should be doing is giving kids opportunities to question things in a non-threatening environment and to practice taking action. We have a long way to go.

While certainly we do have a way to go, there is some evidence in our schools of students taking action of their own as a result of participating in such educational programmes. Judy, an English and drama teacher at Braydon Tech, describes how students discuss the rights of people to be hetero or homosexual without being discriminated against. As a result, two boys 'went to School Council and requested that it consider this as a very serious issue within our school community and address it'. The School Council listened to the arguments and approved the purchase of videos and other material about gays for the school. In a number of schools, students went to their School Council about girls' uniforms, arguing that girls' activity was inhibited by having to wear skirts and dresses. Many were successful. At Wattlehill, a student who was having problems with a male teacher who was 'putting her down in a sexist way' brought the problem to her home economics class. According to Lorna:

> She had a real problem because it was getting so bad she couldn't face class but it was her final year and if she didn't go to class she was the one going to suffer. The class—of boys and girls—actually talked it through and helped her come up with a strategy that was acceptable to her. I felt that it was a direct result of having the issues canvassed in the class before.

Sarah, a Year 11 student at Mt Mullin, comments on the subject of sex-based harassment that teachers in schools have an important role in 'helping students realise about it and why it should change', but, she says:

> Then it's the students as a student body who've got to make it happen. They've got to try and use what the teachers are trying to tell us and what they're trying to teach us about it to our own benefit, 'cause we're the ones who want to make a difference in it. Like, in our school, we're the ones who have to do it, so it's the students who will have to make it work.

Sarah's sense of collective responsibility is to be applauded but we suspect that teachers will need to do a little more than help students 'realise about it'. Awareness is unlikely to bring about action unless it is accompanied by the necessary skills. Lorna suggests, 'If we have responsibility for enabling young adults to think critically and to challenge traditional ways of being, then surely you have an even greater responsibility for helping them develop the practical skills they need and supporting them when they do it in environments where challenge is not encouraged.' She continues, 'If they are going to have autonomy, they are going to have to develop some skills, in being constructively assertive, in negotiation, in developing strategies, and they have to practise them here.'

It must be said, however, that in our schools attention to such skills was not common. Indeed, even when issues of gender were the subject matter of curriculum, there was a reluctance on the part of some teachers to see these new understandings put to use, particularly on the operations and activities of the school. Little wonder then that for many students, 'It's just another course.'

What teachers know and can do

In Chapter 1, we saw the remarkable difference in the extent to which English teachers at Kingwood, ostensibly teaching the same curriculum, dealt with gender. As their students pointed out, 'it depends on the teacher'. And of course it does. It depends upon their commitment to reform, but it also depends upon what they know about gender issues, how informed and skilful they are in matters of pedagogy when gender is involved, and how well they understand and are able to withstand the resistances that bringing such issues to the fore almost inevitably generate. Goodwill and good intentions are insufficient, as we will show.

'It's the spirit of the age—we are more aware'

'A Tradie is probably the last person to come to terms with some of these issues,' says Tom from Braydon Tech, 'but, it's the spirit of the age—we are more aware. We've had people here that have pulled us up and said, "Hey, that's not on." . . . You don't jump up and down or get offended, you say, "Well, I wasn't aware of that, thanks for saying it."' Some issues, however, are not so cut and dried. Recognising there is something to be addressed and wanting to do the right thing is not sufficient. The Tradies at Braydon are faced with a confusing dilemma. Mal Bradford, who teaches technology, has been told that his models are toys for the boys but he cannot think of any models for students to build that are not coded by gender.

> I'm currently looking at a helicopter that would work really well in primary schools. I think a primary girl would like a helicopter as well as a primary boy. But in some people's view, it's still very much, 'Why are they boys' models?' I really don't know how to answer that. I talk to people and say, 'Listen, what can I make that's a working model?' There must be some performance attached to it. One lady suggested, 'Well, can they make a doll—I mean a doll that works?' And I thought, 'Oh no, we want to get away from that, surely?'
>
> So it must work, it must do something. It must involve a range of plastics because that's basically the material that we're focusing on. What can be an equivalent? I recognise that a model yacht is probably gender specific. Well then, what is an equivalent for the girls and really that question cannot, it seems, be answered. What they suggest, in an attempt to answer it, locks us into decorative 'pretty' things.
>
> I don't want to have a programme for boys and a programme for girls. The boys make all these 'whiz-bang' things that fly around and skim across the water. And the girls make these pretty little ornaments, a pixie or a gnome, or something. I think that's working against what a lot of the gender equality has got in mind. Now try as I might, I can't think what is appropriate.

Peter and Tom have been teaching woodwork and electronics at Braydon Tech for ten years. They care deeply about their subjects and their students. Both can name some of the problems quite readily although, as the following conversation shows, they don't see themselves as part of the problem.

> Peter: The problem is that the boys in this school are
>   traditional boys, in many respects. They want to do

things for the girls. If they see a girl struggling with something, they'll go over and say, 'Look, don't worry about it, I'll do it for you.'

Tom: Early on, when the girls lack confidence, they usually say, 'Thanks, that's great, fine.' As they get more confidence and greater knowledge, they get a little annoyed with it, and it takes the boys a while to understand that the girls don't want them to do it.

Peter: There is also the issue of changing girls' attitudes. We live in a very traditional community. Girls have very traditional concepts and it's very hard to break that barrier. Also, in a lot of cases, it's not necessary, to change their attitudes—there's nothing wrong with the things girls do traditionally. But some girls do miss out on opportunities. If they had a diversity of skills and abilities, maybe they could reach their potential, whereas they don't now.

Having said that, both men then move into a strange pattern of denial, pointing to the equal opportunity in the school, the freedom of choice available, their own gender-neutral behaviour. 'Students are students,' they say, 'their gender doesn't matter.' Even though they are men of goodwill and clearly care about their students, their ideas are confused and full of contradictions with regard to the gendered construction of knowledge, skill and achievement.

Peter: The programme is the programme. I'm a bit loathe to make it less than the genuine article for some sort of gender arrangement—unless it was because of some handicapped girls. I think it would make them feel that they're doing less, because they've got to have this special programme. A year ago we tried to put our thoughts together in regard to why do some people have more girls than others. We said maybe the room was off-putting. Like the girls were conscious of their dress so we bought a mirror and put it in the room.

Tom: When they go into the workforce, they're going to have to cope with the traditional way of teaching things and the male attitude and all that sort of stuff. Are we doing them a disservice by meeting them halfway and then turning them loose into this sort of place?

Peter: The girls at the moment are doing well. I don't know whether they understand the theory behind it as well as the boys do but their presentation is wonderful, their practical work is good, their written presentation is certainly as good or even better in most cases than

	the boys. But their conceptual understanding is not the same. They tend to say, 'I don't understand,' and they don't try to understand.
Tom:	I know from my experience that the girls can do it as well.

These stories point to levels of confusion, unease and uncertainty which go unremarked in the policy and advice literature. They show how difficult it is to rearrange one's habitus even when willing to do so. The 'programme is the programme'; disciplines discipline. For many teachers, the ambiguity of the issues and of their own reactions to them can hardly begin to be understood, let alone acted upon, given the inadequate knowledge base from which they are working. Tom suggests that a Tradie is probably the last person to come to terms with some of these issues, but our data suggest that Tradies are not alone in this.

It wouldn't be me

As we suggested earlier, many gender reform strategies assume that ignorance is the major cause of gender inequality and, consequently, that disseminating knowledge will overcome it. Only too often, this is not the case. Some teachers appear to take on certain knowledge but feel no responsibility for change. Geoff at Birrilup describes some reading he has done which convinces him that girls are disadvantaged by multiple-choice questions. In his own experience, girls 'invariably do worse' in multiple choice than they would with other forms of assessment, so that the 'boys leave them for dead'. This is because the girls won't take risks, he says. He discusses this with the Year 11 chemistry students, over two-thirds of whom are boys. They prefer multiple choice, think it would be unfair to have to do short or long answer questions, and say 'let's have multiple choice man!' And so they do. Mary, who teaches English at Kingwood, thinks it is quite useful to have inservice courses and have people come in and talk about 'de-gendering the teaching process', but, she says, 'I don't think they have an effect on my teaching in the classroom.'

It is clear, however, that many teachers do feel an obligation to attend to gender issues once they become aware of them. Sometimes this is a fairly straightforward matter. For example, Yasmin from Braydon Tech recounts how, because girls are fewer than one-third of the students in the school, decisions have to be made about whether girls should be distributed across all classes or concentrated into fewer classes so they are not a very small minority. 'The men will say, "Oh I don't want all boys' classes, they're too hard to handle." They'll say, "Come on, give me a couple of girls." And I used to think, "Oh well, I suppose that's fair enough."' Since then, however, she has attended gender network meetings where 'One of the speakers explained why that's not right and why it shouldn't be and I could suddenly see it.' Now she and others know better and so make a point of saying persistently, 'No, you're not using them like that.'

For other teachers, acting upon their newfound knowledge demands a rather more significant adjustment to the way they regard themselves—professionally and personally—and the way they are. At Kingwood, Jim has taught physics for 30 years and describes himself as 'probably' a male chauvinist who 'can't help it' because of his age and training. 'The idea [of treating everyone equally] and monitoring your classroom interaction doesn't need to be sold to me,' he says, but he doesn't know how to effect the needed changes in his classroom. 'I don't think I'm doing well enough,' he sighs, 'but at this age, I don't think I'm prepared to change my style radically because it wouldn't be me. But I know I don't get the same out of the girls—the same response from them.' The problem for Jim is that he isn't sure whether he should be treating girls and boys the same or treating them differently. This, of course, is a problem he shares with many feminists.

Perhaps the more significant point here, however, is that for many teachers, gaining knowledge on matters of gender is unlike gaining knowledge about their subject area. It is, almost inevitably, self-knowledge as well. It very often requires reassessing who 'me' is. It very often exposes their deepest feelings and the inconsistencies in their own behaviour. Janice, at Wattlehill, believes the 'feminist approach' to home economics taken at her school is the right one and wants to be like Lorna, the coordinator and inspiration for the programme. 'I have Lorna's influence in the workplace but I find it difficult to take home. I'm certainly not a feminist there—I can't do it with the man in my life, for peace.' She used to feel that she could 'separate my two beings, you know, my two roles quite easily', but as she has become more knowledgeable about gender issues, she has found that impossible. Louise, at Eden Park, is 'guilty' of inconsistency between her actions and what she 'knows':

And another thing I was guilty of the other day, now that I reflect on it. I've got one particular male in one class who's very dominant—always manages to get his say in and I've got a couple of girls who also do the same. But you should have seen the different way I treated them. And I know that it is not OK to say to females 'don't be dominating', but I gave body signs that it was not OK and yet I have him body signs that it was OK. So even though I was saying things verbally, my body signs were doing different things. What do I do about it?

She reads a lot on gender issues and thinks it is 'terrific' but laments that, although it 'gives you a hint' about what to do, 'it doesn't really give you a way to undo your own socialisation'. Anita, at Mt Mullin, made the insightful observation that most policies and approaches to professional development make 'an enormous assumption that we can go from being a girl or a boy, with all these documented problems, to being a woman or a man and suddenly the problems aren't there any more'. A few years of pre-service education, she suggests, aren't going to make a new person of you, 'suddenly you're a teacher and you're supposed to have it all under your belt. You are in control and can now change things for your students.' Quite clearly you aren't and you can't.

I thought I was doing the right thing, but . . .

It must also be said, however, that some teachers rather arrogantly grab at some of the ideas associated with gender reform, refusing to imagine that there is much to know. When applying their superficial understandings to deeply sedimented problems, they are shocked to find that it is not that simple and become confused, downhearted and even resentful when their plans go askew.

Some of the male teachers at Kennetton are concerned about the grossly rude, sexist and destructive interpersonal behaviour of the girls and boys who hang out in the back corner of the oval.

There was a group of girls and they would be perhaps not our most academic girls and they tend to hang around out here and they flirt near the boys. But anyway, the girls would sort of 'gee-up' the boys a little bit out here and then finally provoke to a point where they'd get some sort of comment which would be sort of sexual harassment and then come racing over with this report on, 'Oh, they said this to me . . .' So there are a few situations where it gets into a grey area. The girls are sort of, like,

provoking the boys for some attention, but when they get
something that they don't like it's reportable. So you've got to be
very careful, I think, in the way that you support both the boys
and the girls because we don't want the boys to have the feeling
that they can't move anywhere or they can't say anything or, 'Tut,
tut, all this sexual harassment stuff is really painful and has got
nothing to do with rights and feeling comfortable, but is just a
way of girls being able to get at you.' (Dereck, drama teacher)

They arrange for the drama class to perform some role rever-
sals to stimulate reflection and discussion. The role-plays involve
cross-dressing: girls playing boys harassing boys playing girls.
Hips jutting in boys' clothes, the girl/boys' language is crude and
sexually explicit as they strut through clever and funny skits
about abuse. The boys playing girls are either timid and weak or
hyper-sexualised vamps; parodies of femininity. The audience is
seated in single-sex, self-selected groups. The tough boys cat-call
and wolf-whistle throughout and in discussion talk abut the best
moments for titillation, 'Jeez, what about when she said cunt?'
The rest of the class can't concentrate due to their noise. Eventually, the other groups fall silent. The frustrated teachers then
interpret the skits' messages for the students, but it ends up
sounding like teachers moralising about adolescent sexuality and
the whole class becomes resentful. These teachers made the mistake of thinking it would be easy.

Some teachers are able to reflect on their earlier belief that
students would respond to 'reason' and that change would be
easy with wry amusement. As Joan at Banksia laughingly said: 'I
thought if you just told them . . . they'll know all about it, there'll
be immediate change, it'll be terrific. It never works like that
though. Fancy being so stupid to think that it would, it's extraordinary.' But of course it is no more extraordinary than believing
the same thing of teachers. Knowing about gender issues and
relations does not necessarily mean that teachers will be able to
teach about such matters. Sensible teachers also consider questions of pedagogy, students' identities and the power relations
between teachers and students which many adolescents like to
interrupt. They know that many students don't like to 'be told'
but do like to discover their own truths and to share them with
each other. Skilful teachers reflect on the implications of their own
locations for what and how they teach; they don't abandon their
knowledge and authority but they do abandon their will to tell.
They guide students to understandings that they otherwise may
not reach. They are sensitive to the danger of manipulation, but

also to the dangers of abandoning students to the knowledge limits of their own locations. They are very suspicious of all common sense—their own and that of students. Such habits of good teaching are particularly important when teaching sensitive subjects and, as the following conversation between teachers from Eden Park demonstrates, common sense is not always good sense and good sense is hard to come by.

Jacqui: I think being a parent gives a teacher an edge on gender issues.

Louise: I was a teacher before I was a parent but I can't agree. Because your children are your children and you don't know how typical they are of other kids.

Chloe: But you do get another perspective I think. In that they have all their friends around too and so [you hear] all the conversations that go on, not only with your children but with their friends as well.

Louise: I don't know that my middle-class kids are typical of the kids I work with at school though. Most of the kids in our feeder area are from single-parent families, working class and bloody hard slog backgrounds. They're welfare backgrounds . . . I'm always aware of that difference. I suppose that brings in another issue, doesn't it? Whether middle-class teachers don't push middle-class values. I try hard not to make value judgments, I don't know how successful I am. I really try, but . . .

Chloe: You can't do it to them. You can't cause those conflicts in their lives. Ultimately it's their choice, but you can present them with alternatives.

Louise: But the very fact that you present them with an alternative can sometimes throw them into a dilemma. I mean thinking back to the Greek girls that I taught in Melbourne—I'm talking ten years ago when I was reading a bit of feminist stuff for the first time and getting really hot under the collar and going into the classroom and sort of talking off the top of my head with kids. And the girls would get all revved up and then they'd go home and Dad would belt them in the ear and tell them to sit in the corner. I was doing more harm than good. I thought I was doing the right thing, but . . .

Later in the conversation, Louise comments about her present practice:

Louise: I've got two very quiet Asian boys in this group and quite a few times I've said to the whole class, and to

93

them specifically, 'You might find what I've said there in conflict with what your community does, with what your culture says, by all means please say so because I will learn from you. I don't want you to think of me as just the teacher, I want to learn what your culture says about this issue—not just what the white culture, the white middle-class culture says.' They're very quiet but they do tell me in writing in their journals.

Jacqui: I find that issue a bit hard. I guess it's because I don't know where I stand. Teachers here will often let the quiet Aboriginal girls stay quiet Aboriginal girls but will soon squash the very dominating, sexist Greek males because the way they are being treated by the Greek boys affects them personally. I'm still coming to terms with how I stand on this.

Many teachers, having decided to attend to gender issues, learn that sensitivity to matters of gender enhances their work—perhaps after teething troubles. This is particularly the case with the sorts of intractable problems that leave teachers frustrated and mystified. Some teachers are relieved to have a new perspective on old problems and are curious and eager to see whether attending to gender can begin to address them. Those teachers in the learning areas most heavily coded by gender are intrigued about the possibilities and feel a new lease of professional life in some instances. The science teachers at Eden Park are enchanted with using Lego Technics to encourage girls in science. At Fleming, John, who has been involved in trialling new gender-inclusive curriculum materials, bubbles over with enthusiasm:

> I have been so overwhelmed . . . by the insight they have about graphs and the derivative function and what the derivative does . . . They are just so much more powerful than the previous group. Their ability to justify things like the chain rule is breathtaking. [John, mathematics teacher]

This sense of new possibilities is what keeps many teachers working at and through the problems that confront them until they get it, if not right, at least a lot better.

Jean Blackburn said in 1982:

> One role of education is to help young people to understand and reflect on what is, on how it came to be that way and on what

they want to do about it, both at the level of their own lives and in relation to social action. (1982, p. 10)

We think that successful schooling works towards the production of informed, critical, concerned, cultured, creative and courageous citizens who have the knowledge—information, understandings, capacities and skills—to work towards a better world for themselves and for others.

As we said at the outset, knowledge is the core work of schools and, as we have implied throughout, good teachers know about knowledge, learning and learners. Good teachers also know about gender, about its implications for knowledge, learning and learners. They know about the relationship between knowledge and power and they teach powerful knowledge in ways sensitive to the multiple axes of power. In the next chapter, we will show that the interaction of knowledge, power and sexuality is a core part of the gender relations of schooling, a particularly volatile combination which raises many issues for both students and teachers. These are not easily understood or resolved, but while they remain unaddressed and unresolved, students cannot become powerful learners and knowers.

4

Power

It's a 'rubbish bin' suburb. That's what they say about Wattfield. But the teachers at the school don't think so and neither do the locals. However, they are aware that such negativity can rub off on a school and its students. So, the school and community work together to ensure that the kids understand that what they have is rich and unique. As Lorraine Taylor, the EO Coordinator, says, students are encouraged to understand that 'they're an OK bunch of people and that their rich multicultural mix is to be valued'. The school recently developed a policy on sex-based harassment and Tracey is one of three Year 10 students who have taken a leading role in its development and promotion. Tracey describes her involvement.

> I was in a Healthy Localities Project with the Wattfield Council and we did a video on being assertive, domestic violence and harassment. Ms Taylor came to the launch and later asked would I help show kids about sexual harassment. It coincides with an English assignment that I'm doing in which we could choose a topic. Me, Javad and Steven rewrote the policy in kids' words and are doing posters and skits to show them what sexual harassment is.
>
> I was doing some vox pops yesterday—you know, interviews around the school—asking people what they thought it meant and one boy said something stupid. I said to him, 'You know, what—youse think it's part of life?' and he goes, 'Yeah, everyone does it, it's part of life.' I called him sexist and he goes, 'Why, why?' He thought he was right in what he was saying but I didn't.
>
> I've always been against women being hurt and men as well. But now I've talked to people that domestic violence has happened

to so I've got more of an idea of how bad it really is. I've seen a lot more cases.

People didn't know who they could go to, and that they could actually report it, before Ms Taylor took charge and started arranging these classes where kids would be educated. There's a lot of people who still haven't spoken out about things. But among ourselves we talk about it—and things come up in the media—so it's working to a degree and I think it's going to get better.

Maybe for guys, it is hard using the policy against someone. They think it's just girls' things, so they don't want to speak out too much in case something worse happens. They think their friends will hassle them. I think a girl's friend will encourage her if something has been happening but maybe boys might not be so encouraging to their friends unless it's really bad.

I went to see what the younger kids were doing down there in self-defence. Mainly it was just showing us how to be assertive and things like that, you know, how to protect ourselves against people, not necessarily men, just people in general.

The boys were getting pretty annoyed—like there was a meeting and they were saying, 'Why do you get all this stuff, we're stuck outside, we don't do anything.' But I think that they do, because usually the soccer oval is taken up with guys and the football oval is. So they've got enough to amuse themselves. The girls just sort of stuck up for it and said, 'Youse have virtually taken over the school anyway guys, you all think you are so good and you take over.' So we're really putting our foot down for more things for girls. I think the boys will be alright with that after it's been on for a while—hopefully they will. There might even be things that they could do for the boys. Like not all guys know how to defend themselves, so it might be good that they know just how to do it properly when the time comes.

What's influenced me is women getting a little more power lately. It's helped me to be able to speak out. Joan Kirner, the Victorian Premier. And the Turkish Prime Minister, the Canadian Prime Minister, both women at the moment. It shows women more up front. They're getting in there and it's made me speak out a bit more about women's issues.

I like the word feminist. It's positive. I don't think I'm really a feminist's feminist, but I do stick up for women's issues and hate anything along the lines of hassling women. I went to the *Reclaim the Night* march and there were just so many women who were fighting against things like that, they just really spurred me on to speak out more.

No, I'm probably not a feminist as such, but I do speak out about these sort of issues and things like that. I see it as women actually speaking out about what's happening. There's not too

many women who are prepared to do that, you know, especially when they're married or things like that.
I think feminists have more fun. They know where they're going.

'Power can be thought of as running around and through us, like honey, in various states of fluidity and congealment.' This is how Elizabeth Grosz (cited in Caine and Pringle 1995, p. xi) sees it and how we see it in schools. Once conscious of power, it can be seen seeping into every aspect of school life, but also congealing around certain sets of relationships at certain times, in certain places and working in certain interests. Power runs 'around and through' everything in schools—success, knowledge, emotion, responsibility. Further, it is a concept easily spread in analysis, but also potentially messy once multiple understandings and axes of power are recognised. In this chapter we will demonstrate this through the example of sexual harrassment.

In education, the sociologically minded often talk about the 'power (invested) in' certain things—institutional structures or roles, for example. Or they talk about some social groups exercising 'power over' others in and through schools and schooling systems—say, ruling class over working class. Some talk as if only some people in education have power and speak of the 'others' as the almost inevitably 'disempowered'. In this respect, some adopt spatial metaphors and talk about power flowing from the top down, or being located at the centre and not at the margins. Some tell the meta-narratives of power and focus on identifying its big structuring patterns and forces and the ways in which the macro is represented in the micro and vice versa. Others, such as those who draw from Foucault's post-structuralism, prefer to focus on the micro politics of power. They do not deny broad patterns of domination and subordination, but they deny that all power is possessed by one particular group or set of institutions, that it is dispersed from a centre, and that it is primarily repressive. To post-structuralists, power is exercised, not possessed, and best understood through an examination of its local operations. Through the interplay of discourses and the ways in which individuals and groups take up the positions which such discourses offer them, power takes effect and has effects. Power is also understood in other circles as ability, capability, capacity, potential to do things, skill. It involves the power to do or to act rather than the exercise of power over another. It points to the 'empowering' role of education—to the ways in which students can gain 'power through' knowledge, for example, or 'power with' each other through collectivity.

Like feminists generally, feminist researchers and gender reformers in education have found power a tasty but sticky concept. Predictably, they have used it in all of the ways noted above. But they have shown a preference for three conceptions of power, even though more often than not this preference has not been made explicit.

The first and dominant tendency has been to draw on ideas associated with notions of 'power in' and 'power over'. Power is seen to be located in institutional roles, rules and structures and those who occupy the appropriate locations are seen to exercise power over their subordinates through the capacity to make and effect the rules. These locations are seen to be gender neutral except to the extent that males occupy most such positions. The role of education is to get girls and women into those positions via the mechanisms which we discussed in Chapters 2 and 3—largely through access to valued knowledge and to the credentials with the best exchange value. This view of power leads to a push for access and equity for girls and women within existing institutions and structures. In some instances women are seen to bring a different sensibility to their new locations in the power structures; usually, however, they are not. The notion of women having a different sensibility leads to the second implicit view of power in gender reform. But it is worth noting that this first view of power has no particular ethical dimension and it offers no critical view of existing institutions and structures. Further, it collapses institutional power with control and fails to see the limits of such power.

The second tendency draws from a cluster of meanings centring around the notion of power as strength, authority, force, might, stamina, domination, ascendancy, vigour, potency and command. The conception of power here is largely one of 'power over'—typically the power of males over females. The connotations of power here are negative: they connote dominance, mastery, oppression, hierarchy and exclusion by individual men and/or by 'masculine' institutions. As Cox suggests, from this perspective power 'is primarily repressive in its exercise, that is, it imposes prohibitions and sanctions' (1996, p. 21). It is commonly associated with masculine attributes and is seen as antithetical to femaleness and feminism.

This view of power leaves feminists in education in an awkward position, for four reasons. First, it does not offer a very positive view of power. Second, in equating power with the

masculine it implies that to become powerful under current circumstances is to adopt the masculine, and so the sorts of power
of which it is critical. Third, it tells a rather monolithic story of
male power and female powerlessness. Virtue is seen to be on the
side of the powerless and vice on the side of the powerful. This
way of thinking is trapped in a logic which it seeks to defy, and
hence 'powerful' girls and women are viewed with considerable
ambivalence. The way out of this conundrum has been to offer
an alternative version of power associated with the so-called
feminine sensibilities of equality, cooperation, connectedness, nurturance and other 'female' values. This doesn't actually solve the
conceptual problem; maybe it makes it worse. But it does at least
offer an alternative ethic for the powerful. Fourth, this story
cannot accommodate power differences amongst males and
females or other axes of power.

Yet a further perspective emphasises 'power through' the
capacity to do things, to achieve goals, especially but not only in
collaboration with others. This is in contrast to an emphasis on
the 'power over' based on hierarchy or dominance. There are
different 'takes' on this notion of power. For example, access to
certain knowledge and forms of knowledge is seen to enhance
one's capacity to understand, deal with and—possibly—change
one's world. This personal knowledge is seen to be a means of
empowerment rather than a source of power over others. The
feminist agenda here is to ensure that girls and women have
access to this personally powerful knowledge. Other takes on
'power through' emphasise collaborative power (also called
'power with': see Adler, Laney and Packer 1993) and the 'collectivity' of women.

Although the gender reform policy and advice literature has
not done so, much feminist research in recent years has drawn
on post-structuralist notions of power. It rejects the binary logic
and the meta-narratives predicated on unified groups of oppres-
sors and oppressed implied in some of the views of power above.
It is concerned with the ways in which discourses which are
'inimical to women's interests acquire cultural authority' and with
'mobilising counter hegemonic feminist definitions and interpretations' (Fraser 1991, pp. 179–80).

As all these competing understandings of power suggest, it is
Janus-faced. This is best understood through reference to a particular issue. So, in order to expose this Janus face, in this chapter
we will focus on sex-based harassment[1] in schools and gender
reformers' different attempts to prevent it.

Many feminists in education have argued that the oppression of girls and women in classrooms and staffrooms is inextricably linked with sexuality as it connects to power and masculinity (Weiner 1994). Nevertheless, there has been considerable resistance in policy documents and in practice to acknowledging the relationship between sexuality, power and schooling. During the 1990s, however, there has been a discernible shift at the level of government policy and in many of our schools. In particular, the connection of sex-based harassment, and violence more generally, to the construction of femininities and masculinities in schools is being made explicit.

Sex-based harassment and its associated prevention policies, procedures and pedagogies bring a number of issues of power to the fore in a very stark way. We will begin by showing how such harassment is a form of boy 'power over' girls. We will point to the authoritative discourses which are mobilised to make normal, invisible and acceptable such an exercise of 'power over'. We will then show how schools' different ways of responding to sex-based harassment are informed by different notions of power and how different girls and different boys are constructed and construct themselves within such responses. In so doing we will expose the limitations and strengths of different ways of conceptualising power in relation to understanding and challenging sex-based harassment. We will suggest that many cannot see harassment because of the discourses which are available to conceal it. We will also make the case that teachers over-estimate the power of policy and certain forms of knowledge to overcome harassment, overlook the power relations inherent in their own practices of challenging such harassment and the implications that such pedagogical power may have for changing students' sensibilities. We will imply that a better understanding of power's many faces would assist teachers to develop more powerful practices.

Normalising 'power over' and making harassment invisible

> Sexual harassment isn't very much at this school. Oh well, I mean, only in the classroom and the yard. [Year 8 girl, Draymill]

For many girls in our schools, sex-based harassment is a daily occurrence, largely verbal but often physical. For other girls it is more occasional, arbitrary but no less intimidating. Girls describe how it 'makes you feel ashamed' (Year 9 girl, Mt Mullin), and how, 'You sort of take it in and you think about it' (Year 10 girl, Meadowlands) and it 'affects your confidence so you can't concentrate and your learning is affected' (Year 10 girl, Mt Mullin). Tamara, from Draymill, says, 'You think "What have I done? Why do they call me that?"' particularly when it comes from the older boys because, 'that could ruin your reputation even.' This intimidation manifests itself in many forms, from commenting upon girls' bodies and appearance to using explicitly sexual language and actions, leering, or touching girls and rubbing up against them. Often, the harassment is sexist rather than sexual in nature, including derogatory references to girls as a whole or to certain group of girls. At other times, it takes a more general form, such as name calling or subtle physical intimidation such as blocking the way or invading personal space—but is sex-based, that is, it is directed at girls largely because they are girls. It is so prevalent that it largely goes unremarked, even by those on the receiving end.

We asked several hundred students who harasses (teases, bullies) at school and who gets harassed. Harassment is often racially based, but the great majority of boys and girls alike agree that it is primarily initiated and carried out by boys and, while a considerable proportion consider this to be equally directed at girls and 'weaker' boys, most say that, 'it's mostly boys harass girls' (Year 9 girl, Mt Mullin). Many, like the following fifteen-year-old boys from Mt Forest, believe that certain students attract abuse and these 'victim types' just happen to be more often girls than boys.

Who gets harassed?

Lee: Someone who gives the impression that they can't stand up for themselves. Who gives the impression of being a victim. Some people get constantly harassed and they don't usually deserve it.

Shaun: I suppose girls get a lot more sexual harassment and stuff. I don't know just get teased, I don't know why, just seems to happen more to girls than boys.

Grant: There would be more girl victim types than there would be boy victim types.

Lee: I don't agree with that. Do you mean harassment? Girls hardly ever get harassed.

Shaun: Well, only as a joke.

Grant: Yes they do—it's mostly girls. There was one girl they harassed until she had to move classes. They called her names and hit her with rulers. Some people are really sensitive. She was really whiny. Now they are

> organising for someone in that class to do the same
> thing. Now, that's not fair. It's the wrong thing to do.
> She's a bit dippy but it's not the right thing to do. If
> that happened to me I wouldn't be happy. She did
> come to school in pigtails once but that's no excuse.

While wearing pigtails and being dippy may not *really* be an excuse, it appears that, in the view of many, some girls—many girls—do deserve harassment and there are any number of ways a girl can bring it on herself. What the girls who get harassed have in common is that they are girls. There is, of course, evidence of girls harassing other girls—and, indeed, boys—and the incidence of male bullying of males is high. Harassment directed at males by males and that directed at females by females is, however, commonly in terms derogatory to females, such as a boy insulting a boy by calling him a girl or sissy and a girl insulting a girl by calling her a slut.

Within what Sue Lees (1993) calls this 'vocabulary of abuse', the terms 'girl' and 'poofter' ('fag', 'faggot' or 'bumboy') are regarded as almost synonymous and as equally insulting when directed at boys. A number of boys who claim to have been sexually harassed by other boys give as their example that they have been called 'a girl'. When girls are harassed, it is very often because they are girls, when boys are harassed it is not because they are boys but because they are the wrong sort of boys. Mahony (1989, p. 163) puts it bluntly:

> [F]or [the boy] the lesson to be learnt is how to become a real
> man, dominant and not subordinate. For girls, the message is
> different. It is true that they must learn their proper place, but
> this is one of subordination, the 'done to' not the 'doers'.

The story, in Chapter 1, of Jessica and Georgie at Draymill provides a horrifying example of the extent and degree to which sex-based harassment can extend. This is not an isolated case. Girls change classes, truant and leave school in order to escape it. Even girls who are not harassed appear conscious of, intimidated by, and therefore constrained by, the potential to be harassed. Thus sex-based harassment acts as a form of social control which has educational and occupational, and hence social and material, effects on all girls and women, including those who have not experienced it personally.

The extent and the effects of sex-based harassment in schools are now so well documented in the educational research literature (e.g. Jones and Mahony 1989; Australian Education Council 1991;

Lees 1993) that it has to be asked why it needs to be said again. Well, somewhat to our surprise, few teachers in our research schools offer sex-based harassment as a gender issue for their school. There is almost a compulsion in many schools not to see it and not to say it. Nonetheless, the behaviour of (certain) boys and its effect on other students' learning is remarked upon frequently. Its connection to gender, however, is read largely in terms of the unequal distribution of teachers' time between girls and boys and boys' domination of the social and physical space, both of which are seen to disrupt girls' learning. Often, the solution is single-sex classes for girls and girls-only (boy-free) spaces. Even though we are constantly told that it is 'boys in groups' that are the problem and that the 'problem' is a normal consequence of adolescence, the behaviour is nevertheless individualised and pathologised. Remarkably, the sex-based nature of much of the behaviour often goes unremarked as do the power relations between boys and girls.

They don't dislike her as a person

When asked explicitly about sex-based harassment, many teachers simultaneously deny its existence or prevalence and unwittingly describe examples of it. Tom, one of our tradies from Braydon Tech, is a case in point.

> There's a girl in Building Studies at the moment, she's been really intimidated by the boys, who don't dislike her as a person, but really feel that she shouldn't be there. Boys get threatened by having a girl in their place. There is a lot of light-hearted banter about her being there, how she can't do things—it can be very cruel at times. Because she's only one, they figure they can intimidate her and get rid of her. But no, no sexual harassment.

As Jan, past EO Coordinator at Bridgeforth says, 'sex-based harassment is everywhere present and nowhere seen'.

Even in the face of the long-term distress caused to Jessica, Georgie, Nikki and Jodie at Draymill, resulting in Nikki leaving school and Jessica continuing to see a psychologist, a number of teachers regard the sex-based harassment of the girls as 'blown out of proportion'. Others are distressed to think that it had been going on 'before their eyes' and they didn't see it. Yet, according to many girls in our schools, this is not uncommon. How can it be? Is it, as Jessica and Georgie think, wilful blindness? Our data suggest that central to readings of the gendered power relationships between boys and girls is a dominant discourse which naturalises such sexist behaviours as a combination of 'just mucking about' and 'teasing', a normal part of girl–boy relationships and a natural result of boys' sexual awakening at a period of social immaturity.

Robby, Trent and Dan, who perpetrated the sex-based harassment of Jessica and Georgie, captured these themes when the issue was raised by us a year later.

Robby: We learnt a pretty valuable lesson. 'Cause I think we've grown up a bit since that now.

Trent: It just started as a joke and got serious.

Robby: We didn't realise what we were saying. We didn't think like, that 'Oh, you might be hurting them.' We got a bit carried away.

Dan: We didn't set out to do anything bad, it was a good laugh for us. Just a joke. When they would tell us what they thought about us we would just respond more. It became like a sort of debate. Also I've sat with females and talked with a couple of rough, really tough girls here and you can talk like that. But those girls didn't take it that way.

Trent: We got a big ego thing. We had more power over them, like that. Yeah . . . felt dominant.

Robby: Like we were the top of the world—we knew everything.

Dan: In a way I think it was sort of, like, jealousy too. Because we were the only three males in the class and the females were all over the teacher.

Robby: Like in PE, because there were so many girls, if they wanted to play netball we would have to.

Dan: We didn't get to play cricket . . . It was our way of getting back at them.

Trent: Not just because they were favoured but they did their work and got it done. And we were bludgers. We resented them for that, particularly when one got head of the class.

Dan: Yeah, the teachers would say when we handed work in, 'Well done Nikki, she got all her work done.'

Robby: When we razzed them, they would sort of take it, and they used to speak back to us. We tried to make them feel humiliated, to feel as low as we did. Because last year I did not feel good about myself.

Dan: We wanted to bring them down to our standard of work.

Robby:	We wanted to be up there as high as them or higher and be above them. In attacking them sexually we were trying to boost ourselves.
Trent:	That we should be dominant.
Dan:	We were just boys being rough and not really caring.
Robby:	That's a feeble excuse.

The boys, while feeling penitent and ashamed, nevertheless rationalised their treatment of the girls; it was only a joke that went too far, they were unaware of its consequences, and last year they were immature and insecure but now they've grown up.

They're just having a bit of fun

We/they 'were only joking' and 'having fun' is a constant refrain throughout our data from Draymill, as it is from many of our schools.

These kids were just having a little bit of fun, they weren't touching they weren't doing anything except with mainly just doing a bit of teasing which wasn't really doing anyone any harm. [Year 10 boy, Nerringo]
    You just sort of don't think, 'Hey that's sexual harassment', you sort of just say 'Oh well, they're just having a bit of fun.' [Year 10 girl, Bannilong]

Indeed, the Principal at Draymill also described it as a joke, 'at someone else's expense' that 'got out of hand' and then 'became a gender issue'. As the interview with Robby and friends shows, it was a gender issue from the start, nevertheless, defining such behaviour as just 'a joke' or 'fun' makes it acceptable, and even invisible. Even when girls are trying to express their desperate hurt, they use this discourse.

By Year 11 you are sort of immune. When you are younger you get hurt but now we are more of the attitude that we don't care what people think. I mean you do but you get over it. We don't think of it as harassment—it is just fun for them. [Year 11 girl, Mt Forest]

It is clear that these girls do not find it funny and are distressed and confused both by the harassment itself and by their conflicting reactions to it. Over and over, girls describe their feelings of anger and exposure and of being used; fun should feel good but instead it often feels bad.

There are three common subtexts of the discourse which accuses some girls, teachers and policy-makers of 'taking it too far', 'over-reacting' and mistaking friendly fun for harassment. They are, first, that boys are less capable than girls of drawing the line between 'funny' and 'not funny' and so occasionally 'take it too far' and girls and teachers should not make too much of it; second, that girls can't take a joke or cope with the normal give and take of peer relations; and, third, that girls lead boys on and then call foul. Jessica and Georgie are unconvinced.

Jessica: They said, 'Oh, we thought they didn't care. We thought they knew we were just joking.' They just didn't expect that they'd get dobbed in after four years.

Georgie: All in good fun, but this isn't fun. No, it's not funny at all. You know, after a while of them saying those awful things about you, you grow to believe it.

Jessica: I still really have no idea why they did it. Maybe because they were bored.

Georgie: Like they haven't got anything better to do. Yeah. Sort of like, we were there for them—there to be taken advantage of, 'Oh, let's have some fun with these girls.'

As our interview with Robby, Trent and Dan shows, they were only too aware that their earlier behaviour was not a joke between friends; they had been anything but friends and they used sexuality as a means of exerting their dominance. The boys can tell the difference between 'mucking about' within a friendship group and gaining status within their own friendship group by attacking others, although it may not always serve their interests to admit this. Indeed, many boys in our schools, like Grant from Mt Forest who was quoted earlier, consider any interference with their 'fun' to be unfair at the same time that they acknowledge that it is often not funny to the targets.

That's where it comes back to the teachers, they take it too serious. A lot of times it's just mucking around and it's only a joke but I suppose it wouldn't feel like that if you were the victim. But still the teachers always take it too seriously.

Grant's friend, Lee, harangues the 'new teachers who have come in and are all big on equal opportunity'. The only thing wrong with this school, they say, is that the 'sexual harassment policy is over the top' because after all, 'it's only a joke.'

Trying to get their attention

Sex-based harassment is also often seen to be a part of normal relationships between boys and girls, an adolescent mating dance which is complicated within the school setting by the greater maturity of girls than boys during the adolescent years and the sexual and emotional vulnerability of boys at this age. In order to explain why 'popular' girls are often the subject of harassment, some boys suggest that they are 'being macho' and 'showing off toughness and maturity' around those girls because they are 'trying to get their attention'. And many girls buy it. At Riverside, ten girls in Year 9 are shown a video clip of some girls who spoke out in school about being teased by boys. All ten girls are completely perplexed by the video: they appear to regard verbal harassment by boys as a sign of interest and cannot believe that the boys in the video would bother to harass the ordinary-looking girls in the video. 'Why,' they say, 'would the boys be interested in them?' In other cases, such harassment is regarded less sanguinely. A girl at Mt Mullin suggests that boys put down girls as part of the 'competition to see who's the biggest stud with the girls'. At the same school, a boy says that, 'maybe it might be the boy wants to go out with the girl and the girl doesn't want to and he might tease her for it. Have a go at her.'

Teachers also often justify boys' behaviour in coeducational classes, and the need for single-sex classes, on these grounds. 'They're more free when they're just all boys,' says Diane, a mathematics and science teacher at Braydon Tech, 'because they're not having to show off in front of girls or they're not having to be concerned about anything sexual at all, or any of those relationships.' That boys do not 'have to' show off is not contemplated and why boys need to show off not questioned. While not condoning 'extreme' forms of sex-based harassment, teachers often normalise it. For example, Matt, from Rullinga, comments: 'The girls are copping it a bit because the boys are more aggressive and also their sexuality is awakening.' This represents a commonly held view that those who harass are incapable of controlling their sexuality, either because it is a testosterone problem or because they are slow developers lacking in confidence, immature and therefore victims of maturation. It accepts that individual students' behaviours differ on the one hand, but assumes that boys as a group tend to mature later and, while the problem is the collective of boys, the solution lies with the individual's natural development into maturity. Given the well-documented extent of sex-based harassment in adult workplaces, including school staffrooms, and the obvious link to male privilege and to sexism generally, this is a rather odd notion. Indeed, our data suggest that, while harassment is more obviously carried out by younger boys, it often continues in subtle and sophisticated ways as they become older and larger, with many girls reporting that it gets 'more verbal' and also more damaging. But many adults, both teachers and parents, are somewhat reassured when boys behave in this aggressively macho way, since it conforms to 'normal' masculinity—how else will they grow into men? A teacher at Draymill recounts how one boy's mother, when told of her son's harassment of Jessica and Georgie, whispered to her husband, 'Thank God, he's a real boy.' This is not an uncommon response.

Nevertheless, real boys apparently need nurturance and sympathy by teachers and by real girls. This essentialist discourse provides for girls the subject position of being 'more mature than boys'. This is taken up by some girls who become maternal about—or at least tolerant of—male immaturity. One Year 11 girl from Mt Mullin said:

> I think they're immature and unsure about themselves and think they have to impress their friends. And they're worried about being this other person they're not. Punishing them would just make them sillier. You need to make them talk to someone, get all their problems out of themselves.

The essentialist aggression-nurturance dualism within this discourse absolves many boys from responsibility for their aggression since 'boys will be boys'. It also demands that girls take responsibility for dealing with and understanding that aggression since 'girls should be girls'. It thus enables the girls to take the high moral ground and to become powerful through their emotional and moral superiority.

Boys also learn to call upon these discourses which position them simultaneously as victims, powerless in their immature and insecure masculinity, and also as powerful in that same masculinity. Their own sense of powerlessness, say the Draymill boys, was the source of their desire to have power over this particular group of girls. While they say that they were unaware that their behaviours intimidated the girls, in 'attacking them sexually', however, they drew on the discourses of hegemonic masculinity which position boys and men as powerful and girls and women as powerless. Thus their actions arose not just out of their sense of inadequacy, but also out of the pleasure they derived from being positioned as powerful.

At Draymill, the issue is seen to have been resolved since the boys have been punished and other boys (and girls) know it. Furthermore, the behaviour of those three boys has improved. The school is planning to develop a policy to address sex-based harassment in the future. Barry, the Curriculum Coordinator at Draymill, is openly hostile to the prospect:

> A lot of the policies are being engendered by people with a particular bias and I don't trust them. Of course, if you hear a boy calling a girl a slut, or if you hear the girl calling a boy something, usually you stop it but to jump up and down and say, 'These things must never happen' is stupid. It's not an issue. It is something that has always happened. A lot of these policies are aimed at what I would call the middle class. The upwardly mobile, the highly educated, but I don't think their policies relate to the vast majority of the community. I've never seen those policies relate to a canning worker in the factories.

For Barry, it's not an issue because it's always happened. While the behaviour is not acceptable and probably 'went too far', it doesn't have to be dealt with at any institutional level. Many members of the school community, like Barry, continue to construct the harassment as resulting from youth, as something boys 'go through' and (hopefully) grow out of when they become more mature. Indeed, the boys themselves do too.

The irony of this story is that we visited the school because the Principal informed us that their main gender reform programme addressed domestic violence and sexual abuse which, he says, 'is a problem in the community'. This, however, turns out to be a set of guidelines for teachers on dealing with suspected cases of abuse and a welfare/counselling service provided to individual students who, because of their home circumstances, are identified as 'at risk'. These clearly are important activities, but there is no concomitant commitment to the kinds of educational reforms which might reduce domestic violence and sexual abuse in the future. For the Principal and many teachers, no connection is made between the 'everyday' behaviour of boys in school and gendered violence more generally.

It's in their nature to be aggressive to girls

Within this discourse, sex-based harassment is understood by many teachers as resulting from some natural characteristic of masculinity, which at times ('occasionally') exhibits itself in extreme and unacceptable forms. The more extreme forms of male behaviour are seen to be a symptom of a particular individual boy's incapacities or anti-social behaviour and not part of a wider system of social relations which impart power to males in particular ways. At the same time, and somewhat contradictorily, many teachers regard sex-based harassment as 'aberrant' behaviour more typical of certain social groupings (working class), reflecting the stresses of life within particular families or their communities, perhaps unemployment or single parenting.

> They were in Year 10, they could see manhood approaching and what are they going to do and how is a boy to act and them with just a mother at home. I just felt in a way more sorry for them. [Harriet, biology teacher, Mt Forest]
>
> There is their oppression and their total fear and insecurity and the fact that they are beaten and buggered and all the oppressions that can be visited upon these scared little boys and then there's also the masculinity acquired from TV. [Barry, social studies teacher, Bettleford]

Where there is a significant ethnic minority, however, sex-based intimidation is often constructed, by mainly Anglo teachers, as a problem of cultural difference and attributed to 'other' ethnic cultural groups. At Merrilong, for example, many teachers see many school problems as stemming directly from the 'ethnic' boys. They are seen to be powerful in influencing the other boys to be 'like them' and powerful in being so much the dominant force in the school that other boys, along with all girls, are completely subsumed under their influence. The so-called ethnic girls are credited with no power. They are seen to be the ones needing help and encouragement to 'make it' in the school due to their 'double disadvantage' of race and gender. Concentrating on the 'ethnic' (Southern European origin) boys allows sexist attitudes to be constructed only within an ethnic framework. It puts all the blame on the 'ethnic' boys, absolves the 'non-ethnic' boys completely and, indeed, absolves teachers from intervening.

> People are pretty open-minded here. I think they try to accommodate differences by making allowances for the unskilled girls [in sport] or by putting up with perhaps overly aggressive behaviour from the boys, because it's in their nature to be aggressive to girls . . . [Pamela, Physical Education teacher, Merrilong]

111

In other schools, certain 'other' ethnic groups are constructed more positively:

> In relation to harassment, the Indo-Chinese girls are not overtly harassed as much by the other boys as the other girls and most of the Indo-Chinese boys do not sexually harass. It's just not that sort of gender culture. [Bette, personal development teacher, Bettleford]

Whether constructed positively or negatively, this classist and racist discourse places the cause of sex-based harassment outside the school and enables schools to abrogate responsibility for its occurrence within the school. It may not be the case that 'all boys will be boys', but 'certain types of boys' will be.

Some schools have taken it upon themselves

We have demonstrated the power of discourse to control the meanings that surround sex-based harassment and, therefore, what is seen, what needs to be said and what needs to be done. The discourses which naturalise this behaviour enable sex-based harassment to be simultaneously described and denied. Consequently, there is usually little reflection about how the school implicitly or explicitly condones such behaviours.

During the period of our research, however, there was a discernible shift in some schools. The report *Listening to Girls* (Australian Education Council 1991), provided a powerful indictment of the sexist treatment of many girls in Australian schools and received considerable media attention. At around the same time, the Victorian *Action Plan for Girls* (Office of Schools Administration 1991) made addressing sex-based harassment a priority. Together, these provided some stimulus for action by schools in Victoria so that, in 1993, one-fifth of the schools we surveyed had some form of policy or action plan. As the boys from Mt Forest said, some teachers had started to 'spit the dummy' when you 'do something against the girls'. In Western Australia, although a number of our research schools had some education about sex-based harassment, none had a policy or plan which explicitly addressed it and, indeed, some teachers were rather dismissive of the whole notion:

> Some schools in Victoria have taken it upon themselves to develop a gender policy in their school. Kids as young as twelve are going to be suspended if they harass students [make

suggestive remarks or gestures]. We haven't got to that point here. One questions whether one should get to that point. [Mary, English teacher, Kingwood]

Nevertheless, a small number of Western Australian schools had educational programmes to deal with sex-based harassment and others were proposing to work on something in the near future. In both Victoria and Western Australia, the majority of approaches to sex-based harassment largely individualised the issue; only a few linked sex-based harassment to gendered power relations and those that connected it to violence generally did so in a 'non-gender focused' way. What they all did, however, was attempt to enable girls and boys and teachers to *name* sex-based harassment and to develop processes for addressing it when it occurred.

Girl power

Amongst feminists, there are those who—while acknowledging the existence and even the extent of sex-based harassment—are critical of the emphasis placed on the concept by other feminists and on the use of policies or laws to deal with it, arguing that it leads to what they call 'victim feminism' which constructs women as helpless, joyless and oppressed (Wolf 1993). In our schools, approaches to naming and addressing sex-based harassment and the role of policies variously construct girls as powerless or powerful: witness the cases of Stowley, Bridgeforth and Wattfield.

The girls know their place

Stowley has a policy on sex-based harassment which was developed by an EO Coordinator who has since moved to another school. This year, at Stowley, form teachers have given their students two lessons on sex-based harassment. Only one of these teachers has had any part in the development of the policy, only three have experience with addressing the issue and all receive only a five-minute briefing and a set of overhead transparencies. Some are reluctant to teach the lessons, generally because they feel ill-prepared.

Students are informed of the school policy, what constitutes unacceptable behaviour and what sanctions apply for infringements. The task of addressing sex-based harassment is one of containment: student behaviour is expected to change largely due to improved disciplinary procedures. Strategies include individual counselling and behaviour modification contracts for those who transgress. Several teachers comment on the reduction in the level of unacceptable behaviours amongst boys in terms of the number of public and overt instances of sex-based harassment of girls. The policy could therefore be considered to have 'worked'. Our data suggest that—as usual—it is not quite so simple.

Students have been empowered to name and complain about sex-based harassment. Many girls and boys can recite a reasonable definition of what it is, although some, like Mia, feel confused and anxious. 'Nearly everything you could do comes under sexual harassment. I reckon that's pretty silly. I mean even just looking.' Her friend Natalie doesn't agree. 'Yeah, but I mean it's not really. It's like if someone is really yuk and they stare at you a lot, and it's not very nice.' Mia concedes this point and, while not quite sure how far to take it, nevertheless is critical of the way some teachers 'just ignore it', and they 'have to learn what sexual harassment is'. According to Natalie, 'It's the male teachers that have to know the way females get harassed.' 'Or treated,' corrects Mia, still worried by the term.

Most of the girls we interviewed believed that if they reported an offence it would be dealt with, although—like Mia and Natalie—a number did not believe that certain teachers, particularly but not only males, were prepared to see or act on sex-based harassment in class unless the girls actually reported it. The responsibility lies with the girls. And so what is a girl to do?

Their ways of responding vary depending upon time and place. Many use a range of practices—ignoring it, humour, retaliation in kind—and sometimes they decide to call upon institutional procedures for redress and complain to teachers. This, however, can lead to the girls being seen as whingers and dobbers, unacceptable in peer cultures, 'not cool'.

Unfortunately, our interviews suggest that girls at Stowley are positioned by teachers, boys and girls as powerless, as unable to deal with things themselves. The agenda for the policy appears to be to protect helpless girls from hopeless boys.

> The programme might have an effect on an individual case of harassment where it's direct sexual harassment of a girl and there's one to one counselling of that student or as a discipline problem or as a counselling problem. I don't think there's been any general success as far as modifying the behaviour of boys in general. The girls cope by sitting together, by being quiet and

passive, by in most cases just accepting it as the normal state of affairs, by not fighting back. I think it's an inbred attitude. [Don, Curriculum Coordinator, Stowley]

And so, rather than being empowered, many of the girls have been enabled to identify as victims with no personal power or autonomy to do anything about it themselves. The emphasis on authority and discipline appears to underline female weakness and male strength.

This discourse which casts girls as powerless in the face of sex-based harassment ran through many of our interviews with teachers and this was particularly so when the explanations offered for harassment emphasised the 'sexist attitudes' of parents and the local community. As with the teachers at Draymill, teachers at Stowley blame the traditional views of the roles of men and women in the predominantly Anglo rural community.

The school and the community are very patriarchal. The girls know their place. They don't see anything wrong with modifying their behaviour to suit the boys and nor do the people who work with them because often the girls are quiet and unassuming and the problems aren't recognised. [Kay, Library Coordinator, Stowley]

Indeed, some suggest that a multicultural mix would help in reducing sex-based harassment because of the need to learn to accommodate and respect difference.

Trying to explain this gender stuff, especially sexual harassment, is scary, because this is a mono-cultural community. If you live in a mono-cultural community it is very difficult for the community to compare, be challenged and change, because the community is actually what is regarded as being normal. They're not exposed to the flux and change of, say, the western suburbs. [Angie, Year 11 Coordinator, Stowley]

This is rather ironic given that teachers in other schools construct 'ethnic' boys as the perpetrators of the most extreme forms of sex-based harassment.

The approach to sex-based harassment adopted at Stowley positions girls as weak and in need of protection but, at the same time, also as having to take responsibility for reporting and substantiating offences themselves, and yet as weak if they do. These contradictions are not peculiar to Stowley or to Draymill, or to 'traditional' Anglo rural communities, as the case of Bridgeforth shows.

I was sort of angry that they were prepared to put up with it

Bridgeforth is in a more multicultural and suburban community, with almost half of its students from non-English speaking backgrounds. Like Stowley, it has recently implemented a sex-based harassment policy. Bridgeforth, however, offers a more broadly based educational programme which seeks to convince students of the need for the policy and promote it as a matter of respecting the rights of individuals to a safe and comfortable learning environment. Unacceptable behaviour is expected to change largely through awareness raising—that is, by students learning to recognise and name sex-based harassment, to understand it and why it is unacceptable.

Jan, the previous EO Coordinator who was responsible for the development of the policy, felt it was making a difference but described developing the programme as 'harrowing' as she became regarded as the school's 'moral policewoman' and, as one male teacher accused, 'of trying to change normal relations between girls and boys'. A number of the Year Level Coordinators, who were expected to take responsibility for implementing the educational programme and the policy, didn't take it seriously, and refused to deal with girls' complaints, being reluctant to name behaviour they took for granted as harassment and boys as 'sexual harassers'.

> Some of the girls told me that they complained and complained and the coordinators thought it was just boys being boys. 'We won't report it, he's not a bad kid, you know, he is a really good kid,' and 'We should give this kid a warning.' And I said, 'You can't give just a warning. Everyone has to know. Everyone has to know. It must get back to others that it was treated very seriously.'

Jan described her distress at the reaction to the policy of some girls who were loud in stating that it was unnecessary. They saw it as empowering teachers too much to intervene in student peer relationships and allowing 'feminists' to go 'over the top'. Their image of feminists who intervene in boy–girl relationships by speaking out against sexism was that they were anti-pleasure, humourless, extremist and man-haters. It is a position that many girls do not want to take up and, at Bridgeforth, it resulted in their initial rejection of the policy. 'Why,' they asked Jan, 'do you want to change things with the boys? Why do you want to blame them?' This reaction is not uncommon in our schools. Typically it comes from girls who are considered to be 'strong girls' and who reciprocate the verbal and physical harassment in good measure. Some have close peer friendships with the boys whom they feel a need to defend against the relentless force of feminism.

Teachers, in their turn, often position girls who reciprocate and/or participate in harassment as 'bad girls' even when they are reluctant to position the boys who initiate it as 'bad boys'. This positioning of such girls occurs not only because they step out of the role of being the passive and docile good female student, but also because of their mateship with boys and all the sexual connotations arising out of being 'boy mad'. This often means that when they do appeal to teachers about sex-based harassment they are not taken seriously. Many feminist teachers, who might be expected to be sensitive to the contradictions in this, also react negatively to such girls because of their seeming complicity in sex-based harassment and their apparent support of the type of macho masculinity which makes sex-based harassment and other gendered power relations acceptable. Jan commented: 'I can't say that I handled it well at the time. I was sort of angry that they were prepared to put up with it.' In ensuing discussions, her colleague Rachel called upon psychological explanations of the construction of femininity to explain this in terms of the 'girls' desire to be approved of by boys':

> I wonder if this might be partly due to girls being controlled
> through disapproval from an early age—girls being warned not to
> get clothes dirty, held back from exploring—whereas boys aren't.
> If this is so, it may help explain why girls more than boys seem
> to be more dominated by a greater need for approval.

And Jan came to think that 'particularly the tougher more sexually mature girls would feel that way because they are more fragile really and have a lot of investment in keeping the boys happy'. Jan, who continues to run classes, now tries to work with the girls and not on them:

> The next group, I came in with less confrontation. I didn't sort of
> say, 'This is what sexual harassment is, isn't it terrible?' and show
> the video, 'Isn't it disgusting?' which I was assuming they would
> agree with. Instead I talked about what they would consider
> unacceptable. I tried to work from them outwards rather than me
> imposing. I ran it differently. Much more informal. They were
> initially very embarrassed but I got so much more out of them
> than before.

She believes that the improvements in her pedagogy mean that the girls she teaches are increasingly likely to interpret the policy as helping them better control the conditions of their own lives at school.

Jan does not underestimate the task. She argues that too many teachers believe that having a policy deals with the matter. And, indeed, in many of our schools this appeared to be the case. For some, policy development is a cynical exercise about appearances rather than change, but others seem to believe in the power of policy (with sanctions) to change people and are unable to recognise the difficulties using such policies present for many students. As Jan commented:

> I think that teachers underestimate what a risk it is for girls to report it. I mean, we don't even do it as women sometimes. We find it very difficult to say to someone, 'No,' and we are asking fifteen-year-old girls to do it and they find it very difficult to do. Also it isn't sometimes the boys' response it is other girls' responses to them complaining about it.

Raoul, the present EO Officer, said, 'We've tried to make it a process where the girls feel that they can come and report it without repercussions on them for doing that.' He arranged for us to talk to a number of girls whom he described as 'confident', 'popular', 'outspoken' and 'not afraid to stand up to the guys'. These girls, he said, 'are really forceful and really strong about equal opportunity and their rights.' The girls certainly were confident that they were able and popular, that they had bright futures ahead of them and that they had 'equal opportunities' with the boys. But they described sex-based harassment in much the way girls did in many of our schools. For fourteen-year-old Maria, to be sure, dealing with it is simply a matter of 'telling them where to get off because if someone puts me down—which they've done a lot all through my life—there's no way you would see me not saying what I think. Unless,' she laughingly adds, 'it's my mother.' The other girls, however, 'just ignore them. We walk off sort of thing. Sometimes it works.' But, they say, 'when we get upset we tell our [male] friends,' and then, 'that guy gets it handled from there.' Less popular girls, they tell us, are in a more difficult position because they don't have male friends 'to sort it out'. These girls, who continue to characterise themselves as being in need of the protection of a strong male, are the 'strong' girls of whom Raoul spoke. One, who was regularly called a 'Nazi whore', described having reported it to the appropriate year level teachers:

He told me to put him on the Sexual Harassment Policy thing, and so I did and that was that. They just must have, you know, put it somewhere and then it went into the files I think. I didn't know nothing about it after that, the teachers probably did it.

Thus Bridgeforth, at the same time, offers these girls power and strips them of it. Certainly, the girls are *aware* of their rights, but they do not yet have the personal resources to demand and gain those rights, notwithstanding the apparent backing of 'the policy'.

Opponents to the use of the concept of sexual harassment generally, and the use of associated laws and policies in particular, often fail to acknowledge the strength and the courage it takes to say that you have been harassed (Brant and Too 1994). Regrettably, girls (and boys) who use institutional procedures developed to protect them are characterised as weak and powerless victims rather than strong and powerful defenders. In our schools, however, proponents of the use of the concept and policy often make the same mistake. While attempting to raise awareness and understanding, and calling upon students' 'goodwill', many educational programmes offer girls and boys little help in developing the strength, the courage and the skills they need to defend themselves, to experience themselves as powerful and to take responsibility for themselves. Some schools, however, are trying to find a better way. Wattfield is one such school.

We're really putting our foot down

As we indicated in the vignette with which we began this chapter, Wattfield is often referred to as a rubbish bin suburb, but its teachers refuse to accept this characterisation and, in any case, believe that schools should be active agents for change. Tracey and two boys, one Turkish and one Anglo, have been involved in the development and promotion of the school's sex-based harassment policy. They take considerable responsibility for promoting it within and beyond the school, developing posters and skits and video, interviewing students around the school for vox-pops on the issue. A small group of students visit classrooms and explain it to younger students. The emphasis is on encouraging both the boys and the girls to understand the issues and to feel supported.

Girls in the school, much to their delight, are learning how to defend themselves. There is a lunchtime programme in self-defence for Year 8 girls which, according to one of the girls, 'the school paid for with a little bit of money from equal opportunities they had put aside' and 'we wanted to do it 'cause it was for a good cause, to learn to protect ourselves'. Sandy, a drama teacher, described how, 'the girls were getting really disturbed about the way they were talked to by the boys. So we have a girls' lunchtime programme where they plot out how they can defend themselves against that sort of stuff.' Lorraine believes it helps. 'I think the girls are getting better at deflecting that sort of thing themselves and putting them back in their place.' Furthermore, 'the girls are now more likely to support each other'.

Sex-based harassment is prevalent at Wattfield and, with regard to the support provided to girls, there is plenty of resentment and resistance from some boys. 'But,' says Tracey, 'we're really putting our foot down.' Indeed, the girls we speak to—Spanish, Iraqi, Vietnamese, Anglo—clearly feel more empowered to deal with it. They are confident that they can deal with sexist and aggressive behaviour. Witness our field notes.

> They generated a real sense of power through sharing, respecting and valuing amongst the groups. They were able to give voice to their concerns knowing that they would be heard and honoured by the teachers involved. Their teachers commented admiringly on how the girls managed to preserve themselves in the face of sexism and can articulate their concerns. [Field notes, Wattfield]

And, if the use of the policy becomes necessary—which it does—well, it is their policy; it is girls, and some boys, answering back and saying, 'we've had enough'. The discourse at this school is not one of weak girls but of strong—even when vulnerable—girls.

This distinction between weakness and vulnerability is made explicit at Neerbin, where the principal talks about some girls being physically harassed by boys: 'I don't think the girls look on that as happening because they are weak. Rather, they are in a vulnerable situation in the classroom or outside.' The provision of self-defence classes and classes in 'standing strong' against all forms of harassment makes a statement that the greater physical vulnerability of girls is not the same as weakness or powerlessness. It also offers the possibility of reducing the social control exerted by the prevalence of sex-based harassment and other forms of male violence. Barrie Thorne reminds us that, 'In gestures that mix protection with punishment, parents and other adults often tighten their control of girls when they become adolescents' (1994, p. 156). But this can change. As one Wattfield girl said, 'Mum lets me go out now. She never used to but I am allowed now because I can kick and that.' At this school, the hope and belief is that the empowered girls who reclaim their school will, like Tracey, become the powerful women who 'reclaim the night'. This school considers awareness a poor substitute for action.

Boy power

Feminist educators have for some time argued that the responsibility for change should not lie solely with girls and women, but also with boys and men. And in our schools, many teachers are at pains to point out to us that it is time to focus upon boys. Indeed, many EO workers find themselves in uneasy and suspicious partnership with those whose cries of 'what about the boys?' are *not* a call for gender justice.

While often arguing for increased attention to boys, however, both feminist and non-feminist teachers tended only to gesture to difference amongst boys in a tokenistic manner. Difference amongst boys was largely set into dualisms of good/bad boys, quiet/loud boys, aggressive/passive masculinity. Frequently, 'quieter' boys, often the academic achievers, were positioned as being equally passive and victims of macho hegemonic masculinities as girls. These boys were largely ignored by feminist discourses in schools, because their behaviour did not impact upon girls' education.

Boys, however, do differ. Some are, themselves, not the 'right' sorts of boys; others successfully subscribe to dominant forms of masculinity in its most negative manifestations; others decline to participate in hegemonic masculinity.

I am the only kid I know with backwards elbows

Boys who themselves are subject to sex-based harassment in schools are most often those who exhibit a subordinate form of masculinity. Patrick, at Stowley, describes—with some humour—his own experiences.

> I have been harassed at eleven schools now. At every school I have been to I have been the ten-pound weakling. Like, I am the only kid I know with backwards elbows! Because in my job in the school I deal with the locker grills and all that, I get harassed

guaranteed at least every morning. They just feel like throwing rocks at me, pushing me around, shoving me, throwing me into the walls.

At one stage people were writing notes and slipping them into my locker, like 'Patrick is a wanker.' 'Patrick is a poofter.' And all this sort of stuff. I took it to Mr Fiorentino. The writing was tracked down. He got their books off the teachers and they traced it—and it ended up to be a Year 9. And he got into a fair bit of trouble over it. I get harassed a lot because I can't fight someone physically. [Sigh] I can fight them mentally, but not physically.

And Jan from Bridgeforth comments that boys are starting to use their policy.

I also had boys coming up who had been harassed—had been touched and they have complained. So it has been boys as well because quiet boys are also disadvantaged by this behaviour. [Past EO Coordinator, Bridgeforth]

Amy, Student Welfare Cordinator at Bridgeforth, describes the school's concern for a number of boys who had 'copped a fair bit of flak' because they had 'developed their own identity'.

There were some instances of homosexuality and one boy copped quite a lot about four years ago. But it wasn't only that—there were some boys who were very quiet and academic and not macho enough. They've got to be competitive, a sportsperson, drink with mates, the initiator in any sort of relationships with girls. Most of the boys would fit that stereotype and would believe that that ought to be the way that boys should be. And a lot of the students here—particularly the boys—are not tolerant of anything different.

Schools, however, seem even less well equipped to deal with the forms of harassment experienced by boys who are 'different' than they are with harassment of girls. The spectre of accusations of encouraging homosexuality looms large in many schools. A group of girls at Braydon Tech describe how the boys are 'really prejudiced against homosexuals', and 'hopeless in the debate' whereas the girls are 'more open minded'—although other girls tell how they can 'really cut' a boy by calling him a 'poofter'. In a number of schools which undertake 'boys' programmes'—for example, Riverside—the accusation is made by some boys that the school is trying to turn them into homosexuals—an accusation which is sufficient to cause some teachers and some schools to back off. Certainly schools provide a hostile environment for gay boys, in particular.

> I had a visit from an ex-student earlier this week, he had a number of issues last year with his own sexuality. You know, trying to work some things out and he copped quite a lot of flak from the other kids. He was ostracised and ridiculed quite a lot. He came in to tell me, 'I think I'm gay and I'm exploring all that now,' and he said, 'Last year I wanted to deny all of that because I couldn't cope with the sort of pressure that the other kids gave me. And now that I'm out of this environment and out of that, sort of, the mainstream and sort of school and environment, I can sort of look at those sorts of issues.' Yeah, harassment's certainly an issue for the boys as well as the girls. [Amy, Student Welfare Coordinator, Bridgeforth]

But these boys do not appear in the majority and, in our schools, the major focus is those boys who subscribe to, or are complicit with, dominant forms of masculinity (Connell 1995). It is to them we now turn.

We are questioning their whole power base

At Stowley, as we have suggested, the problem of sex-based harassment is seen to be one of containment. Boys are positioned as powerful and as the ones who do the harassing. They have to 'receive counselling' and 'take their punishment' in each case from (more powerful) teachers. Few of the boys we speak to accept or understand how or why their behaviour is inappropriate. According to Hazel, the EO Coordinator, they simply understand that they need to be more careful. 'I think the kids now are aware of it. I don't think that a lot of them have a different attitude to it. But I think that they think twice before they do things these days.'

Tony at Stowley teaches classes on sex-based harassment and is astounded and angry when the boys reject his message. 'My classes on sexual harassment didn't turn out as well as I wanted them to,' he said. 'Basically the problem was that I got boys querying it.' Tony normally teaches mathematics and sport and isn't used to students 'querying it'. That dealing with gender relations might be a little different from other subject areas doesn't really occur to him and he sees the problem as being the boys' lack of logic. 'They were defending their behaviour which was contrary to what I was saying and what we had up on the overhead screen. And a lot of their comments had no reasoning behind them, they were just unbalanced.' His solution, when the boys continued to refuse to see reason, was to make sure they understood the rules 'whether they agree with them or not' and to enforce those rules. At Bridgeforth, Scott had a similar experience to Tony in his first attempt to address sex-based harassment and resorted to a similar strategy. 'Well look, I don't care what you think, this is the policy, and if you are found to be harassing someone, these are the consequences.' Thus both Tony and Scott called upon their institutionalised power to deal with the issue. Scott, however, was dissatisfied with his response and felt it was likely to be counter-productive. He now realises that the boys, 'see it as being something that is threatening to them' and is struggling to come up with a better way.

Scott and Tony each found teaching boys about these matters quite stressful, but neither was subject to the treatment Jan received. In an exercise seeking to make a small group of boys aware of sex-based harassment, she asked them to write down the types of harassment that occurred. In so doing, she positioned these boys as powerful with regard to her femaleness because they became overtly competitive in providing the crudest examples to shock her.

> Here I was trying not to be shocked and it was gaining momentum regardless of me. I was superfluous to what was happening in terms of the dynamics of the group. To be open with them meant they were going to see this openness as a possibility for abuse . . . It gave them an excuse to be cruder and cruder with each other and the abuse started and accelerated. I just stopped it because we were getting nowhere.

As this shows, sex-based harassment can be experienced at any level of formal power. Teachers being positioned as more powerful than students within the school hierarchy does not protect a female teacher from being positioned negatively because of her femaleness. Sex-based harassment is, as Tannen (1995, p. 257) points out, 'a frequent form of insubordination perpetrated by those of lower rank against those above them in the hierarchy'.

Jan is no longer surprised by the extent and level of some boys' resistance. 'I was challenging the way they had always been together, and the way they had worked out their positions. We are not just questioning their relationship with girls, we are questioning their whole power base.'

As Tony says, 'They were all together because they were all boys, they were all backing each other up.' At Stowley and

Bridgeforth, some boys have developed a siege mentality, 'Why are you always picking on the boys?' Labelling the boys as 'bad' has forced them to defend themselves both against the girls and against the authority of school. At Stowley, fifteen-year-old Adrian says rather plaintively, 'Sexual harassment has changed the girls. You never find a boy who has gone to Sexual Harassment—apart from Patrick [the boy with the backwards elbows]. It has always been the girls playing on it . . . and then bang you're dead.' Fellow class member Damian complains, 'Like, now every little thing that we do to someone. Like you won't even mean it. Or even, like, you are only just joking or mucking around, straight away they go to Sexual Harassment.'

One male teacher at Riverside remarked in support of a group of boys who exhibited the most aggressively sexist behaviour in a workshop, 'Sure it's a patriarchy, but that doesn't mean to say that boys have the power.' Having observed this group of boys completely intimidate all those who might offer an opposing voice, we cannot agree that they have no power. Furthermore, the overt exhibition of male dominance and control serves in the interests of all males, even those who do not participate in such acts of verbal violence. However, as we will show in Chapter 5, many boys do not experience themselves as powerful and they do feel put upon. This often exacerbates the very behaviours which need to be addressed. The difficulty, as McLean (1996a) points out, is that these boys do not see the source of their problems as particular forms of masculinity; rather, they see it as girls and feminists. They have adopted a form of masculine solidarity which emphasises the very behaviours that produce sex-based harassment.

Harassment is based on unequal power relationships and, in this case, the inequality in power relationships is sex-based. Our data suggest that those schools with cultures most dominated by hegemonic masculinity (Connell 1987) are also those most likely to adopt a disciplinary approach which individualises cases of sex-based harassment, and treats the issue simply as one of containment through the threat of punishment. Far from addressing the unequal girl–boy power relationships which are the basis of harassment, such authoritarian approaches tend to emphasise them, reducing the possibility of agency for girls and increasing the gender solidarity of the boys. As Connell (1994, p. 12) points out, 'Adult control in schools is enforced by a disciplinary system, which often becomes a form of masculinity formation' and 'masculinity may be constructed through defiance of authority'.

Our studies indicate that the capacity for boys and men to be dominant is not just a matter of numbers but a complex interplay of institutional, student and community cultures. It has become clear to us that many schools in which girls and women teachers suffer a high incidence of sex-based harassment and discrimination do not have a majority of boys or male staff. It appears to us, for example, that at Draymill, where boys are in the minority, a highly masculinist discourse holds sway which serves to reinforce and support the behaviour amongst the male students. There are 'no-go' areas in the staffroom for women teachers and sexist jokes and a quite explicit flaunting of macho behaviour. Toni, the EO Coordinator, remarks that the behaviour of the boys is no more than many teachers indulge in themselves:

> Sexist behaviour is entrenched here. Many of the male staff do not know how to treat women. There is a group who are segregated—they are male, intrusive and aggressive—they're pushing the limits all the time and it reinforces the behaviour of male students who see it as being macho.

It is not uncommon for women teachers to recount stories of sex-based harassment in staffrooms. Even amongst men who have 'grown out of it', the memory of the boy they were is there.

For many boys in such environments, there is only one form of acceptable masculinity available to them and they reject it at their peril. Within this dominant form of masculinity, the need to assert dominance and control and to confirm the pecking order is extreme.

I don't do that sort of thing

It is nevertheless clear that many boys do reject such macho masculinities. 'I don't do that sort of thing,' says a fourteen-year-old from Mt Mullin. 'I feel ashamed for all those boys. Sometimes I tell them to shut up.' For his classmate there is something of a conflict: 'I want to be a bit different to my dad. Like my dad—he wants a boy to be rough, and macho. I don't want to be what he wants me to be.' Armand and James, from our vignette about Brookdale in Chapter 3, do not fit the conventional adolescent macho mould but are 'acceptable' largely due to their sporting prowess. Armand describes how 'I just want to find out about, like, the things that go on between just males and females and the ways you can, like, try not to be sexist and stuff like that. You want to be more polite and stuff like that. I reckon everyone has got a bit of sexism in them.' James suggests, 'Yeah, a lot of boys think that they are the dominant sex and that is all there is to it. We just have more respect.' They attribute their views to a combination of parental influence—'My dad is always having talks with me about that. You know just try to be nice to everybody— and their school's approach to sex-based harassment—'They teach us in the classes that you can get to be more sensitive.' Patrick, at Stowley, hearing his mates defend their own harassing behaviour on the grounds that the girls were complicit, says, 'Hey leave me out of this. I was on the girls' side, remember?' to which they laughingly respond, 'Yeah, you said so.'

At Bridgeforth, a number of teachers have persisted with their efforts and they believe that an alternative is developing side by side with the dominant masculinist culture, one that gives teachers and students within the school more possibilities for change. Jan comments:

> I thought that stopping sexual harassment is not just being a moral policewoman but is about providing opportunities for challenging the way that they both behave. And I think that it has to be a two-pronged thing. Not just the girls. I don't yet really know how we address the boys, but I think that it has got to be a male thing too. Unless we change the way the male culture operates . . . Well you know, we can tell the girls to be as assertive as they want but if we don't challenge that particular male culture . . .

Connell (1994, p. 14) suggests that, 'the school and popular culture may define places in gender relations for boys to occupy but these only become effective if boys take up the offer. Masculinities and femininities are actively constructed, not simply received.' Nevertheless, as he also points out, they 'pick up the cultural patterns and subject positions offered to them'. The promise in the Draymill story lies in Robby, who independently sought out the girls and apologised to them, signalling a desire and even capacity to change, to 'decline the offer of power and pleasure made to them by the gender order' (Connell 1994, p. 18). Jessica and Georgie are not convinced that the other two boys have really 'changed in their attitudes', although they have 'sort of learned they can't actually directly harass anyone. Now they just talk between themselves.' Robby, however, they believe to have changed. 'He's got a lot more respect for women now.' He is able to see alternative ways of behaving which are also a source of empowerment and pleasure—a capacity to relate to girls and other boys on a more equal basis. But this is a possibility only because alternative constructions of masculinity and male–female relations are now available to him.

A number of gender-reforming teachers suggest that addressing sex-based harassment has proved to be the most sensitive and intractable of all gender reform efforts so far attempted. Indeed, as we have shown, addressing sex-based harassment in schools often challenges the very foundations of school organisation and culture. Because the matter is so divisive, there has, in a number of our schools, been a concerted effort to address the issue in a 'non-gender focused' way; it is about 'other people's rights to a comfortable and safe environment', 'human rights' and 'being respectful'. The intention is to put on a non-contentious face. The effect, of course, is to draw attention away from the fact that sex-based harassment is about gender relations within and between the sexes. Predictably, then, few of our teachers, whether gender reformers or not, make explicit reference to power. Neglecting power, however, means the power relations implicit in sex-based harassment and the power imparted by masculinist cultures of schools often go unchallenged. And, as demonstrated, when they are addressed, they are usually not treated in a comprehensive and critical manner which integrates gender equity throughout the daily social practices of teachers and students.

Mac an Ghaill (1994) suggests that schools are masculinising institutions and cultures, and our studies would support this contention. Indeed, both students and teachers commonly tap into dominant discourses of masculinity which justify the denigratory treatment of girls and women as normal and natural. Only rarely in our schools was the behaviour of boys linked to the 'masculinising cultures' of both the school and the community. That is, while a number of teachers recognise that the power relations inherent in schools' structures and processes are as gendered as those of the broader society, most still interpret sex-based harassment as a problem largely about the behaviour of individuals. As a result, very few consider that the school might be complicit in producing the inequalities in gender and power relationships that underpin sex-based harassment. However, as Thorne (1994, p. 171) suggests, 'to challenge male dominance in its overt and subtle forms, we have to change the organisation and content of masculinities and femininities, recognising their complexity and plurality, and altering forms based on opposition and domination'.

The challenges this poses for feminist educators are twofold: how to ensure that a range of acceptable versions of masculinity and femininity are available to boys and girls in schools and how to help them negotiate their way through these alternative and competing masculinities and femininities, and 'take up the offers' that serve the interests of gender justice. In the next chapter, we will show that such challenges bring into play the toxic emotional underground of school life.

5

Emotion

Ensuring that girls' achievements are as visible as those of boys is policy at Nerringo school. Recently Nerringo girls have been particularly successful in the sporting arena. The reaction from boys is mixed and not a few are antagonistic.

Clifford: Most of the boys feel really hard done by because of equal opportunities. It seems to us it has gone a little bit too far. It feels like we're getting downgraded. In class we can't do anything, you don't even get really out of line and you're put straight back in your place. We feel we're second class to the girls. It's the way the teachers act.

Adam: To start with they tried to like even up, like boys were ahead and they tried to even that up to make it even, and now they're just taking the girls ahead further and further ahead, we've just been left in the dust.

Clifford: I don't know how it used to be but throughout my whole schooling life here it's been basically girls have karate lessons, girls have these things and girls go away for sport and all that stuff . . .

Craig: They just tried to even it up and they've taken it too far. Equal opportunity is also for us to do the same things as the girls have been allowed to do. Now it's more like the girls getting everything and the boys getting nothing.

A differently oriented boy, Mark seeks to explain the origin of such antagonism:

Mark: I think an issue lately at this school has been the girls have been getting too much of a go. And I think that's a bit

130

inaccurate, the only reason they've been getting a go is because they're very successful at such a high standard. Perhaps the boys are jealous or something and they feel that they're missing out, whereas perhaps, in the past, the girls haven't had the opportunity and they've been given that opportunity now and they are doing well, and the boys are not really used to it.

The school recently ran a gender equity programme for Year 9 boys and girls.

Mark: We spent two days in separate groups of boys and girls and talked about issues like equal opportunity, mental and physical abuse, alcohol, drugs . . . It didn't just concentrate on girls solely but just general behaviour and how to act in a peer group. It was good. It was covering things that we've talked about a lot before, but you can always experience something different. I think they're beneficial sorts of things.

But Clifford, Adam and Craig remain unimpressed.

Clifford: All we did was sit around and talk about the correct way to treat women and just learn about bodies and everything else, but the girls apparently they went out and kicked footballs and learnt how to drive mowers and learnt how to fix engines and the boys had to talk about girls basically.

Adam: The programme was just to keep us happy, it felt like and the programme like related back to the girls anyway.

Clifford: We weren't taught any new skills, we weren't taught even to do anything that was seen as like basically for girls. Like I'm not trying to be sexist or anything but even in terms of just how to cook or anything like that, which has been seen as women's things. But they taught the girls things that had been seen as male things. The way the school works it would be a lot easier to be a female, you get more opportunities.

Adam: Yes and you get in a lot less trouble.

Craig: The boys have always been taught they're a bad sex. The teachers are constantly on our back which makes it hard for us to do anything. Telling us off all the time does make us angry and doesn't really make us feel that we want to be here. We want to be anywhere else but school.

Clifford: The only times the teachers talk to us in class is just to tell us off.

Craig: We're not as advanced as far in our work as they are. It's not because they're smart, it's because they get more time and they talk a lot and they're always that step ahead of us, so they're always having questions to ask. And as we're waiting for the teacher to come round and help us with our work, they're getting help, they're getting to move on and we're left basically behind.

Clifford: The blokes are basically fed up with the way things go in the school. We feel that we are getting the rough end of the stick.

What has pleasure got to do with gender reform? Or pain, shame, fantasy, empathy, envy, guilt, anxiety or rage for that matter? Lots! Our first purpose in this chapter is to point to the powerful role of emotion in gender reform. We will also show that at one level there is a general awareness of the emotionally charged nature of such reform. Many can name the powerful emotions which it evokes in them and in others. However, there seem to be deeper layers of emotion or more complex psychic processes at work which teachers and students are less aware of and able to artic-ulate; they seem to operate just outside of consciousness and discourse. Further, there also seems to be little consciousness of the social role of emotion. Our second purpose is to identify these powerful emotions and also to explain why gender reform evokes them so intensely. The central argument is that the emotional dimensions of gender reform are under-examined and under-theorised and that the practice of gender reform suffers as a result. Our evidence points to the need for a feminist 'pedagogy of the emotions' (Fitzclarence 1992) which would help those involved to understand why they feel the way they do, what it means for the ways they act, what to do about it.

Teaching and learning are intense emotional experiences in themselves and the operations of schools as institutions intensify these experiences (Salzberger-Wittenberg, Henry and Osbourne 1983). Further, the psychic 'processes of splitting, denial of feel-ings, detachment, projection and collusion are part and parcel of everyday life at school' (Shaw 1995, p. 44). Gender reform in schools builds on this and 'ups the ante'. It is a heady, emotional cocktail.

The interpersonal emotional dynamics in our research schools are complex and varied and far too wide-ranging to be covered properly here. Instead, we will note the ways in which teachers understand the gendered emotional worlds of their students and the implications of this for their gender reform practices. Our concern, though, is with the students' stories about the emotional world of gender reform and about the ways in which it maps on to that of schooling generally.

The policy and advice literature for gender reform is rather restricted and contradictory on matters of emotion. It demonstrates no interest in the emotional worlds of teachers, a limited understanding of the emotional worlds of girls and boys, ignores the emotions set in train by reform itself and it does not understand emotion in wider cultural and socio-historical contexts. A consideration of such contexts is particularly called for given the emotional climate and changing gender relations which characterise 'the age of uncertainty' (Giddens 1994) and 'the age of redefinition' (MacKay 1993). Here we will focus on policy and research on girls and boys.

The policy and advice literature has long attended to the emotional dimensions of students' engagements with schooling and beyond, sometimes in quite explicit ways and sometimes more subtly. The oldest, best known and most explicit focus, beginning in the 1970s, has been on gender stereotyping and its implications for self-esteem. The emphasis has been particularly on girls, but more recently it has included boys; in both cases, stereotyping has been seen to have negative implications for students' sense of self. In contrast, developments associated with proposals for gender-inclusive curricula, non-traditional choices and the single-sex class have, in different ways, drawn their inspiration from ideas about the different psychology of femininity and masculinity. These ideas are most associated with the curriculum policy advice of the late 1980s and early 1990s. Since then, policy has drawn most from ideas associated with the sociology of education and has stressed the construction of gender. Despite some rather desultory gestures towards pleasure and desire, these more recent shifts have tended to neglect emotionality and the psyche.

The research literature shows that these main policy imperatives barely scratch the surface of what it means to be a boy or a girl at school. This literature which explores the psychology of femininity and masculinity points to differential orientations to emotionality, relationships, intimacy and violence. With regard to females it suggests that females are predisposed to attachment, connectedness, collaboration, empathy, nurturance and emotional responsibility, while males are seen to be predisposed to independence, emotional neutrality, competitiveness and aggression. When this literature takes on a psycho/social orientation, males' ways of being are seen to be socially and culturally privileged, inscribed as they are within all dominant fields of public endeavour—including the educational. In contrast, women's ways of being are seen to equip them well for the private spheres of home and family and for lower status servicing and nurturing work—including servicing males psychologically in both the public and private sphere. Further, males are seen to ascribe higher value to their own ways of being, to denigrate those of females but also to ascribe value to females according to the extent of their conformity to females' ways of being. Females are said to absorb such attitudes and so to down-value themselves and what they do and at the same time to service males in such a way as to sustain males' power and their own subordination. Further, males are seen to use their emotional style as a weapon of control. The most sophisticated and sparse end of this literature draws from psychoanalytic theory and points to the role that such psychic processes as splitting, denial, repression, projection, transference and desire play in gender relations and education (e.g. Walkerdine 1985; McLean 1996b).

Such ideas about male and female psychology and gendered power relations are seen to have implications for girls' and boys' ways of being, learning, choosing and interacting at school. These lines of thinking with regard to girls are so familiar that we will not elaborate on them, except to say that this literature is controversial and has been criticised on the grounds that it generalises wildly and that it seems to reinscribe the stereotypes that it seeks to challenge. With regard to boys there have been two main lines of argument. The first ignores matters of the power relations between the sexes, points to boys' and men's emotional and social problems and suggests that many arise from the conventional relationship between emotionality and masculinity. This is seen to lock boys into narrow and restricting ways of being human which have negative effects on their health, their relationships and their perceptions of the value of different curricula and work and therefore on their achievements. Further, dominant modes of masculinity are said to limit boys' and men's emotional horizons and to tilt them towards aggression, repression, conflict and violence, and towards damaging forms of competition and control while at school. The second main line of argument with regard to boys is more sociological. It draws insights from the first, but in the context of feminist understandings of the structural relationships of power between the sexes and the role of emotionality in this and in the different power relations among males.

There is now a rich sociological research literature about

young people's identities, cultures, subcultures and youth cultural forms. This points to the complexity both of young people's lives and of their engagements with cultural 'texts of desire' (Christian-Smith 1993). It shows how socially differentiated gender identities are constructed by discourses in such social settings as schools, the family, friendship groupings, the workplace and fields of leisure and pleasure. Broadly, it is argued that these settings and texts offer a range of ways of being male and female but privilege some as superior and more desirable. It is also argued that young people work with these in order to construct their sense of who they are and how they might best live—they work hard at 'becoming somebody' (Wexler 1992). These studies also break down the concepts of masculinity and femininity along a range of axes including social class, ethnicity, sexuality and race. The emphasis is on both the 'hidden injuries' and the paradoxical pleasures of various, somewhat fluid, forms of dominance and subordination. It is also on the strategies mobilised by young people individually and in groups to negotiate these in what are, to them, self-affirming ways.

The literature on friendship groups, for example, shows that friendship is a consuming feature of much adolescent life and one of the main sources of pleasure and pain during school. Typologies of school boy and girl friendship groups and discussions of inter-group relations are now quite common and point to the cultural clusters friendships are built around and to the pre-conscious forces which may drive group behaviour. The literature shows how hegemonic forms of masculinity amongst boys involve derogating the feminine (the soft, the emotional) and purging it from amongst boys' groups and within the self. For boys becoming men in adolescence, anxiety about identity is a feature of their lives and fear of the feminine lies at its core. This is addressed by some through strong group identification and boundary maintenance and expressed through hostility to difference of any sort—mainly to subordinate males and 'insubordinate' females. There is now clear evidence about the role of misogyny and homophobia in such 'group work' and the heterosexual policing that is involved. Usually this is understood in terms of power relations, but as we will show, there is a great deal of perverse pleasure and repressed anxiety involved. Schoolgirl friendships have often been celebrated in the literature as empathetic havens from the heartless worlds of boys and schools (Gilligan, Lyons and Hammer 1990). While in some ways they are, this is also a rather romanticised view, as some recent studies have shown. These examine the ways in which girls exercise power over each other through the deployment of pleasure, the symbolic and other violence which occurs between girls and the intensity of the emotions involved. For example, Hey's (1996) pathbreaking research on girls' friendships points to the enormous amount of emotional energy which girls invest in girl–girl relations at school, the heartbreak that can arise as a result of friendship crises or rejections and, again, the anxious pleasures involved in the who's in/who's out dynamics of friendship groups. Overall, this literature reveals that the construction and negotiation of youthful identity is hard emotional labour, complex and intense.

Policy-makers and gender reformers have given little serious consideration to the implications of this deep emotional underground for the ways in which gender reform is conceptualised and conducted. No attention has been paid in the policy, advice or research literature to the emotional implications of gender reform itself for students. This neglect is remarkable. Let us show why, drawing insights from all the above.

Remaking the self

Teachers tend to adopt two main somewhat overlapping orientations to students' emotional worlds. Elsewhere we have called these the therapeutic and the authoritarian (see Kenway, Blackmore and Willis 1996). The therapeutic orientation makes students' emotional worlds and personal lives central. The authoritarian orientation either downplays or ignores the emotions, the psyche and students' positionality, treating them as cognitive, rational units who will do what gender reformers think is good for them, think as they are told to think and change as prescribed. Further, the idea that gender education might positively discuss and actively invoke pleasure is almost entirely absent. As students often remark, 'It is so boring, the teachers just go on and on.' Gender reform is seen as punitive, humourless and anti-fun. In Chapter 3, we showed that students tend to resent this approach and, as the following remark shows, they also fear it, preferring pleasurable pedagogies.

> It's just the way you try and bring it across. If you try and bring it across in a way that is light and it's just, like, the tone of voice and the way you say it. If you try and bring it across in a really serious manner and that sort of thing, people are going to just get

scared of it. But if you bring it across and you try and make it sound interesting and just sort of fun in a way, people will be ready to accept it, it won't scare them. [Year 11 girl, Mt Mullin]

Our major, but not exclusive, focus in this chapter is on the therapeutic orientation. Our broad argument is that while authoritarian orientations tend to ignore the personal and focus on the political, therapeutic orientations often attend to the personal at the expense of the political.

Therapeutic approaches to gender reform invite students to remake, reassess and revalue the self. They seek to change students' sense of who they are, what they can do and become and indeed who they need no longer be. Self-esteem is a pivotal and overworked concept put to use in such a wide variety of ways that it explains little (see Kenway and Willis 1990). Fortunately, the self-esteem discourse is not the only discourse teachers draw on and a minority of teachers consider the implications for students' identity. For example, Danni, a vocational education teacher at Mt Forest, recognises fluidity, saying, 'Adolescents are bound to explore a whole range of sorts of images and identities and behaviours.' Angie, a drama teacher from Stowley, makes the case that 'kids build up their defences under old regimes and gender reform challenges such regimes and thus their defences'. She also argues that many students are 'really struggling':

They just can't cope with who they are and where they're going and are coming to terms with their feelings. Gender equity is just something extra on top of that. They feel like, 'Why do you want to know how I think all the time?' They're very sensitive about it and really have trouble expressing their thoughts and feelings about issues like this. Some kids have suffered all their lives at the hands of girls and boys. They build up their defences, for the purpose of self-preservation and survival. They hide away. They do not want to have to look at themselves and their own inadequacies.

Students' manner of defending themselves, she implies, often involves avoidance and denial—boys will often act out and girls will often act in. Boys say, 'I don't want to know about this. This is not an issue for me. This doesn't happen in my home—why do we have to do this? This is rubbish.' 'A lot of girls,' Angie says, 'have learned, even by the age of thirteen or fourteen, a whole lot of ways to actually seal themselves off from a lot of things.' Many boys and girls, she suggests, would rather be who they already know how to be than take the risk of changing. Fear of others' opinions and of isolation and the need for a secure identity are primary motivating forces leading many to adopt safe behaviours and to make safe choices well within gender conventions. While girls' and boys' behaviours may be different, their driving force is similar—gender anxiety and the need to be accepted and to belong.

According to other teachers, it is the differences which must be taken into account when working to change gender relations among students. Take sexual harassment. Generally, teachers are concerned to build trust, but with regard to girls they seek to 'remove the guilt that girls in particular feel when reporting harassment' (Janice, science teacher, Nerringo) and to encourage them to take the risk of disclosure. With regard to perpetrators, the concern is to remove a sense of sexual entitlement and to build empathy as a first step towards encouraging such boys to accept responsibility. Amy, at Bridgeforth, stresses that there is something quite distinctive about male perpetrators.

> A lot of the boys that I've worked with—the perpetrators—haven't been able to put themselves in the opposite role. When you say to them, 'Well, how would you feel if somebody had done that to you?' they can't put themselves in that position and feel or even think how it might feel. I'm speaking particularly about the more macho leaders who've never been bullied or have never been victimised in that sort of way.

Given that much gender reform is based on the importance of empathising with the feelings of others on the logic of 'How would *you* feel if . . .?', such a remark is particularly telling. Our data point to an abundance of guilt and empathy among girls and a short supply of these feelings among boys. The reverse is true when it comes to a sense of entitlement. Taking emotional risks is not a strength of either sex.

Gender-reforming teachers see pleasure in two ways, as either a problem to be rectified through gender reform or a resource to assist it. They express disquiet about the ways in which students' pleasures in and out of school are structured along conventional gender lines, implying that girls and boys should change their leisure and pleasure. But many teachers have no idea what gender-neutral pleasures might look like. In contrast, such teachers will frequently factor gendered enjoyment into therapeutic gender reform programmes as a form of motivation. For example, some teachers seek to use students' pleasures as a way of encouraging them to consider alternative choices or identities. The paradoxes involved in doing this are seldom noted.

Being made to feel

It is not possible to understand the emotional world of gender reform for students without some understanding of the emotional world of their schooling more generally. Students of all ages speak most frequently of 'toxic emotions' (Goleman 1996): nervousness, worry, anxiety, fear and even dread. They fear 'being laughed at', 'making a fool of myself', 'being made to look stupid', 'being stupid', being teased and hurt, being alone and isolated and being betrayed by their friends or their teachers. They speak of panic, of being uncertain, uncomfortable, embarrassed, ashamed, intimidated, shy, lonely and unhappy. They speak of feelings of frustration and bitterness, of annoyance, anger and hostility, of rivalry and jealousy. They also speak of boredom and the regular frustration of 'not [being] allowed'. While such feelings are mentioned in relation to teachers, leaving aside the matter of boredom and discipline, they are most often mentioned in relation to peers. In connection with teachers, many students have a sense of injustice and emotional neglect, of things not being fair and of no one particularly caring. Less often, students also speak of enjoying and being amused by certain aspects of school, of feeling comfortable, confident and proud on occasions, and of warm connections with friends and of the importance of social life, even if it is fraught. Almost all point to the importance of teachers who care, 'understand' and have a sense of humour, as does this Year 10 boy from Mt Mullin:

> We have got a new teacher and she is really good. She looks at
> your point of view, makes you want to get your work done and
> makes you not be *shitty*. For instance this girl today, she was
> upset and she went to the toilets and the teacher told her that our
> feelings come before our work. She was saying that you should
> deal with that and then try and get back on to work. She just
> sees it from your point of view.

You're just a girl in school, that's all

The stories of many girls are different from those of many boys. Girls more readily talk the language of interiors whereas the boys more readily talk surfaces. The girls closely monitor their own and others' feelings—particularly those of their friends and the boys. Their emotional sensitivities are finely tuned; many girls are what Fillion (1996) calls 'intimacy experts'. This means that they often empathise with and nurture others, particularly boys but also teachers, and work hard doing the school's emotional house-work—tending and mending the social fabric, civilising the boys (see further Kenway and Willis with Education of Girls Unit, SA 1993). Girls understand themselves as more emotionally mature than boys and accept a lot more emotional responsibility. Being intimacy experts also means that, if they choose or when partic-ularly pushed, girls can play emotional politics with a fierce perspicacity. For example, knowing how sensitive the issue of sexuality is amongst boys, some girls do not hesitate to tease boys about being gay.

There are many flow-on effects of girls' particular orientations to emotion. Some appear to be 'passion's slaves'. They tend to be ruled by and stay within the tolerance limits of their own feelings. While on the one hand this is constraining, on the other hand it means that these girls engage in a range of quite sensible avoid-ance behaviours with regard to the schools' potentially dangerous places and spaces—the canteen, the corridors, the oval, the smok-ers' corner—and classes with a majority of boys. They are usually good judges of the psychological and possibly physical risks that are not worth taking. This is not sufficiently well recognised by gender-reforming teachers who often want to push them in direc-tions that they—justifiably in some senses—do not want to take.

While the girls do not seem to engage in as much emotional repression as the boys, they frequently read situations from the perspective of 'the other' and thus, at first glance, appear to be involved in some form of denial. The girls frequently 'try to be fair' and to 'give the other side'. As we indicated earlier, despite the irritation, frustration, hurt and stomach-churning humiliation that it may cause them, they quite regularly excuse boys' behavi-our on the grounds of their immaturity and insecurity. At the same time, girls indicate that they don't have much patience with boys.

Mika:	They're all male ego, most of them.
Carla:	Smart-arse.
Mika:	Full of themselves.
Zoe:	They don't want to express their own feelings 'cause they're afraid the rest of them will think that they're dumb or something.
Carla:	They're all trying to be better than one another. [Year 9 girls, Banksia]

Girls also often resent the boys who say girls can't do things, who push them 'to the side' in the school grounds, who 'want us to join in one day but not the next', who overpower them in class, disrupt classes, those who 'don't care' and don't 'take seriously' the things that girls want them to—including, as we will show shortly, some gender reform programmes. But 'boys being boys' can also be sources of fun and distraction.

> Our guys are always taking up a bit more time than the girls. But it gives you a bit of relief. Because if there is nothing funny going on like the boys making jokes and things, it's heavy work all of the time. [Year 9 girl, Edgecliffe]

Girls also often believe that teachers both favour boys and also 'don't take girls seriously'. Even in the context of all of that, they will often adjust to boys' behaviour in ways which seem to go against their own interests. On closer observation, however, such adjustments appear to represent their informed and careful calculations about where their best interests lie.

Whether seeking, gaining, fearing or longing for boys' approval, girls keep boys under surveillance—reading, explaining and excusing them. There is regular speculation about what prompts certain boys to behave in the ways they do. Here is an example which picks up the main themes of many girls' readings of boys' psychology.

> Tamara: The teachers tend to put the boys down, they try and say that we're smarter than them.
>
> Amanda: When the teachers put boys down they will try to act like they don't care. They won't show they are hurt or they'll use it to make them look higher, give the teachers cheek. Teachers put the boys down rather than the girls 'cos the boys try to be the stud, the main actor. They are really loud and they put others down to make themselves look higher. [Year 10 girls, Mt Mullin]

Girls are perplexed and frustrated by the differences between boys alone and boys together.

> Kelly: Boys harass girls a lot. But I've only really noticed it when the guys hang out in all-guy groups. I don't know why. I think they try to impress one another by outdoing their standards until it comes to a point where they just do stupid things.
>
> Sally: My boyfriend, he tries to act really big around the guys but when he is with me he is really sweet. Boys are

> different when they are alone. Why can't boys be OK
> when they are in a group? [Year 11 girls, Rullinga]

As the following comment indicates, this girl at least has some inkling of the pleasure boys get from harassing:

> I feel real bad if I'm harassed. It makes me feel this is their excitement, they're on a high. Their excitement is something that's the other way around for me. They're using me to do something else for themselves. [Year 10 girl, Mt Mullin]

A point too frequently overlooked is that many girls' greatest emotional energy and deepest emotional investments while at school are in same-sex friendships and the social—in pleasurable connections. Much of what girls will and will not do in response to gender reform must be seen in the context of their expectation of female empathy and supportiveness, their longing for painless female communities and the importance of being with their friends. Girls feel most betrayed when their friends particularly, and other girls generally, do not support them after boys have harassed them.

> They laughed at it and I thought they were my friends. [Year 10 girl, Mt Forest]
> They think the boys are going to like them. If they see something happen and it's funny they laugh too so they don't get teased themselves. [Year 11 girl, Mt Forest]

Girls may forgive the boys who harass more readily than the girls who condone and even those who get harassed. This may be apparent to boys.

> Not many of the girls stand up for each other. The girls' friends don't tell the other people to lay off. She's on her own when she's getting teased. [Year 10 boy, Nerringo]

Guys take it hard sometimes too

The boys do not talk so freely about their emotional worlds. Indeed, some took the opportunity to perform their masculinity for us using nonchalance, insults, crudeness, humorous banter, bravado and emotional neutrality to demonstrate their toughness and independence. These boys are very keen to distance themselves from caring, from emotionality more generally and from girls whom they describe as wimps and whingers, 'always running, crying to the teacher', 'screaming on the oval'. Their contempt for 'the feminine' is palpable. When discussing harassment, such boys regularly explain it away as 'just joking' and claim 'everyone knows and gets used to it'. Harassment is a source of normalised pleasure and gratification as well as an expression of power. However, beyond the bravado, some harassers offer powerful insights about the forces which motivate them—jealousy, resentment and the desire to take revenge through humiliation.

Only a minority of boys presented us with tough, misogynist facades; others were surprisingly frank. They talked of the anxiety, embarrassment, shame, frustration, annoyance and pain associated with boys' relentless banter and name calling, pushing and shoving, fighting and beating and of being the wrong sort of boy—for example, being small when only 'big dudes matter'. 'Guys take it hard sometimes too,' said a fifteen-year-old from Mt Mullin. The boys we talked to are preoccupied with boy–boy relations and the verbal and physical violence which characterises them. As other boys' victims, some boys are regularly humiliated. Here is how a Year 11 boy from Mt Mullin explained the different feelings of being victim and perpetrator:

> When a boy is harassed he feels embarrassed, ashamed and don't know what to do. So he just puts his head down and just listens. You can't do nothing. You wouldn't speak again or try anything. Sometimes I have done the harassing. It makes me feel like I'm tough. [Laughter] When I'm with mates. Or if I cause a fight, then all your mates will stick up for you. If you're by yourself, then they might sort of double back on you and you might get a hiding.

Regular boy victims are 'the quiet blokes, the harmless kids, the kid who won't do anything, like tell the teacher or take action against them' says another Year 11 boy from Mt Mullin. Regular perpetrators tend to be the older and bigger boys. But verbal and physical harassment, the constant 'pushing to see who is tougher' and the pressure 'to show your strength' are central features of boy–boy individual and group relations in schools.

For a significant number of boys, the patterns of power and conformity in boys' groups provoke feelings of intense powerlessness and pessimism. As Derek, in Year 10 at Mt Mullin, says, 'They act like idiots. It doesn't bother me, I don't care. If they want to make *dickheads* of themselves, let them.' Yet it became evident to us that when boys say they don't care, they do. Clearly they have learned that emotional neutrality is a powerful weapon for controlling others and defending the self. While boys do not talk easily about caring, friendship groups are an important source of identity and community as well as of evaluation and confrontation.

Ivan: You're either a skeg or a [footy] head, but if you are none of those you are just a geek. A little circle of squares.

Aaron: A dork, a dork. Yeah, basically, and you can't get in.

Ivan: The skegs don't like the footy heads much at all and vice versa. Then there's the smokers, they hate sport and the footy heads don't like them.

Aaron: The smokers are the troublemakers. It can be bad when two groups start fighting each other.

Ivan: I hate the groupings and wondering about them. But you can't do much about gangs. [Year 10 boys, Rullinga]

Many boys feel themselves to be less than girls, believing that girls are more clever, mature and serious, and that they work harder, have more willpower and have less to put up with.

Girls haven't got those big macho friends that have to keep up with everything. They can afford to be a bit smart on the side, but guys have to be macho all the time. [Year 10 boy, Mt Mullin]

However, they are also anxious to point out that girls can be rough and rowdy, that they also tease and fight, that some 'want to be tough too', but that 'girls do not get picked up for these things' and, ultimately, that 'girls get it easy'. These boys feel a sense of injustice with regard to girls' 'favoured' treatment within the school, particularly with regard to discipline.

Being made to feel differently

Let us now consider the emotional dimensions of gender reform practices for girls and boys in schools and note the ways in which they map on to the emotional worlds which we have outlined thus far. How do girls and boys feel about gender reform? What psychic processes does it set in train for them? What emotional effects does it have on differently located girls and boys? Which particular programmes evoke which particular emotional responses?

144

The potent power of familiar and new pleasures for girls

The idea of single-sex classes for girls has become such an ortho-doxy in gender reform that the case about the relative merits of single-sex and coeducation seems closed. Well, almost. Generally pleasant and safe spaces for girls, they offer great benefits. The stories to follow show the potent power of the familiar and new pleasures which they extend to girls. But, as we will argue, they have their limits and some unfortunate side effects.

Most girls are very positive about single-sex classes, spaces and events. Remember the ethnic minority girls in Chapter 1 who talked with such delight of the girls' camp? Echoing the senti-ments of many of their peers around Australia, the Year 10 girls at Blackstone, whom we also mentioned in that chapter, have this to say:

Sue: You learn more, because you feel more confident.
Cath: Oh, our classes [in social studies] are just a lot of fun.
Sue: You look forward to going to class, not, 'Oh, yuk! Social Studies again.'
Angela: Well we just act ourselves sort of thing.
Cath: We speak if we want to speak, we don't have to rely on them. You speak your mind.
Shirley: You can joke around, you can say things without people getting upset.
Cath: If someone's having a problem, you can cooperate together.
Beth: If girls distract you I just tell them to shut up, I want to learn, if you please. [Laughter]

Some single-sex groupings allow girls to 'be themselves' as they work on the curriculum-as-usual. Other single-sex activities pro-vide girls with the chance to 'do girls' things' such as explore the private and the personal. Again, they are encouraged to 'be themselves'. Yet other single-sex activities encourage girls to reinvent themselves through the use of the familiar to get to the new.

Reinventing the self for girls is often associated with reinventing the body. Many girls confess that they are ashamed of their bodies. The daunting prospect of making their bodies available for the hyper-critical male gaze in Physical Education and sport is more than many girls can bear. Further, many girls feel either 'overpow-ered' or obliterated in coeducational sport and Physical Education when the boys either 'heavy' them or 'ignore us altogether as if we are not in the game'. So girls often practise avoidance and deny themselves the pleasures of being physical. Teachers regularly remark on the implications of this for girls' physical and mental wellbeing and devise strategies for helping them to move beyond the gaze and the jock mentality of the boys. Then, 'comfortable' and free to move, many of the girls dare to 'have a go', to take physical risks and are surprised to find how much they enjoy their 'new' bodies—especially the chubby girls, normally the avoidance specialists. As Lyn, in Year 10 at Merrilong remarks, 'Playing sports with the boys makes you feel like nobody—but having all girls around, it makes you feel as if you were somebody.'

Being somebody is better than being nobody, but in the view of some teachers it is not enough. They also want the girls to feel and be somebody powerful. Self-defence is a new experience for many girls and usually very popular. When done properly, it teaches them worthwhile skills, introduces them to the pleasures of physical power and helps them to feel less vulnerable. Witness the eager and serious delight of a group of twelve-year-old Turkish, Spanish and Greek origin girls from Wattfield when they talk of their lunchtime *Girls Take Part* self-defence classes and of the female teacher involved:

Jade: Oh, that was fun. Especially at the end where they had
            a man come. We called him the 'padman' 'cause he had
            to be all padded up. And it was as if he was really
            attacking us and we had to fight back, and that was
            really fun because we could use all our techniques on
            him.
Carmen: Yeah, and so he sort of told us to walk forward and he
            would come and pull us by the hair like a real attacker
            would and we would have to defend ourselves.
Seringe: And it was pretty good. He was rough but I suppose
            attackers aren't going to go, 'Oh, come here. I am
            going to rape you, or something.' [Laughter]
Jackie: No. [Laughter]
Carmen: It was scary.
Jackie: Yes. [Laughter] I was trying to run away from him.
            [General laughter]
Rina: Yeah, it was fun.
Jackie: The thing is there are lots of them [rapists] going
            around now. Lots of the kids are nervous.
Rina: Yes, so we decided to defend ourselves. Because it was
            for free and it was for a good cause, to protect
            ourselves, we wanted to do it.

Gusson:	And now I think I see a car passing, going past, and if I feel like, 'Oh no,' you know, I go, 'I can fight back, I did self-defence at school, I know how to fight back now.'
Jade:	I'm more alert of everything now.
Gusson:	Yeah, you feel more secure.
Jade:	I'm still a bit afraid of it, but not as much.
Rina:	You'd still get a little bit scared and a bit shaky in the hands and with butterflies in your stomach but you know that you can fight back. She taught us all that.

Notions of the non-traditional can be construed in many ways. Some teachers read it in terms of girls traditionally 'most at risk' or who traditionally leave school early. They then work with groups of such girls across a range of activities, some single-sex some not. Joan, the EO Coordinator from Banksia whom we mentioned in Chapter 1, has taken under her wing the school's alienated 'naughty girls'. The dissident voice of feminism has became aligned to the dissident voices of these girls' close-knit, anti-school culture and, as Joan says, they now 'fight for it tooth and nail'. They 'rock along' to all the activities organised by the EO Coordinator. They make streamers and badges on International Women's Day, they talk about girls' issues at assemblies and attentively attend career sessions for girls. For such sessions, Joan has brought back some of the schools' former naughty girls. Former 'ratbags and rejects', these 'role models' have defied their histories and reputations and gone on to 'show 'em' at university and in the world of work.

Carol:	It impressed me when those girls came. They were from this school and they were once ratbags.
Pauline:	They make you really proud.
Carol:	It makes you think there are people who have got somewhere even out of this school.
Marg:	Because you've been a little brat at school, you want to stick it up them and say 'Look what I am now'. [Year 10 girls, Banksia]

Joan has introduced these working class/'under class' girls to non-traditional notions of self and success. She has promised them that 'girls can do anything', that they can reinvent themselves and their circumstances. They have taken her at her word and reconstructed their hopes and fantasies accordingly. Indeed, they have become ambitious as a result, wanting to become engineers and mechanics, journalists and lawyers. Unaccustomed to any positive attention from teachers, they bask in Joan's unqualified support.

These are encouraging stories of the power of gender reform not only to confront girls' sense of isolation, negativity and fear but to offer a range of girls more powerful and pleasurable ways of being in the world. The teaching practices involved show how gender reform can attend to many of the painful emotions described earlier. However, this does not mean that single-sex, self-esteem, self-defence, the non-traditional and celebrating the power of the feminine are immaculate pedagogical conceptions. They may have unexpected and unintended effects.

The problem of the therapy model for the naughty girls isn't simply that in some cases their grades don't match their new fantasies—their lives outside of school don't either. Pauline, the future mechanic, has had to leave the school and her friends to follow her sole parent mother to a nearby city. The mother has left town due to brutal ongoing harassment by her former partner. Pauline doesn't know what the future holds for her any more. Marg, the future journalist, has become pregnant and her fantasies now revolve around motherhood and going to north Queensland to live with her boyfriend and other Aborigines. Carol, her best friend and the baby's aunt, is taking time off school to be with her while she is suffering from morning sickness and shingles. Carol had missed lots of classes anyway in order to look after her invalid, sole-parent father. What purchase does the therapeutic discourse have on these scenarios? Not much. The popular feminist slogan, 'girls can do anything' is premised on the principles of choice, free will and the work ethic. As we suggested in Chapter 2, the liberal fantasy that it is possible to do anything if you feel good enough, want to badly enough and work hard enough has little if any purchase in this situation, and little to do with the grim reality of many girls' lives. Coming to grips with these material realities and assessing what sort of help really helps would have been infinitely more appropriate than feeding their fantasies. In a sense, gender reform both betrays and abandons these trusting girls. Some more of their story raises other issues.

On International Women's Day, Joan organised a special lunch for girls and women only. Some of her girls thought it was 'great' but others, many boys and some male staff were rather cross that males had not been invited.

Judy: My music teacher is a guy who will think of sexism, he will stop men putting women down. But we both agreed that it's being sexist towards men because there isn't an International Men's Day.

Rosemary: But every day is men's day.

Judy: I didn't like the idea of it.
Helena: Yeah, I just went and got some Tiny Teddies for the
            guys because they were missing out. [Laughter]
Mary: We just grabbed handfuls of biscuits and gave them to
            the guys.
Judy: Just because there is one bad guy in the bunch, you
            can't blame them all for being guys, because they're
            really nice most of them. [Year 11 girls, Banksia]

While the girls often empathise with the boys about being left
out, boys seldom reciprocate. Indeed, many work hard to ensure
that the girls feel guilty about having some pleasures just for
themselves. At the same time, they fiercely and often brutally
protect their boys-only places and pleasures—emphasising their
own sense of entitlement while undermining that of girls. Boys
regularly use single-sex events as opportunities to construct a
deficit view of girls as 'too shy, too weak and too worried' to
make it with them in the main game of schooling. They often
mobilise similar constructions of girls who report sexual harassment. Seldom do boys accept culpability and, as a result, girls are
invariably faced with invidious choices between 'ignoring it, fighting back and dobbing'. As the following conversation between
girls at Stowley shows, girls who dob—even girls who are strong
and skilled enough to defend themselves—are constructed as
weak and become the targets of further harassment:

Renee: We told the teacher. Boys think you're cowards, telling
            the teacher, like it wasn't very cool. They think they're
            tough and think we're weak, so they can pick on us all
            the time. But my Mum tells me to stick up for myself.
Raki: But my Mum says no punching. [Year 7 girls, Stowley]

Ironically, in this instance, self-defence classes equipped the girls
to literally fight back but they don't because, as twelve-year-old
Jade says:

My brother would give me an occasional little punch. He goes,
'fight back, fight back!' But it's for intruders not brothers, and
you're scared if you do fight back, you might really hurt him.

There are some awkward dilemmas here for girls which gender
reformers do not help them to work through and which leave
many girls with uneasy guilty feelings that they are somehow to
blame.

Single-sex classes for girls may unwittingly reinscribe the
'myths of female virtue' (Fillion 1996) and female helplessness

which prevail amongst boys—and girls. Indeed, a number of girls feel manipulated and 'put down by special stuff' and resent being made to feel different and inferior 'when teachers make it easier for girls'. As one Year 11 girl from Mt Mullin said, 'This sort of hurts us. Yeah, 'cause it's a little bit sexist. The teachers always seem to think that we need help.' She went on to imply that, while girls may enjoy single-sex classes, some did not necessarily feel challenged in them.

> In the female PhysEd classes some of the females think, 'We can't be bothered doing it, so if we don't like this, then we won't do it.' Those who actually want to do it don't get as much opportunity as they would if they were in with the guys. The guys are physically active. We're just as capable of doing the things as the guys are but just being with the girls and just not doing anything, it just takes all the fun out of it.

Single-sex classes for girls may also act as a nurturing emotional refuge within which less is expected and from which they are not prepared or required to venture. In most of our schools, insufficient attention is paid to the cross-overs between single-sex and coeducation. The possibility also exists that nurturing the girls' sense of being themselves helps to confirm in them the idea that they have a fixed self which is not amenable to change. Further, it is often the case that ensuring that they enjoy themselves and/or feel good about gender reform becomes more important than helping them to understand the role of gender in their lives and to become informed, critical and skilled advocates for change. The naughty girls are not alone in struggling to come to grips with the complexities of gender relations. Observe these sixteen-year-old girls at Braydon Tech trying, without help, to work these issues through:

Lisa: The girls got everything and the boys got nothing. [General agreement]

Sam: Yeah, my brother used to complain about that. He used to complain that the girls got to go on camps but the boys didn't.

Lisa: But then I think a lot of the boys realised that was because girls—well, they get their periods—it was all about like they knew that we were going away to like have talks about things like that. Like boys don't get together and talk about—well, I don't think they get periods.

Erin: They do, they do. [General laughter]

Lisa: Like boys buy those magazines like *Playboy* and all that.

150

Sam:	Like they even buy them at an early age and that.
Rebecca:	Oh, yeah!
Sam:	My brother's only twelve and he's got heaps in his room. [General laughter]
Rebecca:	It's just, I reckon mainly with boys, the only thing that they've got on their mind is just *sex*.
Sam:	Sex and girls.
Lisa:	But once they mature more they don't.
Sam:	Yeah, but how long will that take? [Laughter]
Rebecca:	Too long sometimes.

This conversation and the Tiny Teddies story point to the importance of knowledge about both sex and gender in gender reform. They also point to a matter which much preoccupies girls but which is much neglected by gender reformers—the implications of feminism for boys. While boys cause girls a lot of agony at school, that is only part of the story. They are often brothers, of course, but they may also be sources of entertainment, companionship, friendship and sexual and romantic relationships—a different agony maybe. They are an important, if fraught, part of girls' lives at, and beyond, school. They make connections with girls around such communities of interest and loyalty as generation, culture and sexuality. Indeed, generation often wins out when gender and generation clash. So, when boys complain that they are victims of EO, it is girls who most feel the effects, who suffer and rescue.

When girls ask, 'what about the boys?' and complain that 'this is not equal opportunities', gender reformers tend to dismiss this as misguided. Yet it is blindingly clear to us that girls believe that they have a very strong vested interest in changing boys.

Robyn:	Like in the health class, they just sort of sat back and laughed, and wasn't taking anything serious, but we tried to. If we talk about puberty they would just laugh, they won't take it in as a reality.
Renata:	They'd be making rude jokes at you, but it's all reality, it's no fantasy. Or else they will say, 'Oh, I wonder when such and such gets theirs' or something really immature.
Robyn:	They should understand, 'cause if they don't understand now about girls' parts and boys' parts, then they won't when they get older. They're going to be laughing when they go and have a girlfriend and that.
Renata:	When guys whistle at girls and we were saying how we feel when it happens to us, the guys were saying

that if you walk down the street in a singlet top you
are asking for it. [Year 9 girls, Draymill]

Girls do not want gender reform to cause boys to be cynical,
resentful and alienated, hostile and punitive. They urgently want
gender reform to change boys—at least in certain respects. Girls
want boys to see their point of view, to 'understand how we feel',
to 'deal with their own feelings', to 'stop acting so silly', generally
to be more mature in dealing with emotionality, sexuality and
intimacy. While girls recognise the value of single-sex they also point
out that mixed groups are needed too. Most girls suggest the flexible
use of both but stress the importance of *better* coeducation for the
development of better understanding and relationships.

Jan: Getting to know us as people, not as like you're a girl
             and I like you, but as actual people not objects.
Leone: Everyone needs to hear about this sort of stuff—drugs,
             STDs, contraception and when they are ready for sex.
             You really need boys' opinions. Some boys wonder
             about what girls think and we wonder about what they
             think. [Year 9 girls, Rullinga]

Girls want a different ethic to inform gender reform. Their
remarks indicate that they understand it is 'hard on the men', that
they want more for the boys but that they want a 'fair and
balanced approach', a 'both approach'. As Tahnee, in Year 11 at
Mt Mullin, says, 'instead of saying girls can do other things they
should be saying share everything or every one can do both'. She
would like campaigns for boys which will:

. . . make guys think, 'Do I really want to have a happy
relationship with someone?' It should make them realise that if
they and women are on a sort of equal basis in everything, that
they will have a better relationship, they won't have fights.

As Tahnee's comments suggest, girls want an approach which recognises that they 'are not going back'. This all points to another very
obvious problem associated with therapy models for girls. They
usually do nothing for boys and girls together or for boys alone.

Victims of feminism?

Gender reform provokes intense feelings in boys. Many are confused by it. Witness the remarks of these Year 10 boys from
Birrilup's single-sex science class:

152

Joel: It sort of just happened. It is weird, because everybody is always kicking up a stink about equal rights and that and then they go and do this! Well, they say equal rights, women should be as equal as men and then they go and put them in different classes. They are just, sort of, totally, um, rejecting each other.

Neil: It is unnatural but you just get used to it. After so many years of primary school with mixed classes you used to go, 'Oh, I don't want to sit next to a girl!' But you got used to it, but now it is just so odd because there are no girls in the class.

Gender reform seems to imply that all boys are successful, advantaged and powerful. It asks them to accept, on faith in many instances, the abstract concept of structural advantage based on gender. However, many boys feel the negative force of other relations of power and prestige based on forms of masculinity, class, race and age or, for example, size, sporting prowess and 'intelligence' and achievement. In these contexts, and according to these criteria, many are not obviously successful, advantaged or powerful and certainly do not feel so. Gender reform seems to name them as the cause of problems which many can't empathise with, don't feel responsible for and don't feel they have much control over. It seems to take away things they don't have. Also, it asks them to revalue what they value, to see what they have trouble seeing and to be what they have trouble being. It makes aspects of masculinity problematic in a cultural context where masculinity is seldom made problematic. Further, it makes masculine identity problematic without understanding that a central feature of masculine identity involves a refusal of introspection and self-doubt. It invites boys to be empathetic and emotionally responsible without appreciating that boys generally are not good at either and need to learn to be both. It encourages them to attend to their emotions but the emotion that they are best at expressing is anger and the one they are best at repressing is guilt. And all of this at the time of adolescence when they are least certain of their identity and most striving to find a worthwhile self among the many selves they are expected to develop and project. It is thus not surprising that, as a result of gender reform, many boys feel ambivalent, confused, worthless, blamed, ashamed, anxious, vulnerable, exposed and fearful.

Small wonder that there is no unified boys' voice on gender reform in schools. Most boys struggle to comprehend what it means for them, their relationships with each other, with girls and with their teachers, let alone its implications for their future work and family relationships. Small wonder, too, that only a few say that they feel empathetic and supportive, that quite a few express loud certain antagonism, and that others, by their silence, implicitly and complicitly agree. Boys' obvious responses are well in keeping with dominant masculine codes of conduct. What is so extraordinary is that teachers and others are surprised by this.

There are several common themes in the victim talk of the visibly oppositional boys, most of which are evident in the vignette of the Nerringo boys with which we began this chapter. The most common theme harnesses rationality to the logic of equal opportunity. It makes the case that equal opportunity is a fraud because equal opportunities for girls mean unequal opportunities for boys. Girls' success means boys' failure; strong girls mean weak boys: the zero/sum is one of the dichotomies around which masculinity is constructed (Smith 1996). Sad to say, it is not unusual for teachers to run a similar line. Its roots seem to lie in a fear of the loss of the power associated with masculinity—the castration complex. Aligned with this fearful logic are claims that girls' programmes blame and punish boys, that this is unfair and that teachers and girls should be fair. Such expectations of fairness can be understood to represent the sense of entitlement that is another feature of dominant versions of masculinity (Fitzclarence 1995). Gender reform is seen to be unfair in other ways too, because it misunderstands the essential nature of boyhood. It doesn't understand that boys are 'just joking', 'just having fun' and 'don't really mean it'. Further, gender reformers do not understand that boys also have problems which need attention. While this may well be the case, it is also true that such a line of argument is symptomatic of dominant masculine norms. For, as McLean (1996b) points out, while males typically deny their personal problems they also typically pass them on to others to attend to. Usually those who take responsibility for them are women and girls. Our data show that such thinking leads these boys to feel particularly neglected, resentful and angry, to mobilise a discourse of victimhood, to whip up such feelings in other boys and to seek to rebuild male solidarity around a sense of neglected masculinity which is nonetheless 'under siege and in crisis' (Kenway 1995).

> Dom: All women care about is being equal to men but no one cares about men being equal to women. They don't care.

Theo: Let women do this and that, but no one does nothing, or cares about the men. [Year 10 boys, Brookdale]

Boys' victim talk covers a wide range of school activities. The negative feelings arising from gender reform are mapped on to the volatile emotional under-life that schools help to generate in boys and are intensified. To the extent that sport is considered the last boys' bastion, they feel particularly aggrieved when 'girls get on top' there too. They will project their feelings of being made to feel 'the bad sex', back on to teachers and girls and make them feel in the wrong and worthless too. Retribution is the name of the game. Boys do this in many ways which include such remarks as 'pretty dumb', 'stupid', 'just boring', 'not interested', 'don't care' in relation to any gender reform activity.

Other responses amongst boys include denial and withdrawal. Boys will deny the pain and problems they cause by rationalising them away. They will also deny girls' success by claiming it is not worthwhile. This form of denial may be accompanied by disengagement. Boys may withdraw from the spaces where they feel most vulnerable, most under surveillance and most under pressure to change and go elsewhere. Then, in the places where they feel least vulnerable—the schoolyard, the sports field or outside of school altogether—they may 'up the masculine ante'. Protest involves a reassertion of traditional masculinity. While the oppositional responses of boys are not boys' only responses, they are the most visible and the most acceptable, particularly in masculine cultural strongholds. Such responses overshadow others and stake a disproportionate claim on teachers' and girls' sensibilities. Rather than seeing boys' demanding behaviours as symptomatic of the problems to be addressed and the issues at stake, many accept them at face value. They then blame 'out of balance' gender reform programmes which 'sadly neglect' the boys and call for more boys' programmes.

It is not surprising that teachers and girls are so amenable to boys' victim talk. Many of the boys' claims contain seeds of truth, point to some of the limitations of gender reform programmes and resonate with the therapeutic orientation outlined above and with girls' and teachers' 'will to nurture'. Because teachers do not have access to well-developed ideas about masculinity and emotionality and adequate pedagogies for boys such as those offered in Salisbury and Jackson (1996), they tend to draw ideas from conventional gender reform programmes for girls. Hence we see a recycling of ideas about poor self-esteem and the value of single-sex classes, role models, non-traditional subjects, changing curriculum choices and the like. However, recent thinking on masculinity and emotionality suggests that to base boys' programmes on the same principles as girls' is a flawed proposition. Let us develop this argument by drawing on the examples of single-sex and non-traditional activities for boys.

There are two main examples of single-sex classes and activities for boys associated with gender reform. Some are created as a function of the creation of single-sex classes for girls. Typically these are in mathematics, science, technology, trades and physical education. They offer curriculum-as-usual, have no reform agenda for boys and, as noted in Chapter 2, can be counter-productive in terms of gender relations. Other single-sex classes or activities are created specifically for boys and address such things as personal development, health, careers and gender awareness. There are three subsets. The first involves activities for boys which do not make masculinity problematic—boys-as-usual. The second subset addresses the problems that all boys are seen to have as a function of masculinity—'masculinity therapy' (Connell 1995, pp. 206–12). A third type includes those approaches which address both different masculinities and gender relations. The final subset is the least common, the most necessary and the most difficult. Consider some examples of these different approaches.

Blackstone runs a number of boys-as-usual programmes with a therapeutic orientation. All are blind to issues associated with masculinity.

> We try to address the problems of the weaker boys through the *Breakfast Club* . . . The kids turn up, have some breakfast, and go through self-esteem activities to get a little bit more confidence, a little bit more ego. We also have the *Cable Challenge*. Barry Cable, the footballer, is doing a lot of inspirational self-esteem work. He's going across to the Eastern States with a bus load of kids, going to try them for the Australian Football League. [Laughter] They've got a whole range of schools focusing on self-esteem, 'See the challenge and achieve it.' The spin-off is a whole pile of self-esteem packages, which are delivered to the school. [Bruce, Social Studies Head of Department]

In contrast, schools such as Nerringo, Rullinga and Stowley run masculinity therapy classes and day and weekend programmes which seek to challenge traditional notions of masculinity and the negatives that flow from them and which seek to effect some 'bonding' between male staff and boys. Taking their cue from the men's movement (see McLean 1996b), teachers point to boys' emotional repression and its negative implications for them.

> We try to bring in other perspectives, to show that you don't have to be a footballer, you don't have to drink. We get them to explore the emotional costs of always taking it on the chin. [Mary, English teacher, Rullinga]

As Alan, the EO Coordinator from Nerringo, explains:

> We're getting at that particular view of masculinity which would give boys the impression that they shouldn't express emotions, that they have got to be silent and strong. We're suggesting to them that that style of masculinity has its downside, that there are a lot of problems attendant on that in terms of their own wellbeing. We do a lot of things that relate to communication skills.

Most such programmes are based on the premise that boys are best taught to explore and challenge their own masculine identities by males. 'Hearing it from a male they tend to have more respect for the information,' says Mary. 'They don't think, "Oh well, here is a woman telling us that we have to do this again".' Based on the role model idea, preferred speakers are 'someone they admire', usually a footballer or media personality. In some instances the search is for non-traditional male role models.

> It is really important to give boys exposure to men who are out there doing non-traditional roles and who are also men who they respect and look up to. They need to see that it is not a reflection on their manhood to do that sort of job or to be involved in that sort of activity. They need to see that those who they see as strong men can also have that emotional side to them—is not necessarily a flaw. [Jasmin, social education teacher, Brookdale]

However, not infrequently, boys have to settle for any males who are prepared to be involved for, as Mary observes, 'it is difficult to get good speakers to speak to boys, to be role models, to talk to boys.' Alan from Nerringo points out, 'We try to make it really positive and supportive for them but it is really hard uphill work with the boys.' As he and others have learnt, being positive and critical at the same time is no easy matter.

When on rare occasions remaking masculinity is also aligned with reassessing gender relations, matters are more difficult. Typically in our schools, working with boys to remake gender relations involves the authoritarian pedagogies which most turn students off gender reform—preaching rather than teaching. The following comment from Claire, in Year 10 at Nerringo, gives some indication of the ways in which this is construed.

> They were told how to behave to us girls and how they had to respect us and themselves and emotions. What they said was that basically they just learned about how to respect the girls and they just said it was alright, they really didn't have much to say about it.

So how do boys read and rewrite these approaches to gender reform? On the whole they are most ambivalent regarding curriculum-as-usual, single-sex classes, except in Physical Education. In this case, their arguments for and against single-sex are a curious mixture of hero and victim talk. Consider first their negative views.

Many boys resent being put into single-sex classes, usually without being asked, against their will and, as many believe, against their interests. They feel put down and punished. We have examples of boys bitterly complaining about the loss of girls' support for their learning and good behaviour. Some complain that 'the class is noisy and you can't get work done', that the 'environment's more hostile'. [Year 10 boy, Edgecliffe] Boys claim that they are quieter in co-ed classes and more civilised.

Cameron: I wasn't too happy about it, I'd rather be with the girls because I've found even now the boys are so much naughtier and get into heaps more trouble compared to when we were in a girls' class. You don't dare do it in front of girls. They like swear and fart and burp and just talk about sex and all that, anything really. The girls have gained but the guys have lost out because you know the class has become wild.

Haydon: I think mixed groups would be better, because the boys especially do learn more while they're in a mixed environment, but when you take the girls away, they've only got other boys to show up to, but before they had the girls to like impress. They wanted to at least appear smart and now they've just got their mates that they hang around and play footy with, so they just play up. [Year 10 boys, Edgecliffe]

Implicit in this and many similar remarks is the idea that boys only seek to impress girls, that in an all-boys' class 'there is no one to impress'. However, it is clear that impressing is just as much an issue in boys-only classes, it is just that they 'have to' impress according to other criteria. The following comment demonstrates the point:

> Well like, in the classes where it's boys, the boys talk about boys' stuff. You know, without the girls hanging around listening to them, the boys want to talk about the girls and when the girls are not around, they can say what they want to say about girls. But when there's girls around they can't say anything or they'd be ashamed or something or the girls might get offended. [Year 11 boy, Mt Mullin]

In contrast, boys also claim that curriculum-as-usual single-sex is preferable, although for different reasons. Most boys will not accept that single-sex classes have been created because boys cause problems for girls. More usually girls' problems or problem girls are used to justify the creation of such classes. 'You don't have to stand all their make-up. In the middle of the class they start putting spray on themselves,' says a Year 9 boy from Birrilup. Either girls have a problem with boys or girls are a problem for boys; girls are too weak to stay or girls are so annoying boys want them to go. Either way, girls are construed as deficient and what they do elsewhere is regarded as remedial or as 'girls' things'. Then boys-alone is constructed as the place to be—a place of bantering, bonding and bravado. Here is how the boys in the single-sex classes at East Barton see it:

Gordon: Well, I guess that we don't want to be with girls because they take too long to do all the stuff. The experiments and all that.

Keenan: To get ready and put it all away and they always laugh, scream.

Greg: And act stupid.

Gordon: Yeah and they run around.

Keenan: And they drop the glasses. They are not stupid. If they want to walk around.

Gordon: Yeah, but they get carried away too much.

Keenan: . . . You just get more work down. People get the stuff all done . . . Oh, a lot of the girls pass little notes around.

Greg: Yeah, and they start giggling.

Gordon: And it wastes our time.

Keenan: Yeah, and we can't stand it. Well it is kind of like, man-to-man, type thing. Any man.

Gordon: Yeah, man-to-boy. [Laughter]

Greg: If there are females with you it is kind of . . . I don't know.

Gordon: Stupid, maybe?

Greg: Yeah.
Gordon: Weird. Pathetic.

Many boys argue that boys-only classes give them the chance to do things that they enjoy, that they are not held back by girls' inferior skills—particularly in sport and Physical Education. While many boys claim that they enjoy coed because, in some cases, 'You can hassle the girls and laugh at them,' they also argue that boys' classes, 'seem more fun somehow. You can do more jokes and that.' [Year 10 boy, Blackstone] Joking with the male teachers is seen as a particular advantage, the class is more relaxed and not so strict and students and teacher can enjoy being sexist and uncouth with impunity. Single-sex provides new opportunities for old-style masculinity, for male bravado and bonding.

> I didn't mind it much, I experienced both, the joint and the split up and either way it was pretty good. Although with just the male groups, like you can sort of muck around a bit more, there's sort of more male bonding in a way. Like you can get together at sports time and just muck around and you really enjoy it. Like with the girls in the mixed groups it was perhaps a little bit more competitive. [Year 10 boy, Nerringo]

Intensifying this 'mucking around' and 'male bonding' also becomes a way of protesting at gender reform.

Alternatively, single-sex provides a means of avoiding girls and this is particularly welcomed by shy boys, as these remarks suggest:

Hou: There are no females to laugh at us.
Phuoc: Because we do some things wrong then the girls they laugh and we don't want they laugh. And we just like boys and we don't care. [Year 7 boys, Karrawong]

It is not unusual for boys to feel inadequate when girls are around and to prefer boys-only classes for this reason; however, there is always the fear that if other boys find out about this preference they will censure them for it. After all, in a boys' class they 'might turn a bit queer'. The following remark is not unusual.

Would you prefer to be in a mixed group?
Phuoc: This is embarrassing. They think you are gay or something. You feel weird because of the other guys.

Homophobia becomes a mechanism for policing the masculine self.

Let us now briefly consider other types of single-sex for boys.

160

While boys-as-usual activities are very popular, boys prefer to avoid masculinity therapy and the intimacies of programmes which encourage them to consider—and worse still reveal—their emotions and to critically explore their sexuality. As Louise, a Year 9 girl at Brookdale, pointed out:

> Boys often get stupid at things like drama, boys can't be trusted to take it seriously, they'd be stupid, they'd just puke. Boys can't cope, they'd be embarrassed to sit there while someone was talking seriously about sex, they'd really freak out.

The least popular programmes for boys are those that address issues to do with gender relations. This point is well demonstrated in the vignette at the beginning of Chapter 3 on *Women and Change* and *Men and Change* at Nerringo. Like many of their peers, Theo and Dom resent gathering together to talk about changing their relationships with girls. As we demonstrated there and elsewhere, when it comes to anything non-traditional in gender terms, only the brave boys will volunteer and most boys will avoid what they can.

The dynamics of all the non-traditional approaches for boys (ranging from therapy to encouragement to make different choices) are different from the non-traditional for girls. The crucial difference is the knowledge, activity or field of work. It is not just a matter of the lower relative status of 'girls' stuff' (work on or related to the emotions/the private/the sexual/relationships), it is also the case that hegemonic masculinity fears and despises the feminine and withdraws from it. The non-traditional cuts to the heart of many males' identity—an identity which is fragile at the best of times. It is interesting to note that rarely do boys talk about boys-as-usual single-sex classes as providing them with the chance to be themselves, as do girls about girls' classes. In contrast, such classes seem to provide boys with the chance to find out what it means to be male and they find this out through the bonding effected through sharing traditional masculine pleasures. In terms of gender reform, such classes are bad news. In contrast, the non-traditional single-sex class which does such things as explore emotionality is felt as a double jeopardy for certain boys. In opposing the bonding and bravado mode, it does not provide them with opportunities to develop the male sense of self that they value and it undermines that particular sense of self that many dominant boys bring to it. Non-traditional single-sex classes for boys are thus not safe places for traditional boys.

Because of girls' presence, the non-traditional in coeducational classes produces less anxiety for such boys, although, as our data show, it clearly produces enough anxiety to encourage the boys to erect barriers and perform their gender identity. For boys who already subscribe to subordinate masculine codes, however, girls provide an alternative if ambivalent sense of community and source of support. Those rare few able to negotiate the above difficulties and brave the non-traditional do find that it offers a new sense of self and a new sense of relationality with other males. This is implicit in the comments of the boys at Neerbin who did the coeducational *Gaining the Edge* self-esteem programme.

Hamish: You found things out, things that you really needed to know and that, and you looked at yourself in a new way. Like I think that I have got a fairly low, sort of, self-esteem. It helped me to really look at it in a different way and work towards getting a higher self-esteem and that.

Peter: I was pretty much the same. It just helps. It is great. When I thought about doing it, I just thought, 'I don't care what the other boys think, I'll just do it for me. I will be different for a change.' I felt really good, I suppose. That I could actually do something for myself.

Hamish: Because you weren't like a sheep and followed everyone else around.

Peter: Yeah, because normally you are, like, following the leader all the time and trying to do what everyone else does.

Hamish: They all stick together all the time.

Those boys who indicate an enthusiasm for gender justice seem, like girls, to pin their hopes on coeducation. These boys support the idea of mutually beneficial sharing recommended by many girls:

I sort of didn't see the advantage of having single-sex classes because boys and girls in my opinion have different ways of seeing things, especially in maths and science areas, different input to different questions and problems and I thought if you took away the girls from the boys' classes and you took away the boys from the girls' classes, then it loses that input. [Year 10 boy, Birrilup]

Other boys agreed:

Austin: If you are a fella at school and you don't get to

	socialise around girls it might be bad for you because you are not used to them. You might be scared.
Marcos:	Scared of them. That's right.
Yama:	Well, you get to know them better, you don't feel nervous talking to them. That'd be better for the workplace too. You're not so sexist then. I think that if they had all-boys' classes and all-girls' classes then, later on in life, the male would be more sexist toward the female because they haven't interacted. [Year 10 boys, Birrilup]

We have made the case in this chapter that emotions play a central role in schooling and have many implications for learning, change and gender reform. We have indicated that some approaches to gender reform recognise this but do not sufficiently understand the complexities of the emotions involved, their psycho-dynamics and their social role, hence they are rather innocent about the gendered politics of emotion. We have further shown that most students—even its most fierce opponents in some instances—want gender reform to help them to feel and think differently. However, they do not want it to feel too risky and they want it to be enjoyable and to offer them a sense of agency. As we have also demonstrated, pleasure and fear and the rest of the emotional field of schooling and gender reform are often differently inflected for girls and boys and for different groups of girls and boys. We showed this through the case of the single-sex class and non-traditional activities indicating, also, that what works for girls will not necessarily work for boys. We have implied that, when gender reform inadvertently or otherwise mobilises anxiety, guilt, shame and a sense of powerlessness and injustice in students, it is likely to be ineffective. If it is to fulfil its best intentions, it must work through the many issues associated with such emotions and attend to the differentially gendered matters of empathy, responsibility, pleasure, risk and trust. Equally, it should be understood that boys and girls are both victims and beneficiaries of their emotions. This only becomes clear when one recognises the emotional effects of the social on them and the social role their emotions play for them. In the following chapter we will explore further the ways in which such matters may be addressed through the ideas associated with responsibility.

6

Responsibility

After attending a Women in Education conference, Anita, a literacy support teacher at Mt Mullin, was inspired to run a special breakfast for girls and women in the school. With the support of Zoe, the Deputy Principal, she planned the programme. Girls, women teachers, administrative staff, canteen workers, cleaners—all females were to be welcome. Disconcertingly, as Anita explains, her plan was met with some resistance.

There were some people, mainly women but men as well, who were quite happy with it all. 'Not a problem, yeah, the girls need it, let's do it.' There were a lot who were ambivalent. And then there were the men that got incredibly intimidated by the whole process.

Zoe got accosted in the staffroom one morning before school by a group of these men. I watched it. A couple of the men were really getting into her and being really aggressive, swearing and saying, 'What is this f - - - ing bullshit?' You know, really foul. Oh, but she is so good. She handled it *really* well! I mean, I don't know how I would have handled it. I would probably say, 'F - - - off!' and walk off myself. But she actually sat down at the table, which was really good strategy.

It was the 'fishing guys' table and they were all leaning forward and looming over her and so on. But the Head of Department of Manual Arts—who I wouldn't see as being pro-feminist at all but who is not stupid and, sort of, understands the agenda of the times—was sitting back in his chair and as they got more abusive he physically pushed his chair back further and further. You know, completely removing himself from it. It was obvious he didn't like it but at the same time he was not actually quite prepared to say something. But then there was another teacher there, a music teacher who is very popular, and he spoke out and said, 'I think that this is a good thing.' It took all the thunder and everything away immediately because they had assumed that all the males were, sort of, with them on this.

The breakfast was a great success with the girls in the school but, for Anita, its success was also that 'the whole thing caused people to have to start thinking and actively making decisions—actually having to be vocal about their support and to start to take responsibility'. In support, she offers another incident:

One of the aggressive men started getting into one of the girls who was the host of the breakfast. He told his Year 12 class that, if these sort of things are going to happen, then men should be there or they won't support it. He went on and on for quite a while and she was very upset.

Then she went into her next class which was with another young male teacher. He is in an overlapping peer group with the other chap and I would have thought he was towards the chauvinist side of ambivalent although not an 'out-and-out pain'. Anyway, he was so annoyed at how upset she was that he went to his Head of Department and said, 'This isn't good enough. He shouldn't be getting her so upset.' That Head went and spoke to the first teacher's Head of Department who then spoke to the first teacher. It was just incredible dynamics because these were all male teachers who had really thought that there are no gender issues any more. But they had to become active rather than passive and take some responsibility for dealing with the situation. Things like that occurred throughout the staff. It was quite an amazing uplift of awareness from such a tiny-weeny little thing.

By the time the second activity for girls and women took place, a number of women and men had come 'off the fence' and were prepared to be seen as supportive.

Later, when we had the mini-conference, awarenesses had been raised so we had more committed involvement from women and we also had men being more supportive—they realised that support was needed, where they hadn't realised it before . . . All the women who wanted to attend found men who were willing to give up their preparation time to take their classes. This meant that men were making statements with their time. A lot of the men that I spoke to were basically surprised at the aggression and irrationality of the men that were causing us problems. I think too that they were partly embarrassed to be associated with them. They buy this silly post-feminist belief. They actually believed that things were equal now and then they had to come face-to-face with these, sort of, archaic attitudes. They realised that this behaviour still existed. It put them in a position where they actually had to do something. I think that a lot of the men who were ambivalent realised that ambivalence is not good enough.

Who's responsible? Implicit in this question is the notion of fault: Who did it? What is the cause? Who's to blame? We exhort both young and old people to 'take responsibility' for their own actions, to 'act responsibly', the implication being that they can be held accountable for their actions, that they are 'answerable'. There is also obligation and duty, both informal and formal: Should I do something? What should I do? Who cares? Must I act? Whose responsibility is it? As we shall show, fault and obligation, these dual notions of responsibility, are both central to gender reform and in uneasy tension with each other.

The focus of this chapter is on teachers' responsibility for effecting change in the interests of gender justice; for remaking girls and boys but also for remaking themselves. What is the impetus to taking professional responsibility for gender reform? What causes some teachers to be strongly committed to gender justice and active fighters for gender equity across their school? Why is it that, amongst those who express support for gender equity, some are willing and do make changes to their own practice while others seem unprepared or unable to change? And what causes some to oppose such changes?

Since their inception, government policies for gender reform have not had much to say about educational change processes or teacher development. The feminist research literature on teacher development for change of any sort is almost nonexistent. The literature which does exist usually forms part of gender reform advice packages and largely draws its inspiration from the more general literature on teacher development. Outside of action research, which is a particular favourite, its guiding principles are seldom clearly articulated and are never critically examined. As a result, rather ingenuous ideas about teacher development and school change inform gender reform policies and professional development practices. These embody a range of perceptions about human motivation and change. They have moved from an approach which can be characterised as 'top-down support for bottom-up change' to one which is largely 'top-down', these representing very different policy 'invitations' to responsibility.

Popular in the 1970s and 1980s, the former approach implies that teachers will take responsibility for change if given the right encouragement and conditions, if they work collaboratively, conduct their own research and develop their own knowledge on matters related to gender and their schools—if they 'own' the ideas. Teachers are encouraged to become reflective practitioners and to undertake action-oriented research. It is implicitly built on a model of teacher professionalism which draws on the idea that teachers have a professional investment in improving their practice, that they have a desire for ongoing professional renewal and that, as a result of its emphasis on collaboration, they will feel a sense of connectedness and collective responsibility. The responsibility of the 'change agent' is to facilitate change, not monitor it.

These ideas did not originate with feminism. Rather, they have grown from a broader set of ideas which were fashionable in government and other circles when the wider political climate and the political culture were both favourably disposed towards progressive educational ideas, educational innovation, the democratic devolution of responsibility for school education and also towards redressing social and educational inequality. However, they resonate with popular feminist understandings about consciousness-raising, collaboration, ownership and empowerment, and about the relationship between change and knowledge about educational and social injustice. Within this approach, it is implicitly assumed that teachers will be so indignant—even shocked—by their discovery of the hard facts about gender inequality and about their complicity in producing such inequality that they will feel compelled to change; they will feel professionally obligated and be responsible for bringing about change in the interests of gender justice. Good information, goodwill, good intentions and good practice are linked. It is this way of thinking which continues to inform the work of those involved in teacher development for gender reform.

However times have changed in policy circles. Although some of the ideas about teachers as professionals linger on, such early ideas have come to be seen as innocent and romantic from two viewpoints.

First, anecdotal evidence shows that good information, goodwill and good intentions are not enough and that ideas for gender reform actually encounter some considerable resistance from teachers. Even teachers who are 'well informed' and 'well intentioned' do not necessarily feel obligated to act. And, as we have shown in earlier chapters, many other teachers are not well informed about matters of gender reform and some are less than well intentioned. In the 1990s, many of those who are committed to gender reform in and through schools have become impatient with what seems the inordinately slow progress of local action and piecemeal reforms (Yates 1993). Further, research into the intense subtleties of gender formation in schooling, accompanied by data which show how little has really changed, point to the intractability of the problems. Many of those in gender reform policy circles support fourteen-year-old Anne from the beginning of Chapter 3, when she bluntly states, 'we can't wait'.

Second, the technical rationality which has come to inform all government policies in education has also come to dominate gender reform, which increasingly couches policy in terms of performance criteria. Twenty years down the track we see a complete turnaround in gender reform policy circles. Indeed, ideas about teacher professionalism have now almost entirely given way to those about teacher accountability. Teachers, it seems, will not take responsibility voluntarily and must be required to do so. This has contributed to increased governmental efforts during the 1990s to effect change in a 'top-down' way, through policy edict and monitoring. State systems, schools and teachers are expected to enact policy and to account to governments for what they have or have not done.

Now clearly ideas about accountability produce a very different dynamic. They imply that teachers do not understand, cannot be trusted and must be directed into good practice. It is predictable that teachers' responses to this implication will not be positive, particularly if one takes into account the broader political context of recent times involving major educational restructuring, a mean and lean approach to supporting teacher development for change, and reform fatigue on the part of teachers. All of this makes the job of the gender reformer in our schools increasingly difficult.

In our schools, we met teachers across the whole spectrum from responsible to irresponsible with regard to gender reform. Some passionately embrace the need to help girls and boys make and remake their lives, while others just as passionately reject any need for reform. In between are the majority of teachers, neither passionately for nor against gender reform. Some deny any professional responsibility for bringing about change, while others assume responsibility where and when they see a need, regarding it as part of their obligations as a teacher. In what follows, we consider what motivates each of these groups of teachers and the implications for encouraging and enabling gender reform in and through schools.

Who cares?

It is almost always the case that people in our schools experience gender reform as some sort of challenge. For some, its challenges are welcome and they eagerly embrace a responsibility for bringing about gender reform. For others, the challenge is negative and provokes resistance of various sorts and degrees. Between them, those who embrace and those who reject feminist ideas define the boundaries of the possible for gender reform in schools.

I see that there is something really wrong

Nell Noddings (1995, p. 11) suggests: 'There are moments for all of us when we care quite naturally. We just do care; no ethical effort is required. "Want" and "ought" are indistinguishable in such cases. I want to do what I or others might judge I ought to do.' This describes many feminist teachers in our schools—those who feel compelled to involvement in gender reform, driven by the feeling, 'I must, I cannot do otherwise'. Others also care and see a need for involvement but the compulsion is not so strong; they have a choice which they make in the interests of gender equity.

Many tell us that their interest has arisen from their own histories and not from policy edicts. In school after school, we hear stories of frustration and anger about gender inequalities. Some are predictable family stories of overworked and unappreciated mothers, of fathers who are uninvolved or lazy when at home and of children growing up determined 'not to be like that and not to let future generations be like that'. Ruth, the most active gender equity worker at Riverside, tells us, 'my father would have had his daughters leave school at fifteen if my mother hadn't stood up to him . . . I am grateful to my mother for insisting that I stay at school.' Other stories arise from the frustration and isolation of both training and teaching in fearsomely sexist school departments or of classroom and community cultures where girls are the perpetual minority. 'I get really angry when I teach Physics,' says Ralph from Bridgeforth, 'and I have got, say, only two girls in the class of 25. I see that there is something really wrong.' Less predictable are the good news and redemption stories, and these tend to come from men. Rod, a young teacher at Braydon Tech, says 'I look back on my teenage years and I'm frightened by them. I'm ashamed of my attitudes.' Other male teachers grew up in homes where the unconventional happened and became naturalised, where mothers were in paid work and where fathers automatically shared the household load. They think that this is the way it should be.

These are the passionate teachers. Yearning for gender justice is in their blood. Policy gives them licence and some protection and support, but they read and enact it largely through the lens of their own histories. 'I'm probably tough,' says Linda from Brookdale:

> When I was at high school it was extremely unequal. The boys were treated to everything. It was either sink or swim for the girls. That was what made me become a Phys Ed teacher. I figured I was going to get out there and make it equal in my own classes. But I've also got this tough side that says, 'Well I got off my butt and did something about it. Isn't it time some of you girls got a little bit more assertive and got out there and did something too?'

But these are not the only motivating memories. There are others of being inspired by feminist teachers in universities and by exciting inservice courses. Anita, the literacy support teacher who organised the breakfast for girls and women at Mt Mullin, describes her experience of the Women in Education conference thus:

> I had never been to anything like that before and it was just fantastic . . . I had just not realised how many fantastic and high-flying women were out there. But they were all, sort of, ordinary. I found it very friendly. I mean, I didn't feel any power plays or anything and I felt that the people up the front were just one of us who had got up and was speaking. I found the whole thing essentially very intimate. But just so inspiring. It made me realise that women like me also have to be taken more seriously.

Some are inspired by the very idea of feminism itself,

> I remember at university I enrolled in a course on feminism and I went off to the first class and there was a sea of women, a hundred women or so, and I was the only male. I was really intimidated. But I always wanted to study it. I was just fascinated by feminism. [Dom, Work Education Coordinator, Bridgeforth]

It's many years ago now for me. We studied Friedan's *The Feminine Mystique* and that really did have a profound impact on how I saw the world and suddenly something went click, 'Oh, she's right.' [Scott, English teacher, Bridgeforth]

Teachers like Anita, Dom and Scott are also on a mission but they tend to be both more analytical and better informed about the field than the 'passionate' teachers. Anita is in no doubt that 'inspiration' is not enough.

I think that many women, like myself, have come to their feminist awarenesses because they are analytical and observant and read and think. In my case, it has been very self-directed. I was like it at school but then I lacked all the language and found it difficult to express myself. Still I used to get really indignant at injustices that I couldn't quite vocalise.

Indeed, as we demonstrated in Chapters 3 and 5, inspiration needs to be accompanied by considerable knowledge about gender and by pedagogical sensitivity and skill.

In many cases, strong personal commitments to social justice in general have led teachers to commit to gender justice in particular. Peter, from Edgecliff, believes that, 'Social justice is a concept that . . . should shape curriculum [and] a natural spilling over of that is the gender issue.' His professional identity is tied up in doing the right thing by all of his students.

It's not just a warm inner glow thing that drives it, it's a hard-core principle that you have to maximise delivery, fair delivery to as many individuals as possible, whilst treating kids as human beings.

Scott, from Bridgeforth, believes that, 'to do nothing is to do something' and, furthermore, 'If I'm not addressing those issues, if I'm not teaching girls in the way that they learn best, how can I think I'm fulfilling my responsibility—am I just a teacher amongst the boys?' Others have developed their professional identities around being at the cutting edge—they enjoy the challenges and also see the teachers' role as much more than banking knowledge. Simon, for example, says:

I like to think through an issue I guess, but I'm quite convinced from the literature about girls' education that it is an issue that must be taken up by schools. I'm involved because I believe that injustices are being done . . . It comes down to the reason why I'm a teacher, I guess. It's not just to impart knowledge, I see teaching as being a process of developing people's minds, developing people's attitudes. [Professional Development Coordinator, Banksia]

As this remark implies, being at this particular cutting edge is gratifying both intellectually and politically.

Ray from Wattlehill suggests that 'people become involved from the bigness of their hearts really. And from ambition—an ambition to change the behaviour of people.' Gender reform offers teachers the opportunity to give somebody a chance, to tackle serious and damaging social problems, to see old wounds addressed. This brings forth a sense of agency, feelings of professional pride and responsibility. To put it bluntly, to do such things feels good and feeling good is at a premium in schools under stress.

There is also a serious downside for those teachers trying to undertake gender reform. Often they are ridiculed or have their ideas trivialised and are purposefully and maliciously blocked in their efforts with students and other staff. It is to the sources of such obstruction that we now turn.

Here's your local garbage for the week

At the other end of the spectrum from those who embrace responsibility for gender reform are the openly hostile resistors, those for whom 'the "I must" does not arise, or . . . whispers faintly and disappears, leaving distrust, repugnance or hate' (Noddings 1995, p. 13). These teachers, often but not only men, are also passionate. Some are legends in their own lifetime because of their vitriolic attacks on feminism or because of their failure to understand that certain male styles are no longer acceptable. The School Bursar at Rullinga has a reputation for treating women staff appallingly, regularly leaving administrative staff in tears. He eventually cancels a booking of the local community hall made by the EO Committee for an art exhibition for International Women's Day because, 'no feminists were going to book the hall for such a thing'. At the same school, the EO Coordinator, Marjory, is harassed by a boy who asks her loudly in front of his mates 'Have you got the rags on or something?' The Year Coordinator with special responsibility for dealing with sex-based harassment does not treat her complaint seriously, sides with the boy, and asks the EO Coordinator if she is sure she hasn't imagined it. He becomes vitriolic and loudly abusive in the staffroom when she persists.

Many openly resistant teachers engage in rude and snide public ridicule, mobilise negative humour and rumour, mount aggressive inflexible arguments wilfully blind to the facts, and try to intimidate gender reformers by insulting and haranguing them and booing them at staff meetings. Linda, teacher of English as a second language at Karrawong, describes the sort of irresponsible performance likely when raw nerves are exposed:

> All the senior staff were women. Some of the guys got really pissed off. 'The girlies are running everything around here.' They formed this group called Men's Access. They were very upset about having a girls-only celebration on International Women's Day. So they organised a little group function for themselves where they picked out Miss Karrawong . . . At their morning tea, they ate whole sausages as part of their little ritual . . . They did things like go to a topless bar one night. It was all this sort of gross behaviour.

Some resistors act anonymously and deface and destroy notices or leave nasty messages in pigeonholes. These people are the 'front line troops of patriarchy' (Connell 1994, p. 79). Their rage is unmistakable. Their irresponsibility is extreme.

Others are less overt but no less destructive. The teacher at Mt Mullin in our opening vignette who verbally attacked a female Year 12 student over the breakfast for girls and women is one example. Our schools abound with such stories. Craig, the Youth Education Officer at Kingwood, circulates material on employment opportunities for girls. He remarks, 'I rely on people to pass on information but sometimes the teacher will take the information but not do anything with it—or they will pass it on but say, "Here girls, here's your local garbage for the week." I would say they are hindering that way, not passing on the information as adequately as they could.' What appears to fuel such negative reactions to feminist ideas in schools?

I do believe to some degree your gender equity is to blame

The usual way of interpreting men's resistance is to point to their identity and career investments in hegemonic masculinity and its inscription in education. Certainly many male teachers get most bitter, resentful and hostile around issues of affirmative action for women teachers. This is understood as jobs for the girls and many men believe that, if women apply for jobs, they will automatically get them—even though the data do not support this.

> They get the job simply because they are females. In our faculty there's a person, Bob, who has been going for a promotion for so long he's losing face in the whole system. And there is this lady, I don't know her, probably a wonderful lady, but she was working under Bob as a teacher fifteen years ago. And now she's a deputy principal—female and Bob's still Head of Social Studies . . . And I do believe to some degree your gender equity is to blame. [Mel, social studies teacher, Wattlehill]

Remarkably, he adds:

> In this school the Principal is male and there's one male and one female deputy. Then you've got two heads of department in science both males, social studies are both males, English are both males and maths are both males. But then you have business which is one female. I know it's very difficult for a male to achieve that status in business. There are not enough males in there. And you have home economics which is just a female. Manual arts is a male. Art is usually female here. And so they tend to be in balance.

Ted, at Kingwood, where three of the school's fourteen senior positions are held by women, shows a similar disregard for the data: 'We've got Deidre up here looking after the admin—that's a woman running the office, next year a woman will be one of the senior teachers over in maths, we've got a woman in charge of academic extension. I think that they're pretty well catered for.' Many teachers do not distinguish EEO initiatives for teachers from EO for students and anger towards the former often spills over on to the latter. Many male teachers feel blamed for the sins of their fathers who—unlike them, they believe—had genuine advantages over women teachers. As John at Banksia says, 'You push the females up into those positions of authority. It's like putting all men in prison for what Jack the Ripper did a couple of hundred years ago.' Gary, from Kennetton, who supports affirmative action on the basis that it will 'improve our interactions in schools as a whole,' begs to differ. The feelings may be understandable, he says, but the resulting actions are not, being irresponsible and unworthy of a professional: 'I get annoyed that they actively encourage the troglodytes.'

Changing gender relations are part of this age and have left many men and boys unsure of how to behave in new times which not only require them to rethink their relationships with women but to voluntarily surrender some of their automatic advantages at work and at home. Little is now guaranteed. As Liz, an older teacher at Wattlehill, says, 'bluster covers up a feeling of being threatened in that race to the top where they feel they should go'. She adds: 'They resent it more if a women gets promoted than if one of their male colleagues does—as though women don't really *need* promotion and the ones going for it are those awful sort of pushy women.' There is a prevailing mood of anxiety, stress and insecurity amongst many male teachers, particularly those older teachers most hit by the redefinition of work, marriage and womanhood—the old men confronting the new women (MacKay 1994). Clearly women are also living in the same age, but at least feminism has provided many with a source of psychological support and social and personal interpretation, particularly in education circles. In contrast, as a technical teacher from Kingwood says, 'There hasn't been any campaign to really educate us, speaking from the male perspective. There haven't been people coming in to fix us up.' In a perfect representation of the ambiguity of the times, he then adds ruefully, 'I think that's been a good thing, I think that would have led to more resentment than ever.'

But other matters beyond gender are also involved and at stake. Moving beyond gender reductionism and attending to subtlety and complexity helps to account for the wide variety of resistant responses. This is not to say that gender is unimportant—it often is important, but not always and not only. A range of conscious and preconscious discourses inform teachers' responses to gender reform, some deeply personal, others deeply professional and political. Some are caught up in teachers' lives in very intimate ways at an individual and a group level. John, for instance, is the staffroom comedian at Banksia and the gender reform activists regularly suffer the effects of his bitingly cruel but brilliantly funny critique. On first exposure to this, we were tempted to see it as the most extreme form of chauvinism which is often connected to deeply cynical and alienated teachers, but seeing his dedicated engagement with his students and the esteem in which they held him led us to think again. We learnt that John is struggling to raise a daughter with severe intellectual disabilities, is enraged at the lack of government assistance available to him and others in similar situations, and is deeply resentful of money spent on the relatively more privileged. Things are rarely as straightforward as they seem.

175

They've got a lot to lose

Women's resistance to feminist ideas is also often interpreted in terms of their identity and career investments in emphasised forms of femininity and in the modes of masculinity which such femininity supports. Certainly we came across examples that would support this interpretation. Rachel at Riverside suggests that some women feel personally threatened by EEO initiatives and by women in promotional positions, 'When EEO was introduced there were some very angry men and women. I think that some women felt it was OK not to be promoted if all the people in promotional positions were men'. Emma, at the same school, expresses her anger as the mother of two sons that males are missing out on jobs and opportunities because of preference being given to females. She talks about 'very opportunistic females' who have manipulated the spirit of gender equity behind affirmative action and taken jobs that 'really should have gone to a man'. Some younger women are fearful of the stirring and stigma directed at feminists in and out of schools. Liz, from Wattlehill, says of her younger colleagues: 'Those young women, if they make themselves unpopular, they have got a lot to lose.' She continues:

> We have got some marvellous young women who do really innovative things and they take leadership roles, but they also don't threaten the male ego at all. They do things to avert the threat, so they can be seen as bright young things rather than women who are going places.

And indeed, in many cases such fears are well grounded. Feminist politics as well as women's femininity and sexuality are carefully policed by certain members of staff. Linda, the ESL teacher from Karrawong, tells us of her fears of being 'typecast' as a feminist: 'Because when I was in the Language Centre, we were mostly women over there and when we came here everyone was saying we were lesbians and all this stuff just because we were sort of different.'

Diane, from Braydon Tech, is angry. She appears to find feminism threatening and offensive:

> We had an EO officer and I used to get so angry with her . . . I just saw a totally feminist thing . . . I found out she was buying a whole lot of books through the EO budget. So I took them home. I was so angry. They were all novels, written by women. One was a whole series of short stories but every woman had a bad

176

experience with a man. It was like making the man look really bad. This book was written by feminists.

. . . My definition of a feminist is they really don't like men . . . I mean, it is a fact, they have some problem with a man. I don't have any problem with men, I have a lot more problems with women.

In the past few years the girls are getting everything because they have girls' camps. I'm really anti that feminist type thing, where the girls are getting all the rides and the boys are just being left behind. I mean, I know that the boys have had it—the male race has had it—for so many years, but I wasn't around in those years and I can only look at it now, what's happening today and we've moved well beyond that, I think.

She isn't clear how much 'beyond that' we've really moved:

This is a male-dominated staff . . . Like we have this table tennis table in here, which is a social communication thing. It is male dominated. I get up to play quite often, but it is like, 'Oh, she's a girl.' You know, some men just won't get up and play if there's a female there. I get so angry at some of the male staff here, when it comes to discussing women working. They're quite alright for women to work but once they're married it's a different thing.

But she is quite clear that she wants to 'stay with the strength' and she knows where the strength lies.

I always make a point of sitting at the table with the men. Yeah, see that's how I can have their points of view. What I like about sitting up at the table is there's always some sort of political thing that's going on. The Principal always sits up there, so that's where you learn. If you want to learn about what's going on, you sit up there.

I think about the other women, 'Well, why don't you just come and sit up here all the time instead of sitting down, around the couch, talking about cakes and sewing and clothes and all that.' I align myself more with the men.

Diane immediately agreed when it was suggested to her that the women 'around the couch' actually discussed a wide range of things, mostly professional, but still she has no time for the women who can't see where their advantage lies. Diane's comments capture a lot of the muddled thinking about gender and the stereotyping of feminists amongst many of the resistors to gender reform. The hostility, contempt and defensiveness she exhibits often arise when matters of gender identity and investment are most at risk.

The confused resentment exhibited by many men in

staffrooms, but also by women such as Diane, often is displaced on to gender reformers in the form of blame. They become an identifiable common enemy. Jokes at their expense can provide the pleasurable rush of approval seldom felt elsewhere. The relentless harping and carping and the staffroom 'humour' drives many feminist teachers to distraction. Many such resistant teachers appear to delight in their professional irresponsibility. Not only do they not help the interests of gender justice, but they actually do harm, undermining the efforts of others to an extent disproportionate to their numbers. In many schools, they determine what gender-reforming teachers feel able to attempt and are able to achieve.

Must I act?

> I may readily agree that 'things would be better' . . . if a certain
> chain of events were to take place. But there is still nothing in
> this intellectual chain that can produce the 'I ought'. I may choose
> to remain an observer on the scene. (Noddings 1995, p. 12)

The impact of those who publicly embrace and of those who publicly reject gender reform in schools is often dramatic. These, however, are not the only—or even the dominant—stories in our schools. More common are those of teachers neither passionately for nor against gender reform—stories of neglect, disinterest and apathy, of the 'supportive, sort of' and of the quietly involved.

Almost a luxury

Many teachers simply do not feel that the onus is on them to get involved in gender reform. As Jane from Wattfield says, 'I wouldn't say we have negativity from those staff, just apathy basically, you know, not interested, not important.' They do not actively reject or even argue against gender reform but, in denying responsibility for change, they implicitly ask, 'Why *should* I?' or 'Why should *I*?'

As we have seen throughout earlier chapters, teachers often underestimate the impact that gendered attitudes and values continue to have on students' lives at school and beyond. This may be due to long exposure to the gender equity debate, over-exposure to what some perceive as overly strident pro-feminist views, the complex and confusing nature of the issues, or a fear of what will ensue if the social structures built on male dominance are dismantled. Whatever the cause, the result is that they do not see gender reform as a priority, particularly in a time of stringent government cutbacks for education. They feel overworked, under-resourced and ill-appreciated. As Christina, from Riverside, puts it:

> At the moment that's almost a luxury to have the time to think about what gender equity, affirmative action and all those things mean, let alone get programmes up and running. The more we double, triple and quadruple our personal loads to cover up, the less people know what problems we are facing . . . If you don't have a teacher to teach a class, how can you get a gender equity programme up?

Alan, from Kingwood, is rather more blunt and bitter than most:

> What should I do about it? I feel as though over the last five or six years everything has gone back to the teacher. People say, 'Why aren't you doing something about it?' Why should I do something for nothing, for a pittance? I mean until somebody comes to me and says there's a reward . . . I find there are no rewards and teachers are becoming very disillusioned. We're flat out just trying to keep our heads above water.

Alan is angry. His anger is not directed at gender reform, but at any suggestion that it is part of his charge, his duty, his professional responsibility. 'Why should I go off on a guilt trip?' he says. Unlike the teachers who rail against the very idea that gender reform is needed, Alan acknowledges that 'something should be done' but not that 'I must do something'. Rather, 'they should do something', 'they' being the government, the Education Department. He is critical that change is expected 'without support' and, even if the support is there, 'I'm not prepared to turn around and start seeking out all this information because of the pressure to teach properly in our classrooms. This is just an extra.'

Many teachers express their views in more moderate terms— albeit they may consider gender equity to be an option which they may freely accept or reject. Toni, from Draymill, comments: 'In this school, EO is not understood as a basic curriculum issue— that you've got to be thinking of gender when considering your basic work, the resources we use, the sort of stuff we write on the board.' Danni, from Kingwood, sums it up: 'You can decide not to act, especially if you don't notice yourself not acting.'

For many such teachers, gender reform efforts evoke mixed responses depending on their particular manifestation. Certain feminist ideas are easily tolerated, while others quickly produce a knee-jerk negativity. In Chapter 3, we heard from teachers who were reluctant to change in the interests of gender equity, even when they accepted the need. 'It wouldn't be me,' said one. We also quoted an English teacher who suggested that students were generally willing to discuss gender stereotyping and the like without too much antagonism but, 'the moment you pass any responsibility over to them for the problem, the moment you ask them to act', the trouble begins. This is no less true of many teachers. Indeed, teachers often ask students to change in ways they are unprepared to change themselves—a particularly irresponsible act. When teachers are forced to notice themselves not acting, when it is suggested that it *is* a part of their responsibility to act, tempers often flare. The most acceptable gender reform strategies are those which do not rely on asking teachers to change in any significant way. Witness the comments of Jim from Banksia about staff reactions to a visiting speaker.

> I think they were just about to stampede. A couple of people got up and said what they thought and Viv said, 'Listen I'm not asking you to change your teaching style, I'm asking you to use some examples of females, for instance, things in history that females have done, not just male history.' I could see a few lights going on . . . 'Gee it's that easy.' Everyone thought they were being asked to change the way they live, change the way they do things.

Passing the responsibility over to teachers for the problem of gender inequality and injustice makes them 'faultable'—both for what they do and what they do not do—and many do not like it. Acknowledging an obligation to change their practice seems tantamount to accepting blame for existing inequalities. Denial is a common response.

I wouldn't throw myself in front of a train for gender equity

For many teachers, calls to positively discriminate destabilise their sense of themselves as good teachers. Certain of those who deny responsibility for bringing about change claim that it actually goes against the grain of teachers' responsibilities, which are to give all students individual attention and also to treat them all equally—where, paradoxically, equally often means 'the same'.

Dave Blakeney, the principal at Kingwood, tells us his daughter is 'brilliant' and 'topped her school' in Year 10 but chose lower level mathematics and science courses in Year 11. He interprets this in gendered terms.

Sometimes girls, and Rhonda was one, will choose below their capabilities because in spite of the fact that she has done well, she always feels that she mightn't have done as well. Whereas boys in the same situation will go in reverse . . . As far as choices are concerned, boys will tend to shoot above the line, whereas girls will tend to shoot below the line.

He is disturbed that his daughter's school felt no responsibility for querying her decision, 'If Rhonda had been Robert in the same situation, I bet you I would have at least had a phone call about it.' He continues, 'This issue worries me because I think sometimes . . . we don't make quite the same running for some people as we do for others.' By his own analysis, this is a situation that should be addressed by schools. Since he knows better, we presume he will ensure that Kingwood does better—but it seems not. 'I think probably the same thing happens here at Kingwood,' says Dave, 'in the sense that we say people are free to choose.'

How does Dave construct this denial of responsibility? Adroitly, he moves from his analysis of the gendered nature of students' choices and of schools' responses and calls upon the discourse of teacher autonomy, 'I see my role as more of an encourager than a director.' He then shifts again to a discourse about individual differences.

I've always tended to see all these equity problems from the individual differences standpoint rather than rights for women or rights for Aboriginals. I felt it was more meaningful to me to work that way. You weren't terribly depressed if you failed in three out of four because at least you succeeded with one.

Many teachers at Kingwood also call upon the discourses of individual difference and free choice to absolve themselves from responsibility for addressing the gender differences which they themselves identify within the school. The 'transitional' programme is intended for Year 11 students who are unlikely to benefit from a more academic programme and who wish to enter a trade. Alan, the transition studies teacher, comments:

I'd like to see more girls in the course. I look at the person as an individual first and these individuals have certain specific problems—some of them happen to be male—some of them happen to be female . . . I make a point of telling them it's open for boys and girls. I explain the things that girls do and the things that boys do—to show it's wide open for both genders. But I'm not sure what to do. I think it's just the way the cards fall. I don't think it's a case of girls not coming into the course because of any gender issue. I think it's just a case of their own personal situation. I'm not sure why there are more boys than girls.

But, for Dave, the appeal to individual difference and free choice is too slippery—after all, he does know better—and so the ground shifts again and the needs of other 'more needy' groups are called upon to explain his disinclination to address matters of gender.

> The gender issue certainly is an issue of equity but I don't believe it is the big issue. I have a greater concern for Aboriginal education in terms of equity—even though I've been very unsuccessful in that area. I recognise their disadvantage as extreme. I wouldn't throw myself in front of a train for gender equity in quite the same way as I would for others.

Fortunately for Dave, he will not be forced in front of a train in the near future. The 'others' he describes himself as having an affinity for are 'Aboriginal education' and 'migrant education', but there are no Aboriginal students at Kingwood and the 7 per cent of students from minority ethnic backgrounds are almost all from middle-class professional families who 'have a good attitude to work and integrate easily into the school'. Many teachers who decline to engage with gender reform, however—like Dave—do so on the grounds that other social justice issues such as those associated with race, class or disability are more pressing.

Calling upon the needs of 'other groups' has proved a powerful strategy for silencing the demands for gender equity in a number of our schools. Increasingly during the 1990s, it seems to us, EO workers choose to 'play down' the emphasis on girls in an attempt to make their messages more palatable. Jan, from Bridgeforth, recalls spending several anxious months planning an inservice day on gender-inclusive curriculum because 'a minority, but a strong one, made me feel that they didn't approve of it, that it was a load of rubbish.' Eventually she decided not to mention gender until halfway through the day. 'Actually,' she says, 'it worked out really well because I just talked about social justice issues and then we did lots of activities on how people learn and different styles of learning and then I worked into it saying that, well, gender-inclusive curriculum is basically inclusive curriculum'. Thus, in order to get gender reform accepted amongst all staff, gender-inclusive curriculum becomes 'inclusive curriculum' and pedagogy is legitimised as simply 'good teaching'. Unfortunately, this often subverts gender reform by enabling teachers to reassure themselves that they are doing the right thing without addressing gender relations at all. At Bettleford, for example, members of the Mathematics Department use group work, amongst other 'good teaching' strategies. They believe, therefore, that they are being 'gender inclusive'. Georgina, an active member of the EO team, comments wryly:

> They think they are doing a terrific job . . . If they think that is all you have to do . . . While that is good, they are still not aware of how they operate. There is one staff member who greets his class, 'Righto guys,' and I say there are girls in the class. He says, 'They know what I mean,' and I say, 'Exactly'.

Nevertheless, taking the focus off gender and putting it on to social justice appears to present a less threatening and more palatable face to reform. Indeed, Jan's strategy was perhaps prophetic because Bridgeforth School has now changed the title and role of the EO position and the committee to 'social justice' in order to include forms of inequality other than 'just gender'. Scott regards this as 'a more embracing approach [since] we've tried to include all of the students that we have at this school, whether they be male, female, what nationality they are, their backgrounds'. According to Joan, the EO Coordinator at Banksia, a similar 'strategic' change has occurred there. The strategy, however, is not without risk. As Teresa, another teacher at Banksia, says, 'I think people have been using the broader social justice needs as an excuse and now with Joan in charge of eight social justice areas, not a lot will be achieved in any of them.' Indeed, Joan is coming to realise the subtlety and the intractability of many of the problems that she is trying to tackle. She cannot develop her knowledge in all these areas and in the absence of knowledge she is unlikely to be effective in any. She cannot do it all.

Speaking of feminist educational analyses of the 1980s, Arnot (1995, p. 166) has suggested, 'It was precisely in the spaces created by concepts such as freedom of choice, teacher autonomy and child-centred education that sexism was repeatedly found unchallenged and often thought "natural".' Our data suggest that this comment is relevant to many Australian schools in the 1990s. Further, we would add to that list the concepts of 'disadvantaged groups' and 'social justice in general'. The first, as we have seen in earlier chapters, allows schools to shift responsibility for many of the problems students have at school to their home or their culture, which can then be asked to accept the onus to change. The second means that issues of gender can be submerged under a welter of other issues. Gender reform challenges all the cultural baggage about gender that individuals bring to school; it is highly disruptive of social and therefore power arrangements in schools. Teachers 'face the possible unravelling and remaking of aspects of their personal world as well as the professional world they inhabit' (Ruddick 1994, p. 128). It is little wonder, then, that gender reform is threatening to schools in ways that reform for 'other groups' is not. Social justice clearly is the underpinning rationale for gender justice; nevertheless, 'social justice in general', as it is understood in many of our schools, is used to dilute the threat of gender justice.

You will have to be concerned with gender equity

We have seen in this and earlier chapters the myriad of ways in which teachers and principals distance themselves from the responsibility to reform themselves or their schools. And yet, with all of this, many non-'feminist' teachers, male and female, do decide to undertake at least some of the work of gender reform. Such teachers 'accept the initial "I must" when it occurs and even . . . fetch it out of recalcitrant slumber when it fails to wake spontaneously' (Noddings 1995, p. 13). What brings them to feel obligated to act?

As we showed in Chapter 3, raising teachers' awareness about gender issues often does encourage them to re-vision and revise. Stories such as the harassment of Georgie and Jessica at Draymill touch deep sensibilities in teachers. As one says, 'We were quite horrified at the types of things that were going on. We were all feeling a little bit guilty to think that these things were going on in our classrooms and we weren't aware of them.' A number of teachers are now developing a sex-based harassment policy and associated curriculum-based educational strategies for the school.

Many who feel alienated by the sexism of their colleagues feel unable to closely associate with feminism without risking their own masculinity. As Alana at Bettleford comments, 'We do have guys upon the staff who are supportive in private, but they generally do not stand up publicly and say so'. Some men are forced out of their inaction by events such as those in the vignette about Mt Mullin with which we began this chapter. At the time of the first breakfast, Zoe, the Deputy Principal, invited the main protagonists of the anti-breakfast males to her office to discuss the matter. One refused but several came and Zoe offered her help and resources to any who wanted to do something for the boys. None took up her offer. Twelve months later, however, another group of men—shocked and distressed at the extent of their colleagues' vitriol—actively sought advice from boys' programmes elsewhere and ran a conference to assist boys to address issues of masculinity and power. Some subordinate males, in particular, seize the opportunity to work with boys who, like themselves at school, lose out in the masculinity stakes. The 'very macho' head of the Manual Arts Department who physically distanced himself from the aggressive behaviours of his colleagues in the staffroom has become actively involved in the schools' emergent sex-based harassment programme. Thus some of the men at Mt Mullin now recognise that, by their silence, they had condoned and perpetuated discriminatory attitudes and behaviours and that 'ambivalence is not good enough'. They *can* be held morally responsible for actions they don't personally take, for harm they don't personally cause, they *are* obligated to 'get off the fence'.

Other stories are more modest, even mundane, but nevertheless stimulate action. Jemma, at Bannilong, is concerned about lunchtime activities being restricted to sports. She searches her mind for something that will attract both boys and girls who are not sporty. Her embarrassment is obvious as she explains that she chose Bingo.

> That's the only thing that I could think of that would get boys and girls in a non-sporting atmosphere. It is hard coming up with ideas like that and bingo seems so dicky, I can't think of any other way to do it. I was embarrassed to even put it on the bulletin to attract the kids, but I had kids coming up this term and saying 'is bingo still on?' It's the only thing that I've come up with that boys and girls who aren't sporty will do together. It was wildly successful.

Tony, a mathematics teacher at Stowley, has never thought of gender issues much. Recently he became responsible for the school's lunchtime programme, noticed that girls were not actively involved and felt he should do something.

> With the sports equipment I give out, there's 'girls only' stuff. Even if all the other equipment is gone and a boy comes up, I say, 'No, I'm saving that for a girl.' I do get more girls coming up and asking me for stuff. I think I have actually seen a change.

I've noticed boys and girls getting on differently in the yard. Those basketball courts we've got outside, you would never have seen a girl there and this was only months ago. Now, I would say there are more than 50 per cent girls playing with guys and there's sort of a respect for one another. And in such a short period of time you see boys playing netball, which is a so-called female sport.

Tony is now involved in the school's sex-based harassment pro-gramme. As we suggested in Chapter 4, his authoritarian approach may exacerbate the very behaviours he wishes to change, but he is on a steep learning curve and he has taken on the duty of professional growth.

Cath, senior teacher of science at Eden Park, sees her profes-sional responsibilities as centring completely on improving her own science teaching and that of her department and this has led, recently but almost inevitably, to the issue of gender. When she first came to the school, teachers complained that there were girls who did not know what a one-sided razor was, let alone ever used one. 'I asked them how much practical work they did and they said, "Oh we haven't done any yet," and this was halfway through the year! How irresponsible!' She has now encouraged the teachers in her school to become involved in a Girls and Technology Project, 'I think that if you are really interested in everything to do with the area you are teaching in then you will have to be concerned with gender equity.'

Many teachers agree with Cath and without fanfare engage in gender-equitable and gender-reforming curriculum practices. They quietly persist with efforts to get girls into interesting and challenging work experience settings; refuse to use sexist texts, or use them but assist students to read 'against the grain'; offer boys and girls new ways of thinking about men and women—perhaps by having them interview their grandmothers and other female relatives about their experience of wars; ask students to reflect upon their gendered interpretations of 'hero'; investigate gen-dered patterns of participation in certain positive and negative health practices; try to make the industrial arts environment more physically inviting for girls by playing music and washing aprons; engage girls and boys in non-stereotypical use of instruments in music; deal with derogatory and disrespectful gender-based remarks; and have equal intellectual and social expectations of girls and boys. These kinds of activities are rarely given the label of a 'gender reform programme'—indeed, often it took some considerable effort to find out about them during our visits since they had become everyday practice for some teachers and as a result went unremarked. These small acts nevertheless lie at the very heart of change in schools. Such teachers are neither the heroes nor villains of gender reform but, through their own behaviour, they provide models of what a more gender-just world might look like.

Whose responsibility is it?

Implicit in what we have written so far is the view that dealing justly with matters of gender is the professional responsibility of all teachers. There are, however, many demands upon teachers in schools and all cannot be expected to take equal responsibility for gender reform programmes. Feeling responsible for everything places one under an unbearable burden which is more likely to induce guilt than action. Furthermore, what is the general responsibility of everyone often becomes the responsibility of no one in particular. There are, however, certain roles or offices in schools which might reasonably be expected to bring with them particular duties of care in regard to matters of gender equity. These include the senior administration of the school, such as principals and deputies, curriculum coordinators, student welfare coordinators, as well as those in designated EO positions. Many who hold these positions of responsibility, however, approach the issue with considerable ambiguity and ambivalence.

He just didn't want to know about it

In school after school, we hear stories of principals and other school administrators who are 'supportive—sort of'. Quite a number appear to have no idea about what is and is not happening in their school, showing a disconcerting disregard for their leadership responsibilities. 'I imagine there is enough happening in the area of gender,' says Dave, Principal at Kingwood. Some express their 'in principle' support, but choose to stay behind the scenes. Some express sympathy and empathy for gender-reforming teachers in private, but decline to provide it in public. For example, Jemma at Bannilong describes how the Principal urges her to confront those departments which have not taken on gender-inclusive pedagogies but is unwilling to 'take sides' in public.

At Rullinga, Marjory, the EO Coordinator who is harassed first by the student and then by the Year Coordinator to whom she reports the incident, reports it to the Vice Principal. He refuses to support her and suggests she is making too much of it, 'He just didn't want to know about it'. She then approaches the Principal, who suggests that, although she is right and he is sympathetic to her case, she should probably drop the matter. 'You know what will happen. If I do anything your life will be unbearable in this town. He [the Year Coordinator] is a very powerful person around here.' Thus the Principal warns her of the potential and considerable personal risks *she* takes in seeking to make issue of this person's position with regard to EO. What he neglects to mention is the personal risks *he* would take in making it an issue. Rullinga has a masculinist culture amongst both staff and students which connects strongly with the culture of the small rural township. It is not in the interests of the Principal to challenge this culture, to assign responsibility—both obligation and blame—where it is due. It may destabilise the power relations upon which his personal and professional status rest. His authority and responsibility within the school cannot be separated from his close association with male-dominated community sporting activities and Rotary— in which the Year Coordinator is actively involved.

Connell (1995) points out that while many individual males may not fit particular dominant versions of masculinity, they have considerable investment as males in maintaining these hegemonic masculinities which portray that which is feminine as 'other'. Very often this investment outweighs any responsibility to female teachers and students or to gender reform. This theme runs through our data. Male principals, and male teachers generally, who do not and would not themselves engage in hegemonic forms of masculinity, nevertheless draw the patriarchal dividend 'without the tensions or risks of being the frontline troops of patriarchy' (Connell 1995, p. 79). By their inaction, they become complicit. As the case of Mt Mullin shows, this can change—but all too often it does not.

While the details vary, the denial of responsibility with respect to the needs of female and/or feminist teachers, female students and gender equity generally is not uncommon amongst 'leaders' in our schools. There are, of course, exceptions and, within our schools, these are predominantly although not universally amongst female leaders. Our evidence suggests that many women in leadership positions in schools work actively to alter the power relationships and discourses embedded in the gender regime of their school's cultures. One female teacher at Stowley, for example, speaks of how sexist comments have become unacceptable in the staffroom since the 'new regime' of the female principal, and about the significant shift in how the staffroom culture works.

Notwithstanding the exceptions, many gender-reforming teachers feel betrayed by those in positions of special responsibility in schools—those from whom they have a right to expect both leadership and support. And if they feel betrayed, how much worse is it for those students whose needs are similarly neglected? The harassment of Georgie and Jessica at Draymill provides just one example. Not only did the Principal fail to act until a parent threatened legal action, but the action when it came was ill-informed and partial and, indeed, underlined the masculinist status quo, defining the girls as the ones with the problem.

This 'betrayal' occurs at all levels of leadership and in many ways. We have already described the Year Coordinators at Bridgeforth and at Rullinga, to whom both teachers and students are expected to report cases of sex-based harassment but who 'laugh it off', and the Curriculum Coordinator at Draymill who refuses to countenance the suggestion of a curriculum-based approach to the issue because 'it's always happened'. There are also the cases of co-option and distortion of the gender reform agenda in self- or other interests. Consider the following examples. The Head of Department at Kenneton wants a piece of science equipment for the school and decides to apply through 'girls' money' even though there isn't any direct link to girls. He explains, 'I know we have a far better chance of getting it if girls are mentioned in the application'. The Heads of Department at East Barton and Kingwood set up single-sex classes and drop them once their Masters theses are written. The EO Coordinator at Kenneton applies for the position because he needs to demonstrate commitment to EO to rejuvenate his stalled career but plans to undertake research in the school to demonstrate that 'the feminists' have got it wrong. And we have the Head of Department at Wattlehill who, in front of a high-level officer from the Education Department, teases two women teachers for coming to school 'power dressed' but does not remark on the male teachers who are also 'dressed up' for the occasion. After all, 'it is only a joke,' he says. As Van Nostrand (1993, p. x) suggests, 'It is evident that the crucial juxtaposition of gender, power, collusion, and leadership . . . has essential and poignant significance for many people.'

None of us is perfect

As we have suggested throughout this book, schools vary widely in the extent to which they provide a climate for reform in the interests of gender equity. When in an apathetic, unsympathetic or hostile environment, gender-reforming teachers find that school days are lonely and long and commitments are sorely tested. Many EO Coordinators, in particular, become preoccupied with questions of style and strategy and with identifying the tolerance limits of their colleagues. Credibility is always at stake and many worry constantly about how to avoid any negative fallout which might undermine them and their work. Some are so anxious about intimidation and negativity that they are timid in the extreme. This has unfortunate implications for their work with colleagues, as the following remarks by Megan, EO Coordinator at Mt Forest, demonstrate:

> I don't want to get known as someone who stands up and ear bashes them. I know they don't like that. None of us is perfect and who am I to go around telling them they are not? I am happier to keep the issue before them by short gentle reminders. I have reported back to them on the sexual harassment survey. It is on the wall over there. I announced that I was putting the sexual harassment policy of the government on the board and that it would be there if anyone wanted to look at it. I don't suppose that they looked at it but it just puts it in people's minds . . . I don't feel confident.

Megan is a vulnerable junior teacher, untrained for the job, unsure of her own politics and terrified of a backlash. In her role as EO Coordinator she has certain formal obligations for bringing about change but she defines these as relating mainly to students and not to staff. She feels quite powerless in her relations with staff. In not using her power, however, she also abrogates her responsibility. Megan is not typical but she is not unusual either.

Disconcertingly, many EO workers see professional development about gender as successful if they get through the day without too much bad feeling. Changes in practice are regarded almost as a bonus. Jemma, at Bannilong, has 'spoken at odd times at staff meetings about gender inclusive curriculum, but that's a bit of a brick wall.' She says:

> I've done all the easy bits, but I really feel that sort of curriculum reform is the hard slog. I mean it's necessary but goodness knows how you approach it, you can't force it or you'll get antagonism.

> There's obviously a problem there which you can't
> change—bearing in mind that you want to keep the whole thing
> happy, friendly and all the rest of it.

For many coordinators, the responsibility they feel for keeping 'the whole thing happy' weighs heavy on the heart and mind. It outweighs all other considerations—including the need for change. Bronte, at Stowley, tells us about an inservice on gender-inclusive curriculum which he ran and which he believes was 'fairly successful'. He also tells us that some of the staff treat gender-inclusive curriculum as a bit of a joke but denies, it seems even to himself, that this is a problem, 'I don't think that they really mean it. They just want to say something about it and get it off their chest. They don't hold any grudges or anything.'

Many who are committed to gender reform for their students are unable to deal with the concomitant responsibility to reform teachers. They feel uncomfortable with making their colleagues feel uncomfortable. As Megan says, 'None of us is perfect and who am I to go around telling them they are not?' And this gets to the heart of the problem—the relationship between those two notions of responsibility: fault and obligation. If I don't feel responsible (that is, to blame), can I be held responsible for undertaking change? Mac an Ghaill (1994, p. 179), in his analysis of masculinities and schooling, has suggested that 'there is a real tension here for the gender and/or sexual majority between not feeling guilty, and not taking responsibility both for the cultural investments one has in oppression and the privileges that are ascribed to you and that you take up as part of a dominant group'. As we suggested in Chapter 3, this tension dominates much of the work that gender-reforming teachers undertake with their students, although it is rarely made explicit. Our data suggest that it is no less central in work with teachers and will need to become much more explicit in the teacher development work of those trying to bring about educational change for gender reform.

Most of the key people are there

A considerable number of our schools had specially designated committees with EO responsibilities. The status and support for these committees varied both across and within schools during the period of our study.

In many of our schools, EO committees have little formal

status, functioning largely as 'interest groups' which meet at their own discretion. In others they are a recognised part of the committee structure of the school with established responsibilities and regularly scheduled meetings. Whether formally or informally constituted, as Scott at Bridgeforth suggests, they are often 'largely a committee of concerned female teachers with the odd sympathetic male'. Often a source of energy and inspiration for gender-reforming teachers, they provide members—often junior female teachers—with a sense of belonging and responsibility and the possibility of effecting change. They are also often regarded by non-members as a clique and function largely on the sidestream of the schools' main activities—thus the EO Committee at Banksia was variously described as 'just a women's action committee', 'a bunch of radical women' or, more unkindly, 'the ladies taking care of themselves'. When regarded in this way, the potential such committees have for mobilising broad-based support within a school is severely hampered.

As we indicated earlier, in a number of our schools, 'EO' changed to 'Social Justice'. The new Coordinator at Bridgeforth, Raoul, has worked tirelessly to have the Social Justice Committee become a sub-committee of the School Council with established membership of 'all the major people who define policy in the school'. Jan, the previous coordinator, found the old structure 'very frustrating' and is convinced that this is an improvement.

> I think that we should have been much more political. It needs to be accepted as part of the whole curriculum. You really needed to have key people, like the Curriculum Coordinator and the Administration, involved—with all the legitimacy that brings. Then you will get everyone involved.

Scott agrees: 'Unless you are prepared for it to be seen as a side issue to your school curriculum, it needs to be integrated into whole school planning. I think that it has become a more integral part of the school culture.' By agreeing to EO becoming Social Justice, Joan, the Coordinator at Banksia, undermines the opposition and also recruits to the committee the welfare and integration workers and, perhaps more importantly in terms of the power politics of the school, the school's more progressive male teachers. The Social Justice Committee has drawn in more 'movers and shakers', thinkers and debaters. It has became a group that is not 'put off by opposition'. It too is now a sub-committee of the School Council and hence able to put policy up through the system. At both Bridgeforth and Banksia, and a number of our other schools, the committee has come out of the sidestream and into the mainstream. The intention is to foster more widespread commitment and involvement. All to the good.

As we have already suggested, however, the risk is that, in the process of broadening the scope of such committees, the web of understanding and experience built up by EO workers about *gender* will dissipate and with it, so will the impetus to gender reform. Furthermore, there is no guarantee that the committees so formed will have any commitment to addressing gender equity or that they will become advocates or goodwill ambassadors for reform. To the contrary, some members are quite open in their intention to take the focus off gender. Megan, at Mt Forest, explains: 'The previous principal thought that we should get away from it just being girls' issues. In the past we have had some people who have pushed very hard for girls and I think that is another reason for choosing social justice.' This approach does not necessarily bring EO in 'out of the cold'.

New promotional structures and criteria during the early 1990s in Victoria required teachers to demonstrate commitment to EO. Often EO positions attracted special conditions and allowances and became part of the promotional structure. Raoul comments that this had some unintended and unfortunate consequences.

> The people who had done Equal Opportunity in the past were
> not eligible because many were the more junior members of staff.
> So you had senior teachers who had never given a stuff about
> Equal Opportunity taking up the positions because it was
> considered a way of getting promotion or because of their
> position in the school.

As a result, not only have some previously 'passionate' teachers lost heart but those now 'involved' often are quite ignorant of the issues and include active and passive resistors to gender reform. Linda, from Karrawong, points out the counter-productiveness of such policies which rely on compliance to effect change:

> People learned how to say the right words but I don't think they
> really won minds. You can't change attitudes by changing the
> rules. I think you fall into a trap if the only way you can
> convince people to do something is to tell them that they have to.
> We didn't win the ideological battle, we just changed the rules.

Now, in the mid-1990s, she suggests that some of the rules have changed again and 'all these guys that have been closet sexists feel vindicated because they can see that they are going to be ascending again'.

The extent to which the rules have changed again is unclear; what *is* clear is that recent accountability-driven policy approaches to change have largely relied on 'creating structures without cultures' (Hargreaves and Earl 1994, p. 5). Some clever strategists, however, have worked within the structures to try to change cultures with respect to gender.

Lorna convenes the Social Justice Committee at Wattlehill. She is an unapologetically committed and active feminist who knows and is amused that men in the school find her reassuring. Geoff, a social studies teacher says, 'To me Lorna is a very moderate person. I think she honestly believes in gender equity as opposed to female rights.' Lorna has wooed a number of 'uncommitted' people within the school to become members of the committee. Liz comments that: 'We used to get just two or three men who would come along . . . actually, I must admit one or two came along just for a bit of a stir, but they soon got involved.' Robert, a Head of Department, joined, not to 'stir' but 'because I've got great respect for Lorna and the things that she does'. His social justice concern, he says, is the academically less able but since joining the committee he has become much better informed about gender issues and has become convinced of the need for action. He says he can now see the inequities amongst male and female staff members, and the way certain male teachers 'continue to put down women teachers and also female students'. He now believes that gender equity for students in schools cannot be achieved without addressing the culture of the school as a whole. Robert thinks that Lorna's approach has been pivotal:

> Lorna is playing a very important role in getting gender taken seriously within this school. She does this by being non-aggressive, by being very professional and by slowly and surely and politely enabling people to take notice and change their attitudes in the process.

Lorna laughingly tells us that she sees the role of the committee as largely educative—'educating the committee, that is'. Many teachers genuinely do not see the problems that gender reform is intended to address. Lorna's understanding of 'critical theory' means she takes seriously the notion of 'enabling' teachers, as well as students, to 'take notice' and 'see'. As Senge (1992, p. 9) suggests, what is needed is for people 'to learn to carry on "learningful conversations" that balance inquiry and advocacy

[and] expose their own thinking effectively and make that thinking open to the influence of others'.

As Lorna and others at Wattlehill point out, Lorna couldn't achieve this alone. The school has had a long history of innovation, beginning twenty years ago with a Principal who was the first in the state to offer adults in the local community the opportunity to participate in classes alongside students and then set up childcare facilities within the school to remove one inhibition to women participating. The school was also an initiator of School Councils and participatory decision-making, involving staff, students and parents. The two Principals who have followed him have carried on the tradition of 'giving teachers a lot of freedom to pursue their own programmes and ideas' (Arnie, Manual Arts teacher) and 'giving teachers trust and responsibility' (April, English teacher).

We support people who want to do things

The form of leadership practised at Wattlehill is characteristic of those of our schools most active in gender reform. For example, at Nerringo, whose girls' football team featured in Chapter 1, there is a wide range of gender reform programmes and a general tenor of support for change which is somewhat at odds with the generally 'traditional' nature of the community. Alan, the EO Coordinator, represents the views of many teachers in the school when he says that the key enabling characteristic of the school is that the administration has consistently and publicly supported gender equity over seven or eight years and that 'part of the culture is that we learn new things, we try out new things, and we support people who want to do things. It's terrific.'

Our data suggest that responsible leadership in schools involves creating the kinds of environments that empower women and girls and men and boys 'to do things' and which enable them to learn as they do. Those in leadership positions in schools who do actively support gender reform do so in a variety of ways: legitimating gender equity reform through good policy frameworks and providing material resources to facilitate it; being open and receptive to innovation; providing structures which enable female and male teachers to participate in, and have some control over, change processes; facilitating the development of the school as a learning community; keeping up with the literature and debates themselves; and listening to students. Eden Park is one such school. Claire Stevens, the Assistant Principal, describes the decision-making process as participatory and democratic:

> There are established procedures within the school for individual members of staff to put up ideas to the rest of the staff which are then discussed in small groups. Consultancy groups of six to eight people from a mix of subject areas meet informally once a week. Following discussion in the consultancy groups, the idea is then presented at a whole school staff meeting for formal debate. By this time there will generally be a two-thirds majority in favour and then the project can be run. This process enables neophyte teachers to gain support for their ideas too. Ownership of programmes is essential to their successful implementation; not all ideas should come down from the top—rather, they should come from the staff.
>
> Students also have input into determining the shape of things. Almost all teachers use some form of evaluation at the end of their courses. This may be in the form of an informal discussion with students about course content, methodology and resources or with a more formal evaluation form which the students complete. The principal also holds regular morning teas with different groups of ten to twelve students, just to get their views.

Claire firmly believes in the value of these structures, 'To have them available is important. It really is. Otherwise things fall apart. They're just too difficult on your own. You just have to have the support of your colleagues.' Staff are actively encouraged to read journals, study and participate in inservice and, on the whole, they seem well read and considerably more knowledgeable about current thinking regarding gender than teachers generally in our schools. Hargreaves and Earl (1994, p. 5) suggest that 'creating cultures and structures together seems to establish much more positive contexts for implementing . . . change'. At Eden Park, gender reform is so much a part of the culture of the school that some teachers are unable to identify its beginnings, explain how it came about or conceive of a school being any other way. And the structures support the culture.

When there is a critical mass of committed people and a sympathetic environment in a school, teachers gain professional satisfaction from their gender reform work. 'This is a young innovative staff,' says Maria at Eden Park. 'There is a different feeling here. We embrace a lot more of the new thinking.' For teachers such as Maria, the invitation to responsibility is irresistible.

We have implied throughout this book that schools have a responsibility to pursue gender justice in and through education. Successful gender reform in schools is dependent upon teachers and administrators understanding and accepting this responsibility in a number of senses.

The first is a sense of *obligation* and hence goodwill towards the task of gender reform generally—supporting the work of others even when not actively involved themselves. Many teachers do show such goodwill, but as we have seen, many do not. Some revel in their irresponsibility, others decline to 'go public' in support and hence allow the minority voices of dissent to inhibit change. Clearly gender reform seeks, in one way or another, to unsettle the hierarchical polarities which distinguish between male and female, preferred and stigmatised femininities and hegemonic and subordinate masculinities. It seeks to unsettle the identities formed and dividends paid around them. It is predictable that such reform will provoke strong feelings, positive in some quarters, negative in others. Our data suggest that successful policies and practices are sensitive to this and are thus strategically more powerful.

The second sense of responsibility involves a preparedness to accept *culpability* in the processes that produce and reproduce inequality in and through schooling. It is in this sense that teachers have a responsibility to be knowledgeable about matters of gender: they need both a critical knowledge of self and of the complex interplay of gender and power in schools and society more generally. Such knowledge does not demand of teachers that they 'feel guilty'—wallowing in guilt is both easy and unhelpful—rather it demands a genuine commitment to monitoring and removing discriminatory practices including those associated with complicit masculinity and femininity. It also demands that schools model a better world for their students. As Karen, the Principal at Bridgeforth, says, 'Kids learn what's accepted and expected in this place and we hope that they will take it with them beyond school. So we have a responsibility to ensure that what we model *is* a better place.'

The third sense is that of *accountability*. We can and should be held responsible for the effect of our own actions and inactions on our students and colleagues. In this we support Toni, quoted earlier, who sees thinking about gender as a 'basic curriculum issue' and part of your 'basic work' as a teacher. Our data suggest that those who support gender reform feel a professional obligation to be responsive to perceived needs and actual situations, commit themselves to looking after the interests of each one of their students, and recognise that this demands that they 'make good' the existing circumstances by providing both a 'gender just' education and an education which pursues gender justice. Policy and accountability are inextricably linked, but policy needs to focus on fostering the desire for change by enabling teachers to see the problem for which gender reform is the solution (see Hargreaves and Earl 1994).

Finally, responsibility must be understood *collectively*. To suggest that schools have a responsibility for gender reform is not to suggest that each and every teacher should or could participate in gender reform programmes in the same way or to the same extent. Rather, the collective of teachers within a school must take responsible action. In addition, sustained change is unlikely to result from the cumulative work of individuals; rather it requires organisational change—both structural and cultural. Part of the duty of those with special leadership responsibilities is to build that community or collective sense of responsibility in schools—to support teachers and students to create the kind of whole-school learning communities which enable and encourage change in the interests of gender justice.

Conclusion

In the Introduction we made several promises. We promised to fill the gap in the research literature which has left educators with few close-up accounts of what happens in schools when the people who normally work there try to change gender identities and relations and to address the associated inequalities and injustices. We promised to show what gender reform looks and feels like and what it means to variously located schools, teachers and students. More specifically, we promised to show how gender reformers read and rewrite gender reform policies and advice in the context of the everyday life of schools. We also promised to disclose how others in schools read and rewrite the work of gender reformers and with what ultimate effects on gender identities and power relations.

In so doing, we sought to 'voice the unvoiced' in the policy process, to offer narratives which made the perspectives of teachers and students central rather than marginal. We promised to attend particularly to the interests and concerns of teachers and students and thus to consider how our research may enhance gender reform practices in schools. It was thus that we sought to assess the merits and otherwise of particular policy imperatives on the ground: to move beyond feminist truth telling in policy texts to 'test' such truths in schools and so to reinvigorate policy.

We mentioned that we were frustrated with two current modes of feminist research in education: feminist theorising which has few empirical referents in schools and research into the micro gender politics of schools which fails to acknowledge wider

199

patterns of power and change. We promised to do some theoretical work from an empirical base and to do it in such a way as to point to the micro gender politics of schools and to policy patterns across schools. We thus promised to offer an accessible 'descriptive analysis' of feminist post-structuralism and, through it, to contribute to the development of a feminist theory of and for change in education. We have done our best to keep these promises.

In all our chapters, we showed what gender reform looks like 'in the flesh', indicating that it did not usually look much like the 'crude, abstract simplicities' (Ball 1994, p. 19) found in advice manuals, policy documents, or indeed certain popular theories. We made it very clear that there was seldom a perfect match between policy prescriptions and educational practices. Indeed, as we showed in Chapter 1 and continued to show throughout, there was almost always a 'mysterious gap' between the hopes represented in such theories, policies and suggestions for practices and what happened in schools. The gender reform policy process was fractured and indeed fractious due to the competing interests at stake and the deep identity issues involved, but also due to the interweavings of disparate discourses and the uneven relationships of power which sustained them.

As we illustrated in each chapter, gender reform in schools was multi-vocal, dynamic and contextually inflected, operating within a web of other discourses. Gender reformers sought to work within, against, around and through the different tolerance limits of many different discourses in their efforts to remake the meaning of success, knowledge, power, emotion and responsibility and so to remake the meanings of masculinity, femininity and, indeed, feminism. Many pushed hard against the limits of the practical and the possible. Equally, as we showed, in their reading and reworking of the discourses of gender reform, other teachers and students pushed gender reform to its limits and exposed some of its limitations.

In Chapter 2 we discussed the ways in which gender reformers contested conventional notions of success and how some such contestations backfired and others remained marginal. We pointed to the ways in which dominant definitions of success associated with 'the academic' both narrow its meaning and select, particularly, certain social classes of males for future powerful class locations. We showed how this dominant discourse absorbed even the mildest feminist challenges to it and reinscribed the dominant. We offered two examples: the campaign to 'multiply girls' choices' through mathematics and the mobilisation of the educational panic associated with the 'under-achieving boy'. We pointed to the ways in which the discourse of the 'under-achieving boy' was able to dominate gender reform policy circles in the mid-1990s because the popular meaning of gender equity in earlier decades had solidified around achieving success for girls in mathematics and science. Hence, when girls appeared to become successful in these fields, boys appeared to be 'at risk'.

Through the example of the campaign to 'multiply girls' choices' through mathematics, we showed policy *as* discourse and *in* discourse (Ball 1994). Policy working *as* discourse offered regimes of limited and limiting truth which constructed students in particular ways and which led many schools to uncritically change their practices and students, their 'choices'. The stories of variously positioned girls, however, also showed this policy to encourage girls into mathematics and science *in* discourse. We showed both how this discourse worked as a criticism of other versions of success and of other cultures and how it was critically reworked in accordance with girls' other concerns and desires. We went into the history of gender reform in schools and into schools' ongoing struggles around issues of success to find the roots of the panic around the 'under-achieving boy'. We showed how gender reform was often misread and misrepresented and how inappropriate comparisons between boys and girls were made which together gave the impression that boys generally were failing and that gender reform was to blame. Through this example, we showed how discourse was mobilised in certain interests: how representation and power came together to eventually harness the press and governments in the interests of privileged boys—not all boys.

We examined gender reformers' struggles to identify 'really useful knowledge' in Chapter 3, considering the different ways in which knowledge is configured in gender reform discourses: knowledge as it participates in asymmetries of power, knowledge as a medium of exchange (e.g. for a credential), knowledge as information to motivate change, self-knowledge and knowledge of the requisite skills to effect change. We continued our discussion of the campaign about girls and mathematics and showed how, in the name of gender equity, knowledge was misused to persuade and how, as a result of single-sex classes, new and unfortunate knowledge about gender relations was produced. Here we stressed the significance of 'the knowledge teachers don't know they teach'. We also pointed to the ways in which conventional school knowledges—namely maths, art, English, history, home economics and manual arts—were understood, deployed and critiqued with regard to matters of gender by teachers and by gender reformers.

We showed how teachers construct knowledge about gender for students—how some try to neutralise it in the interest of classroom control and their own comfort, while others try to connect knowledge and action in students' everyday lives. We attested to students' different responses to such approaches and offered the provocative and moving example of the teacher who made a difference because she 'asked' students to 'wonder about things' and to 'explain themselves'. Through examples of teachers struggling with the implications of gender reform for their classrooms we showed how raising their awareness of gender was not enough to effect change. We made the case that teachers' knowledge about the social construction of knowledge, skill and merit was crucial to reform, but that their knowledge about their own gendered identities was also crucial. We made distinctions between valued and valuable and comfortable and uncomfortable knowledges, showing how teachers do and must negotiate their difficult parameters. The most powerful knowledge for gender reform, we indicated, includes knowledge about power, about how to act differently in the immediate, everyday world and about how to be an advocate for change.

We began Chapter 4 by identifying different sociological understandings of power: power in, over, to, through and with. We pointed to theories which stress the meta or the mini narratives of power, the multiple axes of power, power as oppressive, power as productive. We observed that, in the discourse of gender reform, power-in, power-over and power-to perspectives have dominated and little attention has been paid to the ethical or epistemological issues for practice which such understandings invoke. Through the use of a post-structuralist perspective and through a consideration of many different stories of sex-based harassment and of gender reformers' attempts to address such harassment, we showed how various expressions and views of power were manifest in schools and in gender reform. We disclosed how normal practices of harassment were and how they were usually a search for and expression of power by boys over girls, over other boys and over teachers. We also demonstrated that teachers, girls and boys often naturalised and normalised boys' harassment of others and that such normalisations often made their search for power marginal or invisible. Inherent in the discourses conventionally drawn on to account for and explain boys' harassment of girls and each other were arguments about boys' lack of power—their immaturity, their biology, their normal boy-ness or their ethnic boy-ness. Such notions often led to teacher and student denials of the existence of sex-based harassment and to a process of blaming those who did see it and 'cop it'.

We also showed how different gender reform approaches to addressing the issue of harassment offered both girls and feminists some rather paradoxical positions to occupy. These included positions for girls as powerless and in need of protection, but also as sufficiently strong and mature to deal with the problems associated with reporting, or as inviting and inciting harassment and thus with few rights of redress. Wishing to avoid such positionings often led girls to see teachers as too interventionist in adolescent affairs and to seek to deal with harassment themselves. In many cases the power of discipline and of policy were overemphasised by teachers and the power of pedagogy was underemphasised. We offered some examples of good policy and pedagogy for girls and for boys.

Chapter 5 pointed to the powerful emotional underground of school life and of gender reform. We began with accounts of the ways in which the gender reform policy and advice literature has addressed the emotional dimensions of change and their subsequent suggestions for practice. We then drew attention to literature which points to the emotional effects of the social on males and females and to the social role of their emotions. We clarified teachers' conventional understandings of students' emotional worlds at school and pointed to some astute observations which single out issues of gender anxiety, the desire to belong and to be treated as 'somebody'. We revealed that such feelings were experienced by many students. We showed the ways in which gender reform mapped on to this emotional under-life through the examples of single-sex and non-traditional activities for both sexes. We pointed to the ways in which such activities often provided girls with new ways of becoming somebody. But we also showed how these had some unintended side-effects. Those approaches which did not attend to the material differences between girls seduced then betrayed them; single-sex classes for girls were often read by boys as reinscribing them within traditional modes of femininity and sometimes girls used single-sex classes in this way too.

We pointed to the complex psychic processes involved in boys' responses to gender reform. We indicated that certain boys' negative responses to gender reform were not a good guide to decision-making and were best seen as symptomatic of the problems to be addressed. Equally, we revealed that boys were both victims and beneficiaries of their emotions. We demonstrated that certain boys used the emotional dimensions of gender reform to help them to reinvent dominant forms of masculinity. We explained too that gender reform mobilised boys' anxiety, guilt and shame and the sense of powerlessness and injustice that many feel at school. We suggested that the reformist methods developed for girls did not necessarily work for boys but that, either way, emphasis on the emotional sometimes led to a neglect of powerful knowledge. We explained that young men and women at school have a powerful investment in being treated as agential and responsible but that gender reform often infantilises them. We made the case for a pedagogy of the emotions.

Chapter 6 addressed the crucial issue of responsibility for reform among teachers. The chapter began with the observation that responsibility has at least two dimensions involving both a sense of fault and of obligation and suggested that both have been evident in gender reform policies. It then showed how, across time, teachers have been positioned within policy with regard to their obligation to be responsible. In early gender reform policies, they were positioned as freely choosing responsible professionals. However, in more recent times, after the slow progress of gender reform became evident, such approaches changed. Teachers were then positioned as implicitly irresponsible requiring performance criteria and accountability measures. We implied throughout that neither position is adequate. The rest of the chapter pointed to teachers' different responses to policy's 'invitations to responsibility' and answered the questions 'What motivates teachers to respond so differently?', 'What different forms does responsibility take?' and 'What school structures and practices encourage teachers to accept responsibility?'

At the fervent extremes were those who embraced and those who rejected responsibility. Policy supported the former but their motivation tended to come from their personal and professional histories. Those who rejected responsibility had a surfeit of ill-will and lacked professional responsibility. They sought to de-legitimate and disrupt gender reform. Their influence exceeded their numbers and contributed significantly to the timid behaviour of many of those who had assumed the responsibility for reform and who had a formal responsibility to support it. In between these extremes were the majority of teachers, neither passionately for nor vehemently against gender reform. While many denied responsibility and exercised some very 'creative strategies of non-implementation' (Ball 1994, p. 20), these were the teachers most likely to be influenced by policy and by the school environment. In this chapter we pointed to the difficulties involved in encouraging such teachers to accept responsibility for current constructions of gender and for changing them and suggested that part of the difficulty lies with the tension between the two notions of responsibility: fault and obligation. We also suggested that educating is better than legislating for reform and that communities of responsible practice must be carefully crafted through the development of complementary structures and cultures. We concluded by stressing that the responsibility for gender reform involves the development of a sense of obligation, culpability, accountability and of community support.

Overall then, we told multiple stories around the discourses of success, knowledge, power, emotion and responsibility. We pointed to the different meanings of these concepts in policy and research, to the many ways in which people in schools worked and reworked these and to the range of factors involved in these re-inscriptions. Studying these re-inscriptions proved valuable. It pointed to the limitations and dangers of the slogans and the quick-fixes of gender reform. It also pointed to the host of new issues for consideration which inevitably arise when gender reform 'truths for practice' are implemented. We showed that this was the case with regard to the 'truth' campaigns around, for example, 'maths multiplies your choices', the under-achieving boy, single-sex classes, non-traditional 'choices' and sex-based harassment. Our stories of each attested to the need to be alert to the ways in which reform is regularly reinscribed as it is woven into the fabric of school life and into the lives of students and teachers. Meaning can seldom be pinned down. This is not necessarily a matter to mourn, for it points to possibility, not closure.

Concentrating on re-inscription meant that we offered a view of gender reform 'from below'. We described its look and feel, drawing particularly on a teachers' eye view of policy and a students' eye view of teachers' work for gender reform. This view from below is important for both policy-makers and teachers. It encourages them to consider in advance the positions which their texts offer their imagined readers and to observe the different ways these positions inscribe and are reinscribed. A view from below alerts policy-makers to the long and busy roads between the meta-narratives of policy and the micro-physics of power in schools. In particular, it invites them to demonstrate a better understanding of the pedagogy of teacher and student change. It challenges them to attend to complexity, contingency and contra-diction and at the same time to undertake the inevitable broad-brush policy work of abstraction, simplification and compromise.

A view from below also alerts gender reformers to the differ-ences that make a difference. It encourages them to be much more attentive to students, to school and teacher cultures and to local issues and needs. It encourages them to see that students and colleagues are positioned very differently by the dominant and subordinate discourses of the school and elsewhere. It encourages teachers to avoid a one-theory-fits-all approach and to explore where students and colleagues are coming from and why they read and rewrite in particular ways. They can then assess the extent to which they need to reassess their own practices and re-educate themselves.

Overall, in this study we exposed gender reform's intimidat-ing complexity. Looking at such complexity up close tends to obscure its main patterns, which may register only as traces or appear to disappear. Theory helps us to stand back from this apparently disordered complexity, to adjust our focus and assess the bigger patterns.

Our research confirmed our conjecture that the particular reading of feminist post-structuralism announced in the Introduc-tion could be a useful theoretical lens through which to examine gender reform. It also confirmed our hunch that it could assist in the development of feminist theories to support change in schools. Its particular strength is its acknowledgement of the complex ways in which institutions, meaning, power, human identity and gender come together. It acknowledges contesting discourses and practices, it recognises the dynamic interweaving of social and cultural forces, and it therefore can readily be deployed as a theory of and for change.

Feminist post-structuralism led us to conceptualise gender reform as a political process of making and remaking meaning in schools in ways which sought to challenge the unequal gender settlements of particular schools and their localities as well as those of wider society. Further, it led us to portray gender reform as a discursive field within which meanings about gender reform itself were constantly negotiated and contested; a field in which truths are made and remade. Gender reform was a subordinate discourse in policy circles and in the schools of this study and post-structuralism led us to show that feminists in schools were doing inter-discursive work; trying to disarticulate the conventional and dominant meanings of success, knowledge, power, emotion and responsibility and to rearticulate their meanings in more humane ways. Post-structuralism also led us to consider gender reform policy texts as the raw materials from which fresh meaning may be made by gender reformers and others in schools. Further, their 'texts' may be the raw materials from which fresh meaning may be made by other teachers and students. It also helped us to recognise that other teachers and boys and girls are also involved in the politics of discourse and to focus on the ways in which they reworked gender reform into other discourses that mattered more to them. It led us to search out the ways in which the meanings of gender reform were negotiated, revised, contested, appropriated and resisted. However, it also led us to notice when and how discourses within gender reform fixed or narrowed identity, meaning and reason in ways which prevented teachers and students from being and seeing otherwise.

As we implied throughout, a sense of the dangerousness of truth does not mean there is no necessity for 'truth'. Clearly feminists must speak with some certainty and authority to many people in schools who, as we showed, view knowledge as fixed, who offer their own knowledge as fact, pure and simple, and who often want technical solutions to complex problems. The challenge is to speak with certainty and a certain uncertainty. This is apt in the age of uncertainty and redefinition.

Through our empirical work, it became possible to see some of the limitations of feminist post-structuralism; to identify what so far it has tended to neglect in terms of educational theory and practice. As noted, post-structuralism calls attention to complexity and instability. Although the various texts of gender reform were encountered somewhat promiscuously by individuals and groups in schools, there were also certain regularities in their responses. We wish to draw attention here to those associated with emotion, with age and history, with school culture and with powerful pedagogies.

Our data pointed to the powerful role of emotion and of psychic processes in the reform process. It showed how destabilising gender was very disruptive, particularly for those who had invested heavily in particular types of masculinity or femininity. However, despite an increasing interest in psychoanalytic theory and in desire and pleasure, we found that feminist post-structuralism in education did not provide us with much appropriate conceptual assistance on such micro-micro matters. We now want to include in the theoretical apparatus of feminist post-structuralist approaches to policy, pedagogy and curriculum, a lexicon which can guide inquiry into and understanding of the emotional effects of the social and the social role of the emotions in schooling, and which can help us to properly consider the development of a feminist pedagogy of the emotions to assist the production of really powerful knowledge for gender reform.

Our research also led us to understand the collective importance of the fluctuating relations of power between teachers and students, the changing gender/generational gap between teachers and students, and the 'nature' of contemporary adolescents. These call for a contextual and historical sensibility—a sensibility rather lacking in feminist post-structuralist micro-analysts and in policy-makers. As we illustrated, some teachers, gender reformers among them, had a very dated view of gender which took little account of the processes of gender redefinition and uncertainty which have occurred within schools and beyond over the last two decades. The gender/generation gap was reflected in the refusal of many to countenance the different views of gender expressed by many students who were keen to address gender issues, but to do it their way. Further, the adolescents in these studies did not like to be told and they particularly did not like to have the things they did and valued criticised by older generations. Peer relations were generally considered far more important than teacher–student relations. Equally counter-productive were approaches which failed to recognise that adolescence is a time at which young people are shaping their identities in the context of individual—and, indeed, economic and cultural—uncertainty and instability. In our view, generation is a primary structuring discourse which may transgress as well as transcribe those associated with class, gender, race, sexuality and 'ability'. It is our view that hearing what students say when they answer back will help feminism to stay alive.

In concentrating on discourses, post-structuralism tends to overlook the broader patterns which emerge as the ongoing result of discourses in conflict and concert. It tends to see through rather than to see culture. But our research led us to believe that school culture plays a crucial role in reform. Without their re-culturing, some schools will continue to reproduce outdated gender relations and identities. In general, those schools and departments which were most successful were open to and refreshed by new ideas and encouraged energetic intellectual exchange and change 'from below' (from new and junior staff) as well as from outside. Their priorities and practices indicated that they supported, encouraged and celebrated difference and the entitlements of all students, but that they did not support differences built on dominances or entitlements based on those structures of power noted above. They recognised the importance for learning and identity of the head, the hand and the heart. They encouraged all students to accept responsibility for their behaviour and to take initiatives for change. They recognised that schools owe girls and boys the right to feel welcome, cared for and safe as well as the right to be educated about life as it is and as it might become if it were to fulfil their best hopes. The teachers in these schools recognised the importance of changing their practices and themselves. Their schools modelled a better society.

The schools and departments which failed at gender reform were insular and actively subscribed to traditional and hierarchical versions of power and of masculinity. They were structured in such a way as to endorse the culture of male entitlement and indicated by their priorities and practices that the needs of males were more important than those of females and that the needs of some males were more important than those of others. These schools and departments operated mainly at the level of hyper-rationality, discipline and control. They avoided empathetic and affiliative behaviours. They were repressive in their teacher–student relations and did not offer their students opportunities to develop wise judgments or to exercise their autonomy in responsible ways. Further, they operated in such a way as to marginalise and stigmatise certain groups of students and of staff. Gender reform in such schools tended to be achieved only by stealth.

Attention to the patterns of discourse across the many schools, teachers and students of this study pointed to the general effects of gender reform policies. Apart from all those things listed in the Introduction, we showed that in schools they provided an important charter for reform, guides for new thought and action and a language for change. They raised the general awareness of gender issues in schools, attracted financing, staffing and professional development for teachers and extension activities for students, and legitimated the actions of activists. They also helped to bring like-minded people together and to attract others to undertake gender reform, reconfiguring many people's thinking and practice and some institutions. Their importance cannot be over-estimated.

During the final stages of our research, however, it was clear that, as schools came increasingly under siege as a result of government cutbacks, the tightening of government controls, the narrowing view of the purposes of education, the intensification and trivialisation of teachers' work, the push of market forces and the retreat from social justice policies, they were increasingly disinclined and unable to support gender reform. Their cultures were becoming more like the second type of school noted above. Indeed, as our final visits indicated, gender reform was on the wane almost everywhere. Governments' retreat from gender reform points to the need for self-starting, self-reliant 'DIY feminism' (Bail 1996), and for some very astute new forms of policy and political work.

Post-structuralism has other benefits and costs when it comes to suggestions for powerful pedagogies. It indicates that gender reform must be overtly educative and help students and staff both to identify the dominant narratives which have helped to shape them and to deconstruct the cultural excuses which are used to justify the status quo. However, deconstruction was not enough in our schools. As noted, the most successful programmes undertook this destabilising work in environments characterised by respect and support. But also, they assisted students and staff to draw out some positive counter-narratives, helped them to build both alternative sources of strength and status and new communities of support for other ways of being male and female. They guided and encouraged students and staff both to discover their own informed truths about gender and to develop their own responsible practices for change in the light of local circumstances. They treated people as agents rather than passive recipients of reform: orienting them towards action. They encouraged students and staff to develop a vision of a better world around them and to make the many small changes necessary to achieve that world. Many students and staff at such schools and even at some others were 'hungry for change', they could not wait and were 'not going back'. As Jan at Banksia said firmly:

> I can see us, this generation, growing up to be less sexist than kids from, say, five years ago. It's because we've been brought up at our school to be equal and that's the way it's going to work out.

Notes

Introduction

1 For a valuable discussion of narrative methods in research and the many approaches and issues involved, see Casey 1995–96.

2 A Commonwealth Project of National Significance 1990, *Broadening girls' post school options, A review of the field and issues identification* awarded to Jane Kenway and Sue Willis. See Jane Kenway and Sue Willis 1995, *Critical visions: Policy and curriculum rewriting the future of education, gender and work,* The Department of Employment, Education & Training, Canberra, ACT. A Commonwealth Project of National Significance 1990–91, *Broadening girls' post school options, Project two: Case studies,* awarded to Jane Kenway and Sue Willis with the Education of Girls Unit of South Australia. See Jane Kenway and Sue Willis with the Education of Girls Unit of South Australia 1993, *Telling Tales: Girls & Schools Changing Their Ways,* Australian Government Publishing Service, Canberra. Australian Research Council Award 1990–92, *Gender Reform in Schools: The reception and effects of equal opportunity programs for girls,* awarded to Jane Kenway and Sue Willis with Leonie Rennie and Jill Blackmore. Jane Kenway with Merilyn Evans 1991, *Working for Gender Justice,* Ministerial Advisory Committee on Women and Girls, Victoria, Australia.

3 In Australia, gender reform happens at Commonwealth, national, state, regional, local, school and sub-school levels. In this sense, then, it can be seen as a broad cultural process, which consists of many smaller cultural processes, all of which intersect.

4 Australia has been unusual in gender equity policy formation due to the institutionalisation of gender equity for women and girls resulting from a combination of strong top-down 'state-centric' policies at Commonwealth and state level and bottom-up grass roots feminist activism in schools and unions. *Girls School and Society* (Commonwealth Schools Commission 1975), the first national report on the education of girls, coincided with the first International Women's Year. Since that time, most Commonwealth and state public-sector departments, particularly in education, have had women's advisers, advisory committees or gender equity units which inform policy and undertake professional development and material production for dissemination. This has resulted in an impressive record in Commonwealth and state-level policy development often backed up by funding programmes. While the states have differed in the way in which they have informed, adopted and adapted Commonwealth policies, policies have built sequentially upon earlier state and Commonwealth policies. Commonwealth and national policies and plans include, *Girls and Tomorrow: The challenge for schools* (Commonwealth Schools Commission 1984), *The National Policy for the Education of Girls in Australian Schools* (Commonwealth Schools Commission 1987), *The National Action Plan for Girls 1993–97* (Australian Education Council 1993) and *Gender Equity: A framework for Australian schools* (Ministerial Council on Employment, Education and Training, and Youth Affairs 1996). For discussion of the shifts in thinking in policy circles during this period, see Yates (1993) and for a discussion of shifts in the language of gender reform and a listing of Australian Commonwealth and state reports, policies and other publications, see Gilbert (1996).

Chapter 4

1 Although the term sexual harassment is more common, we have adopted the terminology 'sex-based harassment'. There has been some debate about the appropriateness of applying a term such as 'sexual harassment', with all of its connotations and legal associations, to schooling K–12. In its *Equal Opportunity Action Plan for Girls 1991–93*, Victoria described gender-based harassment as 'the unwanted imposition of behaviour that is based on sex stereotyping' and included within it both sexual and sexist behaviour. The 1993 *National Action Plan*, however, adopted the term sex-based harassment to include both sexual harassment and gender-based harassment where the latter also includes the type of bullying directed at

some males who have a subordinate style of masculinity. In our schools we found that the term 'sexual harassment' was almost always used by students and teachers alike even when the school policies distinguished sexual harassment and gender-based or sexist harassment. In this chapter, we have adopted the national terminology of sex-based harassment except where the use of one of the other expressions is more clearly appropriate or we are referring to usage in particular schools.

References

Adler, S., Laney, J. & Packer, M. 1993, *Managing women*, Open University Press, Buckingham.

Allard, A., Cooper, M., Hildebrand, G. & Wealands, E. 1995, *Stages: Steps towards addressing gender in educational settings*, Gender Equity in Curriculum Reform Series, Carlton, Curriculum Corporation, Carlton, Australia.

Alton-Lee A. & Denson, P. 1992, 'Towards a gender inclusive school curriculum: Changing education practice', in S. Middleton & A. Jones (eds), *Women and education in Aotearoa*, Bridget Williams Books, Wellington, NZ, pp. 197–221.

Arnot, M. 1995, 'Feminism, education and the new right', in L. Dawtrey, J. Holland and M. Hammer with S. Sheldon, *Equality and inequality in education policy*, Open University Press, Clevedon, UK, pp. 159–81.

Australian Education Council 1991, *Listening to girls: A report of the consultancy undertaken for the review of the National Policy for the Education of Girls*, Curriculum Corporation, Carlton, Australia.

——1992, *Where do I go from here? An analysis of girls' subject choices. A report of the consultancy undertaken for the Australian Education Council Committee to review of the National Policy for the Education of Girls in Australian Schools*, Curriculum Corporation, Carlton, Australia.

Australian Education Council/Curriculum Corporation 1993, *The national action plan for the education of girls 1993–97*.

Bail, K. 1996, *DIY Feminism*, Allen & Unwin, Sydney.

Ball, S. 1994, *Education Reform: A critical and post-structural approach*, Open University Press, Buckingham.

Belenky, M. Clinchy, B., Goldberger, N. & Tarule, J. 1986, *Women's ways of knowing: The development of self, voice and mind*, Basic Books, New York.

Blackburn, J. 1982, 'Some dilemmas in non-sexist education', *The Secondary Teacher*, vol. 1, pp. 10–11.

Brant, C. & Too, Yun L. 1994, 'Introduction', in C. Brant & Yun L. Too (eds), *Rethinking sexual harassment*, Pluto Press, Westview, UK, pp. 1–31.

Caine, B. & Pringle, R. 1995, *Transitions: New Australian feminisms*, Allen & Unwin, Sydney.

Casey, K. 1995–96, 'The new narrative research in education', in M. Apple (ed.) *Review of Research in Education*, vol. 21, American Research Association, Washington DC, pp. 211–53.

Christian-Smith, L. 1993, *Texts of desire: Essays on fiction, femininity and schooling*, The Falmer Press, London.

Collins, C., Batten, M., Ainley, J. and Getty, C. (1996) *Gender & School Education*, AGPS, Canberra.

Collins, G. 1995, 'Art education as a negative example of gender enriching curriculum', in J. Gaskell & J. Willinsky (eds), *Gender in/forms curriculum*, Institute for Studies in Education and Teacher's College Press, New York, Ontario, Canada, pp. 43–58.

Commonwealth Schools Commission 1975, *Girls, school and society*, Report by a study group to the Schools Commission, November, Canberra.

——1984, *Girls and tomorrow: The challenge for schools*, report of a working party on the education of girls, July, Canberra.

——1987, *The national policy for the education of girls in Australian schools*, Canberra.

Connell, R. 1987, *Gender and power: Society, the person and sexual politics*, Polity Press, Cambridge.

——1994, *Knowing about masculinity, teaching the boys: Educational implications of the new sociology of masculinity*, paper for the Pacific Sociological Association conference, San Diego, April.

——1995, *Masculinities*, Allen & Unwin, Sydney.

Cox, E. 1995, 'Girls and boys and the cost of gendered behaviour', *Proceedings of the Promoting Gender Equity Conference*, 22–24 February 1995, Canberra, pp. 303–11.

——1996, *Leading women*, Random House, Sydney.

Edley, N. & Wetherell, M. 1995, *Men in perspective: Practice, power and identity*, Prentice Hall, London.

Evans, J. 1995, *Feminist theory today: An introduction to second wave feminism*, Sage, London.

Fillion, K. 1996, *Lip service*, Harper Collins, Sydney.

Fitzclarence, L. 1992, *Representing painful experience in a post-modern curriculum*, invited address to the Research Perspectives for the Drama Classroom Conference, Deakin University, Geelong.

——1995, 'Education's shadow? Towards an understanding of violence in schools', *Australian Journal of Education*, vol. 39, no. 1, pp. 22–40.

Foucault, M. 1977, *The Archaeology of Knowledge*, Tavistock, London.

Fraser N. 1991, 'The use and abuse of French discourse theories for feminist politics', in P. Wexler (ed), *Critical theory now*, The Falmer Press, London, pp. 98–118.

Gaskell, J. & Willinsky, J. (eds) 1995, *Gender in/forms curriculum*, Institute for Studies in Education and Teacher's College Press, New York, Ontario.

Giddens, A. 1994, *Beyond left and right: The future of radical politics*, Polity Press, Cambridge.

Gilbert, P. 1996, *Talking about gender: Terminology used in the education of girls policy area and implications for policy priorities and programs*, AGPS, Canberra.

Gilbert, P. & Taylor, S. 1991, *Fashioning the feminine: Girls, popular culture and schooling*, Allen & Unwin, Sydney.

Gilligan, C., Lyons, N. & Hammer, T. 1990, *Making connections: the relational worlds of adolescent girls at Emma Willard School*, Harvard University Press, Cambridge.

Goleman, D. 1996, *Emotional intelligence: Why it can matter more than IQ*, Bloomsbury Publishing, London.

Hargreaves, A. & Earl, L. 1994, 'Triple transitions: Educating early adolescents in the changing Canadian context', *Curriculum Perspectives*, vol. 14, no. 3, pp. 1–9.

Hey, V. 1996, *The Company she keeps: An ethnography of girls' friendships*, Open University Press, Buckingham.

Henry, M. & Taylor, S. 1993, 'Gender equity and economic rationalism: An uneasy alliance', in B. Lingard, J. Knight, & P. Porter (eds), *Re/forming education in hard times: The labor years in Australia and New Zealand*, The Falmer Press, London & New York, pp. 90–106.

Jenkins, A. 1990, *Invitations to responsibility*, Dulwich Centre Publications, Adelaide.

Johnson, R. 1983, 'What is cultural studies anyway?' *Anglistica*, vol. 26, nos. 1/2, pp. 7–81.

Jones, C. & Mahony, P. 1989, 'Introduction', in C. Jones & P. Mahony (eds), *Learning our lines: Sexuality and social control in education*, the Women's Press, London, pp. ix–xvii.

Kenway, J. 1991, 'Feminist theories of the state: To be or not to be?' in M. Muetzelfeedt (ed.) *Society, State and Politics in Australia*, Pluto Press, Sydney, pp. 108–45.

——1995, 'Masculinities: Under siege, on the defensive and under reconstruction?' *Discourse*, vol. 16, no. 1, pp. 59–81.

Kenway, J., Blackmore, J. & Willis, S. 1996, 'Pleasure and pain: Beyond feminist authoritarianism and therapy in the curriculum', *Curriculum Perspectives*, vol. 16, no. 1, pp. 1–13.

Kenway, J. & Willis, S. 1990, *Hearts and minds: Self esteem and the schooling of girls*, The Falmer Press, Sussex.

——1995, *Critical visions: Policy and curriculum rewriting the future of education, gender and work*, The Department of Employment, Education & Training, Canberra, ACT.

——1996, *Critical visions: Policy and curriculum rewriting the future of education, gender and work*, AGPS, Canberra.

——with Education of Girls Unit, SA 1993, *Telling tales: Girls and schools changing their ways*, AGPS, Canberra.

Lees, S. 1993, *Sugar and spice: Sexuality and adolescence*, Penguin, Harmondsworth.

Lewis, S. & Davies, A. 1989, *Gender equity in mathematics and science*, Curriculum Development Centre, Canberra.

Mac an Ghaill, M. 1994, *The making of men: Masculinities, sexualities and schooling*, Open University Press, Buckingham.

MacKay, H. 1993, *Reinventing Australia: The mind and mood of Australia in the '90s*, Angus & Robertson, Sydney.

Mahony, P. 1989, 'Sexual violence and mixed schools', in C. Jones & P. Mahony (eds), *Learning our lines: Sexuality and social control in education*, The Women's Press, London.

Marginson, S. 1993, *Education and public policy in Australia*, Cambridge University Press, Cambridge.

McLean C. 1996a, 'Boys and education in Australia', in C. McLean, M. Carey & C. White, *Men's ways of being*, Westview Press, Boulder, pp. 65–84.

——1996b, 'The politics of men's pain', in C. McLean, M. Carey & C. White, *Men's ways of being*, Westview Press, Boulder, pp. 11–28.

Miles, S. & Middleton, C. 1990, 'Girls' education in the balance: The ERA and inequality', in M. Flude & M. Hammer (eds), *The Educational Reform Act, 1988: Its origins and implications*, The Falmer Press, Basingstoke, pp. 187–206.

Ministerial Council on Employment, Education and Training, and Youth Affairs 1996, *Gender equity: A framework for Australian schools*, AGPS, Canberra.

Noddings, N. 1995, 'Caring', in V. Held, (ed.) *Justice and care*, Westview Press, Boulder, pp. 7–30.

O'Doherty Report 1994, *Challenges and opportunities: A discussion paper*,

Inquiry into Boys' Education, NSW Government Advisory Committee on Education Training and Tourism, Sydney.

Office of Schools Administration, Ministry of Education, Victoria 1991, *Equal Opportunity Action Plan for Girls in Education: 1991–93*, Melbourne.

Ruddick, J. 1994, *Developing a gender policy in secondary schools*, Open University Press, Buckingham.

Salisbury, J. & Jackson, D. 1996, *Challenging macho values: Practical ways of working with adolescent boys*, Falmer Press, London.

Salzberger-Wittenberg, I., Henry, G & Osbourne, E. 1983, *The emotional experience of learning and teaching*, Routledge, London.

Sawicki, J. 1991, *Disciplining Foucault: Feminism, power and the body*, Routledge, New York.

Senge, P. 1992, *The fifth discipline: The art and practice of the learning organisation*, Random House, Sydney.

Shaw, J. 1995, *Education, gender and anxiety*, Taylor & Francis, London.

Smith, G. 1996, 'Dichotomies in the making of men', in C. McLean, M. Carey & C. White (eds), *Men's ways of being*, Westview Press, Boulder, pp. 29–50.

Tannen, D. 1995, *Talking from 9 to 5: Women and men at work: Language, sex and power*, Virago, Berkshire.

Teese, R., Davies, M., Charlton, M. & Polesel, J. 1995, *Who wins at school?: Boys and girls in Australian secondary education*, Department of Education Policy and Management, University of Melbourne, Melbourne.

Thorne, B. 1994, *Gender play: Girls and boys in school*, Open University Press, Buckingham.

Van Nostrand, C.H. (1993) *Gender-Responsible Leadership: detecting bias, implementing intervention*, Sage Publications, Newberry Park, California.

Walkerdine, V. 1985, 'On the regulation of speaking and silence: Subjectivity, class and gender in contemporary schooling', in C. Steedman, C. Unwin & V. Walkerdine (eds), *Language, gender and childhood*, Routledge and Kegan Paul, London, pp. 203–42.

——1989, *Counting girls out*, Virago, London.

Weedon, C. 1987, *Feminist practice and post-structuralist theory*, Basil Blackwell, Oxford.

Weiner, G. 1994, *Feminisms in education: An introduction*, Open University Press, Buckingham.

Wexler, P. 1992, *Becoming somebody: Toward a social psychology of school*, Falmer Press, London.

'What about the Boys?' 1994, *The Gen*, March, pp. 1–5.

Willis, S. 1989, *'Real girls don't do maths': Gender and the construction of privilege*, Deakin University Press, Geelong.

Willis, S., Kenway, J., Rennie, L. & Blackmore, J. 1992, 'Studies of Reception of Gender Reform in Schools', *Curriculum Perspectives*, Newsletter Edition, June, pp. 3–12.

Wolf, N. 1993, *Fire with fire*, Chatto & Windus, London.

Yates, L. 1993, *The education of girls: Policy, research and the question of gender*, ACER, Hawthorn.

Index